WOODWORKING
Mistakes & Solutions

WOODWORKING
Mistakes & Solutions

R.J. DeCristoforo

STERLING PUBLISHING COMPANY
New York

Library of Congress Cataloging-in-Publication Data

DeCristoforo, R. J.
Woodworking mistakes & solutions: professional secrets for
the home craftsman/R.J. DeCristoforo.
    p.   cm.
  Includes index.
  ISBN 0-8069-3886-2
  1. Woodwork—Amateurs' manuals.   I. Title.
  TT185.D433 1996   96-24178
  684' .08—dc20   CIP

10   9   8   7   6   5   4   3   2   1

Published by Sterling Publishing Company, Inc.
387 Park Avenue South, New York, N.Y. 10016
© 1996 by R.J. DeCristoforo
Distributed in Canada by Sterling Publishing
c/o Canadian Manda Group, One Atlantic Avenue, Suite 105
Toronto, Ontario, Canada M6K 3E7
Distributed in Great Britain and Europe by Cassell PLC
Wellington House, 125 Strand, London WC2R OBB, England
Distributed in Australia by Capricorn Link (Australia) Pty Ltd.
P.O. Box 6651, Baulkham Hills, Business Centre, NSW 2153, Australia
Manufactured in the United States of America

Sterling ISBN 0-8069-3886-2

To all of us woodworkers
who like to do it right the first time.

Contents

Introduction

Some woodworkers believe that expertise in woodworking is acquired through trial and error and that becoming a good woodworker is a matter of learning from mistakes. While the second generalization makes some sense, assuming that the mistakes are not repeated, the idea of achieving woodworking expertise through trial and error is incongruous. For one thing, we're not in a research lab where it is routine to experiment with procedures to prove or disprove them. While experimentation can be part of woodworking enjoyment, step-by-step experimentation when working on a project can waste a lot of time and material, and can be frustrating.

My feeling, which certainly is not original, is that woodworkers gain knowledge when they adopt the role of student. In essence, we learn from the experiences and the mistakes of others, and so are prepared to avoid them. We may be amateurs when alone in the shop, but there are a host of fellow enthusiasts who are happy to share their experiences, willing to tell of mistakes, and eager to suggest problem-solving methods and techniques for avoiding mistakes that have been proven by on-hand application.

There are two aspects to woodworking. The *engineering* aspect deals mostly with planning and construction (including measurement and layout) and assembly. The *creativity* aspect has to do with design and appearance, to which we react subjectively. We can originate designs or work from plans offered by others, sometimes opting to make changes that please our own senses. In the engineering aspects there is rarely room for compromise. You can't stretch a board that's cut too short or widen one that was ripped too narrow—not without some penalty, as you will see. There are acceptable variations with many joints, but it is essential that the components fit precisely.

There are mistakes of the mind and of the hand. Those of the mind occur when we neglect to give the task at hand proper attention. Being preoccupied can cause "small" errors that lead to big mistakes since they are often overlooked, such as making a cut on the wrong side of the dimension line so the board is shorter or narrower by the gauge of the saw blade.

A typical mistake of the hand is wrongly marking a dimension point. That is one reason why we are so often cautioned to "measure twice, cut once." But there is more involved.

It is also important to take the time to be *sure* of a measurement. This may slow you down a bit, but it will help to induce a pace that helps to achieve accuracy and more enjoyable woodworking.

In the following pages, I describe both hand and mind mistakes, and how to avoid them. Also examined are other factors that play a part in the engineering and creative aspects of woodworking: how wood moves; how to make accurate dado, mortise-and-tenon, miter, and dowel joints; how to fine-tune table saws, radial arm saws, and other power tools; how to plan projects properly and avoid assembly errors; and techniques for preparing a surface for a finish. There is also a chapter that contains plans for many of the jigs that are important accessories in my shop. Despite the fact that power tools are accurate and have a good amount of built-in control, it is often advisable to build an accessory that guarantees precision, additional safety on a particular application, or allows you to produce any number of duplicate cuts or parts.

The intent of this book is to identify areas where mistakes are likely to happen so they can be anticipated and avoided. It doesn't matter whether you are installing storage shelves in the garage or reproducing a classic dining table; success in both cases and for any woodworking project depends on being aware of possible areas where mistakes can be made and avoiding the need to repeat tasks and waste wood

R. J. DeCristoforo

1

Measuring and Marking: Where It All Begins

How you "measure up" in the phase of woodworking that involves marking lines, dimension points, etc., so the parent material can be transformed into accurate project components, will determine your woodworking success. Casualness is a principal error. There are always arguments about what should be allowable tolerances for error in woodworking. While these tolerances are not as essential as they are in a machine shop, where work is done to the thousands of an inch, they are still critical.

If a miter joint is to form a 90-degree corner, each of the cuts must be 45 degrees, period! On a square or rectangular frame, a slight mistake is multiplied by eight, which adds up to a disastrous error, as you discover at assembly time. The truth is, it's just as feasible to work accurately as it is not to. Careful marking and layout are not difficult techniques. There are many devices that help, but they depend on you to use them correctly and carefully. These devices are discussed below.

MARKING AND MEASURING TOOLS

Measuring Tapes

Measuring tapes rate highly as basic measuring tools. They're compact, easy to use and carry about, and are available in many lengths. The minimum length for a tape used in a wood shop is 8 feet, since that's the longest dimension of a standard plywood panel. Common graduations are in sixteenths and eighths of an inch, but some are marked in both metric and inch dimensions so conversions can be made while you are working.

The widths of the tape range from $\frac{1}{4}$ up to $\frac{3}{4}$ inch. The widest ones in longer lengths are more suitable for construction work. The narrowest $\frac{1}{4}$-inch versions seem a bit flimsy. The happy medium for in-the-shop woodworking is a coved, $\frac{1}{2}$-inch-wide tape; the cove allows the blade to be extended a reasonable length without bending. A locking mechanism that will secure the blade at any extended position is essential. Having to hold the tape steady while marking dimension points is a nuisance and leads to inaccuracies.

A measuring tape has a hook at its free end that the user brings to bear against the edge of an object being marked or measured. Generally, the hook is slotted and attached with rivets that are just tight enough to secure the hook while allowing it to move to-and-fro. If this weren't so, it would be inconvenient to use the tape for inside measurements. For the tape to be accurate, the movement of the hook must be limited to an amount that equals its thickness.

It's difficult in these days of shrink packaging, but if you can do it before buying the measuring tape, test the accuracy of the hook by using the tape to measure a 12-inch rule or the blade of a combination square. It's also good to check the measuring tape for accuracy against another measuring device you're sure is accurate before starting a project. After all, tapes get tired or refuse to be good after they are dropped or abused. A fellow woodworker went all out; he had a machine shop mill him a shiny piece of steel *exactly* 12 inches long that he keeps wrapped in a soft, oiled cloth! He checks his measuring tape against this steel. But even if the hook on your measuring tape is not accurate, it's easy to adjust by carefully bending it a bit with pliers.

Many times, especially if the tool has been around a while, I simply ignore the end of a measuring tape or rule. Instead, I line up an arbitrary graduation mark, like ½ or 1 inch, at the squared end of the workpiece and subtract that amount from the reading on the tape when I mark where I wish to cut. I find that making the mark in the form of a V instead of scratching a line helps me, for example, to place a square accurately (Illus. 1-1).

It's possible for two tapes to give you different measurements. Therefore, always use the same tape throughout the construction of a project. If you have a partner working with you, share the tape or, at least, check his against the one you use to be sure of similar results.

When you read the scale on this and any other measuring tool, look directly down on the graduation mark. Your line of sight should be at right angles to the marking point regardless of the work situation. Any other viewpoint can distort the reading and cause inaccuracies.

Measuring the thickness of material with a measuring tape isn't the best practice, especially

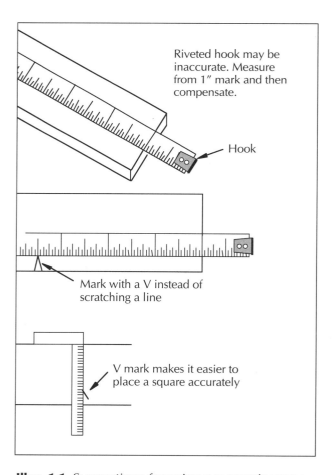

Illus. 1-1. Suggestions for using a measuring tape.

on thin material where you have to read graduations that are partially, if not wholly, obscured by the hook. Also, graduations on common tapes are not fine enough so you can easily be aware of slight differences in material thicknesses. To be sure, it's best to use a caliper at such times and when checking joint components like tenons (Illus. 1-2). Calipers are also usable for inside measurements, so they are good tools for checking the dimensions of a mortise, the diameter of a hole, etc. Another plus is that the sliding component of the caliper is removable, and that makes it available as a depth gauge.

The *folding rule* (Illus. 1-3), commonly called a *zig-zag rule* because of the way it is opened and closed, is preferred for particular measurements by some woodworkers, especially carpenters and cabinetmakers. A popular unit extends to 6 feet and folds to a compact 8 inches. A plus is that they are fairly rigid even when fully extended. When the unit incorporates a sliding extension, as many of them do, it is handy for inside measurements; the reading on the extension is added to the sum of the opened blades.

Thus, the tool is suitable for measuring the height and width of openings for doors, drawers, and similar installations. Since the extension is removable, it can be used as a short rule or as a gauge to check the depth of holes or mortises.

A calibrated straightedge (Illus. 1-4), commonly called a bench rule, will complement other measuring devices. These tools are available in lengths up to 8 feet, but a unit that is 24 or 36 inches long is a good choice for the workshop. In addition to measuring, a straightedge is practical for drawing long lines and for checking the evenness of edges and the flatness of slabs. I keep a short one on hand since I find it more convenient than a measuring tape for marking dimensions that are less than an inch or so.

Steel Squares

The term steel square covers a variety of tools, all of which resemble the example shown in Illus. 1-5. There are carpenter squares, rafter squares, homeowner squares, and other types. Many of these squares can be used to provide a good deal of information.

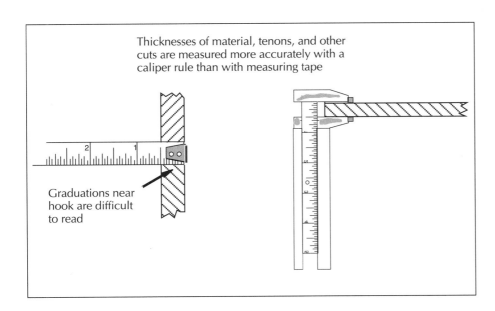

Thicknesses of material, tenons, and other cuts are measured more accurately with a caliper rule than with measuring tape

Graduations near hook are difficult to read

Illus. 1-2. Calipers are easier to use than measuring tape and more accurate when measuring thicknesses.

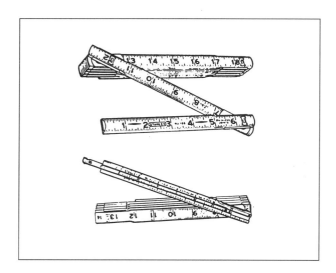

Illus. 1-3. The folding or zig-zag rule.

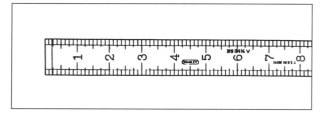

Illus. 1-4. A 12-inch bench rule.

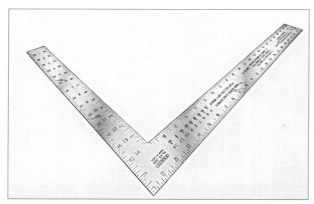

Illus. 1-5. All steel squares look like this one, but they may be marked for particular applications.

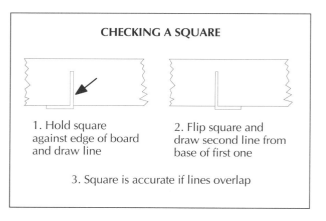

Illus. 1-6. Checking a square. Always do this before using the square.

A steel square's "body" and "tongue," respectively 24 and 16 inches long, can both be used to draw long lines, whether at some mid-point or 90 degrees to an edge, and to check the trueness of edges and surfaces. The tool is especially useful for checking the squareness of inside or outside corners on large projects, and for ensuring that large frames have right-angle corners.

Illus. 1-6 demonstrates how I check the accuracy of a square before putting it to use. If necessary, I adjust it by doing a judicious amount of touch-up with a draw file.

Techniques with a Square

You don't have to worry about fractions when it's necessary to divide a board of odd width into a number of strips of equal width. Place a leg of the square across the board at an angle that will allow the diagonal line to be divided into even inches by the number of strips that are needed. For example, assuming four strips of equal width from a board that is 11¼ inches wide, place the tool at an angle that provides a

12-inch reading. Marking the board at 3-, 6-, and 9-inch graduations provides equally spaced guide points. The technique, of course, is not limited to squares; any calibrated straightedge will serve the same purpose.

Any diagonal line that is drawn from the 12-inch mark on the tongue of a steel square to a point on its blade will establish a particular angle. Illus. 1-7 tells what graduation points to use on the blade for most commonly used angles. Since the angles will be complementary, they can be established from a vertical plane as well as a horizontal one. Just mark a perpendicular line from the tongue's 12-inch graduation.

In addition to drawing angles, this system can be used to determine the correct cutting angles for multisided figures. Illus. 1-8 lists the dimension points to use for segmented projects ranging from those with 3 sides to those with 20 sides. Following this chart will ensure accurate results but, as always, it's essential to work carefully, marking dimension points exactly right.

Marking Pencils

The pencils used to mark the lines and dimension points are as important as any layout tool. The prosaic carpenter's pencil, which has a roughly rectangular body and broad lead, is adequate as long as a lot of the lead is

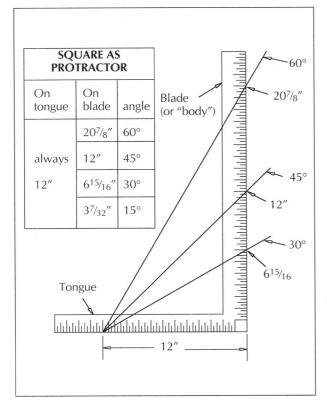

Illus. 1-7. How to use a steel square as a protractor. All base points are at the 12-inch graduation.

SQUARE AS PROTRACTOR		
On tongue	On blade	angle
	$20^7/_8''$	60°
always	12″	45°
12″	$6^{15}/_{16}''$	30°
	$3^7/_{32}''$	15°

USING SQUARE TO FIND POLYGON CUTTING ANGLES		
No. of Sides	Tongue Dimension	Blade Dimension
3	12″	$20^7/_8''$
4	12″	12″
5	12″	$8^{25}/_{32}''$
6	12″	$6^{15}/_{16}''$
7	12″	$5^{25}/_{32}''$
8	12″	$3^{31}/_{32}''$
9	12″	$4^3/_8''$
10	12″	$3^7/_8''$
11	12″	$3^{17}/_{32}''$
12	12″	$3^7/_{32}''$
14	12″	$2^3/_4''$
16	12″	$2^{13}/_{32}''$
18	12″	$2^1/_8''$
20	12″	$1^{29}/_{32}''$

Illus. 1-8. The chart indicates the dimension points to use for polygons with various number of sides.

exposed and brought to a chisel point by sharpening and then honing on fine sandpaper. But even then, its use should be confined to straight lines. The #2 lead pencil, common for writing, may also be used, but it wears quickly and must be sharpened frequently to produce clear, sharp lines. Pencils with #4H or #5H lead hold points longer and produce suitable lines. Mechanical pencils, those used by draftsmen, are a good choice since they can be fitted with leads of different hardness. The problem with mechanical pencils, especially when they are kept sharp by using a draftsman's rotary sharpener, is that their points break easily, and excessively frequent sharpening becomes a nuisance. I like using them, but being aware of this problem, I allow the lead to make its mark without bearing down on it. Another practice is to rotate the pencil when it is used to draw a long line.

Whatever pencil is used, it should be held at an angle so the point of the lead contacts only the bottom edge of the scale (Illus. 1-9). It's obvious that inaccurate lines occur when the pencil is held vertically. Another error is to place the rule flat on the work and then make a short, heavy line to indicate the dimension. The right way is to hold the rule at a slight angle and to slide the point of the marker down the graduation line so what you get on the work is a small dot (Illus. 1-10). This works best when the rule has incised lines that serve as grooves in which the point of the marker can ride, but, regardless, working so is far better than using small scratches to indicate dimension points. You can't use this technique when working with a measuring tape and some other measuring tools, but the critical factor is to mark dots, not slashes.

Using a Knife as a Marker

When doing marking that allows no room for error, such as defining the lines of the mating part of a joint , a most suitable marking tool is a sharp knife (Illus. 1-11). The advantages of using a knife are that it forms an extremely fine

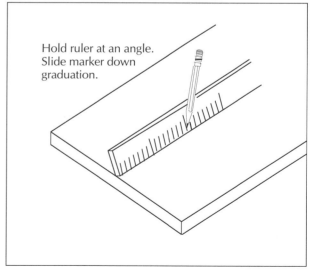

Illus. 1-10. The accurate way to mark with a rule and a pencil. It's best to establish a point, not a scratched line.

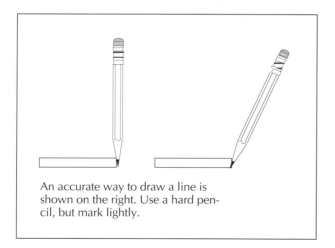

An accurate way to draw a line is shown on the right. Use a hard pencil, but mark lightly.

Illus. 1-9. The right and wrong ways to use a marker. The right way is shown on the right.

Illus. 1-11. A knife forms a fine line and severs surface fibers, so the saw cuts will be cleaner.

line, and it severs the surface fibers of the wood, helping to produce smoother cuts when sawing. The latter advantage isn't limited to joints; an incised line promotes smoother sawing even when doing sizing cuts, especially when they are cross-grain.

Utility knives are the types of knives that are used for marking. Their blades have various shapes, but the one that is most suitable for this purpose is long and narrow, with a long taper, like the knife shown in Illus. 1-12. The point of this knife makes it easy to stay close to a guide and to function in tight quarters, and it's easier to use accurately when doing work like making cutouts in patterns (Illus. 1-13). For the latter application, it's wise to tape the pattern to a piece of dense hardwood.

Often, when you need to mark a part for a dado or rabbet, it's better to use the companion piece as a gauge rather than measure with a scale. You can position the part to be inserted accurately by butting it against the rip fence of a table saw or by using a strip of wood or square (Illus. 1-14).

Preventing Errors When Using Marking Tools

When marking a cutting line parallel to an edge, we often use our fingers to gauge the edge distance. This is not a good way to work because the pencil will form a thick line and our fingers will follow any irregularity in the edge of the work (Illus. 1-15). It's always better to use a square so the line will be straight regardless of the board's condition, and will be square to the work's edge (Illus. 1-16). However, it is important that you make sure the blade is locked in the head and that the tool is held firmly against the edge of the board.

Another way to ensure that you draw straight lines is to use a *marking gauge,* a tool that is extremely accurate when marking lines parallel to an edge (Illus. 1-17). Marking gauges are made so they can be equipped with a lead or a short scriber. The required edge distance is set by measuring from the point of the marker to the tool's head. The beam, the component on which the head of the gauge moves to and fro, may be graduated, but use it only for an approx-

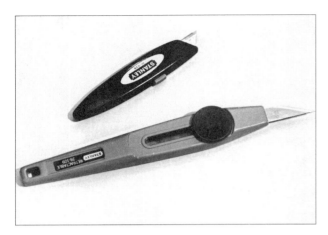

Illus. 1-12. A good knife for marking has a narrow, long-tapered blade. Always retract it into the handle when it is not being used.

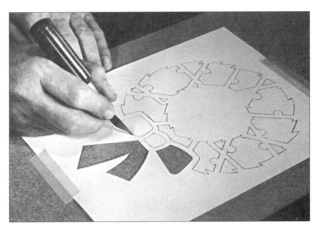

Illus. 1-13. A sharp knife is a must when you are cutting patterns for scroll-saw work. Taping the pattern to a hard surface such as hardboard will help make clean cuts.

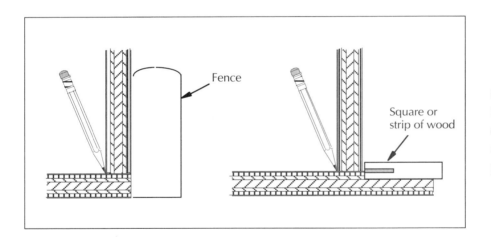

Illus. 1-14. Marking cutting lines for rabbets and dadoes can be done accurately by using the insert piece as a gauge and guide.

imate setting; determine the final setting by using a scale to measure from the head to the point on the marker.

Don't set a lead or scriber to project any more than is needed to mark the work. Use the tool so it rides on one of the flat faces of the beam. If you hold it vertically, the point of a lead will broaden quickly or break; a scriber will dig in, especially when you are marking cross-grain.

Errors can happen when you bring a square to a dimension point and then bring the marker to the square. It's more accurate to place the point of the marker directly on the dimension point and then move the square to meet it (Illus. 1-18).

When marking a board for cutting it to length, don't mark two terminal lines because it will double the chance for error. Instead, start by squaring the end of the board so that you need to measure just once (Illus. 1-19).

Illus. 1-15. We often work like this to mark a line parallel to an edge, but this isn't a very accurate technique.

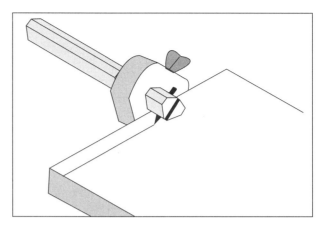

Illus. 1-17. Using a marking gauge is a good way to draw straight lines on a board. Once the distance from the point of the marking gauge to the head is set, the tool can be used to establish the same line on any number of parts.

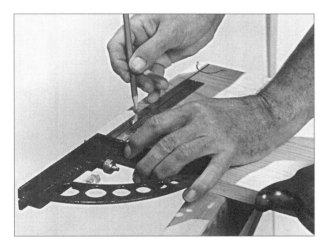

Illus. 1-16. Using a square to draw a line parallel to an edge. It lessens the chances for error.

CREATING CURVES, ARCS, AND CIRCLES

By working with a variety of templates and other simple design tools, and by doing geometrical constructions, a draftsman can create unlimited forms, do layouts accurately, and add a special arc or curve to a project or component.

The woodworker can profit by using the same tools and techniques when planning and executing his own creations.

It isn't difficult to draw a straight line with a ruler or straightedge. With the right templates, curves and arcs are just as easy to draw. For curves, there are several options, the most common and useful being *French curves,* templates that are available in many shapes and sizes (Illus. 1-20). You don't need too many of them to be able to construct or duplicate just about any curve. For example, you can use part of an edge of a French curve as a guide to join three dots marked at random to form a uniform curve. These tools are ideal for jobs like marking the curved areas of table aprons, making designs for shelf supports, or creating patterns for scroll-sawing.

To speed up production when a pattern is symmetrical about a centerline, draw half of it on a sheet of folded paper, and use this half pattern to trace both sides by flipping it for a second tracing. It's usually more practical to mark

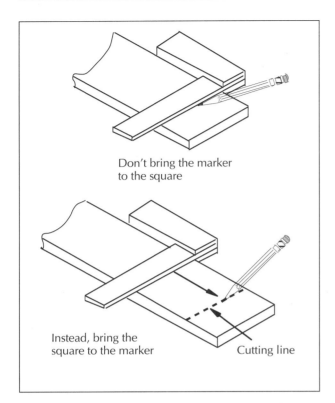

Illus. 1-18. Don't bring the square to a dimension point and then bring the marker to the square. Instead, place the point of the marker directly on the dimension point and then move the square to meet it.

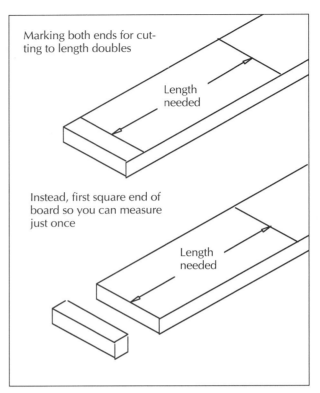

Illus. 1-19. It's better to square one end of a board and then mark it for the length that is needed.

asymmetrical patterns directly on the wood. If duplicates are needed, use the first one as a template to mark other wood. When the material is thick enough, it can be resawed into several pieces. Another technique is to make a pad of several pieces, and then saw the assembly as you would a solid block. This technique is described in greater detail on pages 33–36.

Flexible curves are thin strips of metal, usually lead, that are encased in plastic. They are easily bent to create a particular shape or to conform to an existing curve that you may wish to duplicate (Illus. 1-21). While they don't rival

Illus. 1-20. There are numerous templates used by draftsmen that are practical for woodworking layouts. The one being used here is for drawing ellipses. Having only half-shapes gets more on a template.

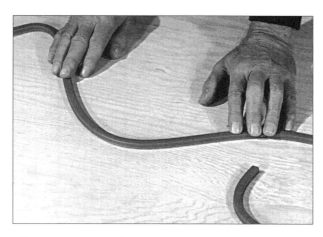

Illus. 1-21. Flexible curves will hold any shape. They are used to create curvatures or to transfer them from an existing project when duplication is the object.

contour gauges, tools that can conform to fine details in products like molding, they are flexible enough to bend around pretty tight radii.

When a flexible curve isn't available, you can improvise by using a slim strip of wood or plywood as shown in Illus. 1-22. It won't offer complete flexibility, but has often solved layout problems.

Another way to trace a profile, one that's used often when the end of a part must be shaped to fit the contours of a molding, is to use a pair of dividers or a compass as shown in Illus. 1-23. (Dividers and compasses are discussed below.) Hold the tool almost perpendicular and move it so, in essence, its points will always be square to the contour.

Circle-Drawing Tools

Tools for drawing circles and arcs are known as *dividers* or *compasses*. If there is a distinction, it's mainly that dividers have two metal points and are generally used for marking metal, while a compass has one metal pivot point and uses a pencil or a piece of lead for marking. Thus, the latter tool is more suitable for woodworking. Some versions can be used either way—a knurled screw in one leg of the tool will grip either a metal point or a pencil. In addition to its basic function of marking, a compass is used to step off measurements and to divide distances into equal spaces along a straight or a curved line.

A compass can be set in one of two ways for marking a circle (Illus. 1-24). One method is to

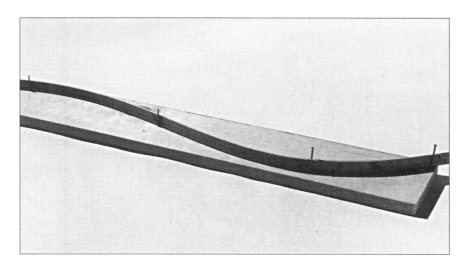

Illus. 1-22. A slim, narrow strip of wood or plywood can be used to lay out curves. Use slim nails to keep the strip in place.

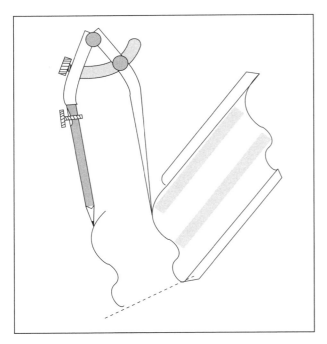

Illus. 1-23. Using a compass to duplicate the contours of a piece of molding.

the other one for the radius needed.

Draftsman's circle templates are a good choice for small circles and for rounding inside and outside corners without having to locate the center point of the layout as you must do when using a compass (Illus. 1-25). When they are used on paper or wood, the indentation caused by the pivot point of a compass is eliminated. Also, because they are precisely made, they provide accuracy with minimum fuss.

Circle templates are available in a fairly wide range of diameters. Some have only half circles to keep the size of the template manageable. One that is a standard part of my layout equipment is only $7\frac{1}{2}$ x 10 inches, but I can use it to create 62 sizes of circles with diameters ranging from as little as $\frac{3}{64}$ inch up to $7\frac{1}{2}$ inches.

Drawing Large Circles

There is a limit to sizes of circles that can be drawn with a compass or template, and that's where a *beam compass*, *trammels*, or improvisations of these tools come in. We've all tried the technique of stretching a string between a nail and a pencil and found it wanting. An improvement is to drive two radius-spaced brads through a strip of wood, or, to create a more permanent tool, to drill the strip of wood

mark two points, spaced to equal the radius of the circle, and then set the tool's points on the marks. A better way, since there are less steps to take, is to adjust the tool directly by placing both points on the correct graduations of a rule. Don't, however, work from an end of the rule. Instead, place the pivotal point on the 1-inch mark, and spread

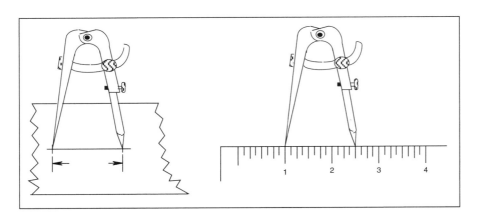

Illus. 1-24. Two methods of setting a compass for marking a circle.

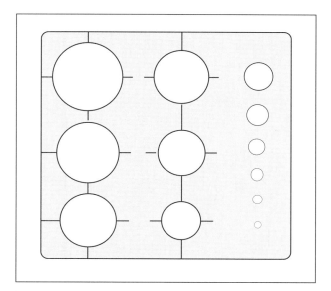

Illus. 1-25. Draftsman's circle templates can be used to accurately draw small circles and to round inside and outside corners.

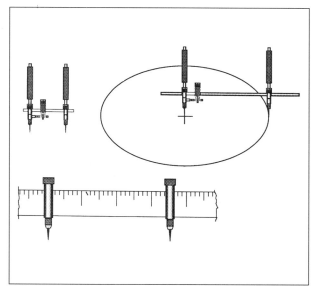

Illus. 1-26. A beam compass (top) and trammels. Both are used to draw circle and arcs that are too large for dividers or a compass.

so it will hold a pencil snugly and then, as needed, install the brad-pivot at a correct point.

The beam compass is a precision instrument with a pivot and marker that can be positioned anyplace on its steel rod (Illus. 1-26). Its pivot point is actually an assembly that includes a fine-thread screw adjustment for extremely fine settings. Standard rods are 6 and 12 inches long, but longer ones can be used so the compass's capacity is virtually unlimited. It's an expensive tool, out of the price class of a compass, and that's to be considered for a tool that isn't required too often.

A more economical and practical solution for woodworkers is to provide trammel points that can be mounted on something like a yardstick (Illus. 1-27). The trammels, commonly made of aluminum, will grip either metal or lead points, and they can be mounted on any strip of wood whose dimensions match those of a regular yardstick. Thus, even circles with

diameters greater than 36 inches are feasible.

MARKING HOLE LOCATIONS

The most accurate way to mark a hole location

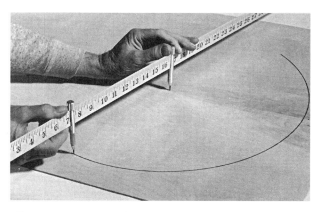

Illus. 1-27. Trammels that are designed for mounting on a yardstick, or a similar bar of wood, are economical and practical.

is to draw lines that intersect where the hole must be. This leaves little room for error. *Don't use a knife or scriber for this type of marking* because you may cause blemishes that finishing won't hide. Instead, use a hard pencil, *lightly*.

The same crossing-lines system can be used to determine the center on the end of a cylinder. In this case, a center finder that you can make, as shown in Illus. 1-28, should be used. Cradle the workpiece in the V of the jig for one line, and then rotate it about 90 degrees before drawing the second line.

Accurate marking will be negated if you don't follow through by correctly preparing for the drilling. All holes, whether in wood or metal, should be started by first forming an indentation with a center punch or prick punch (Illus. 1-29 and 1-30). If you do not do this, there is no guarantee that the drill bit will enter where it should. When using the punch, hold it at an angle as you place its point on the mark, and then tilt it to a

vertical position before tapping it with a hammer.

The next consideration is to be sure the drilled hole will be square to the surface it enters. This isn't a problem when working on a drill press, but supplying a guide, like the one in Illus.

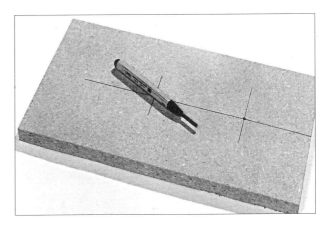

Illus. 1-29. Always use a punch to form indentations when preparing to drill holes. This makes it easy to place the point of the drill bit where you want to drill the hole and does much to keep the bit from wandering.

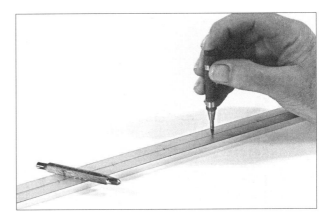

Illus. 1-30. Special punches are available for marking metal. The one being used here is spring-loaded. Pressing down on the cap snaps the point against the work.

3/4 x 8 x 8"

45°

1/2 x 1/2 x 12"

Illus. 1-28. How to make a center finder for round stock. It can also be used to draw diagonals on square pieces.

1-31, is an advantage when you are working with a hand drill or a portable electric drill. The lines on the guide, drawn with a square, are lined up with the intersecting lines on the work. The small hole through the guide makes it usable for all jobs since the idea is to use it for pilot holes that can later be enlarged to the right size. Once you have a true pilot hole, it's not likely that you will err when changing to a larger bit.

You can eliminate layout, and possible errors, when it's necessary to drill centered holes into the edge of a board by making the centering jig that is detailed in Illus. 1-32. It's a simple design, but it requires careful construction anyway. Make the beam from a piece of maple or birch and then, on the beam's centerline, drill the guide hole and those for the nails. Additional holes for the nails will provide more flexibility in how the jig may be placed. Since frequent use of the tool may distort the guide hole, it's a good idea to install a steel bushing that has a $1/16$- or $1/8$-inch center hole. Secure the bushing by pressing it into an undersize hole or by using epoxy.

Dowel Centers

One of my thoughts in the area of woodworking layout is that any time you can minimize the process by introducing a mechanical means of establishing contact points, you reduce the possibility of error. One method I use is to drive small brads into carefully marked locations in one piece and then, after clipping the heads off the brads, pressing the part against its mating part. Thus, for example, when drilling holes for dowels, I establish compatible hole locations while making a layout on just one piece. This is an area where *dowel centers* can help. These are metal plugs with a centered point that are made to fit various sizes of holes. To use them, first mark hole locations on the part and then insert the centers in the holes you drill for the dowels. Then, place the second part in correct position and press it against the centers. The points on the centers will mark the locations of the holes that are needed in the mating piece (Illus. 1-33). There are ways to ensure that you place the parts correctly as you press them together. On an end joint, for example, place one part snugly against the inside corner of a square, and the other against the square's leg. The angle between the parts will be maintained at 90 degrees as you make the contact.

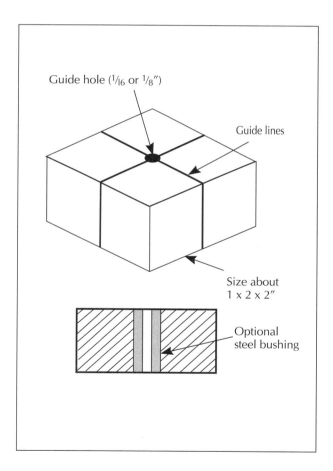

Illus. 1-31. This simple jig will help you drill straight when drilling holes. The jig is placed so its guide lines mate with the intersecting lines on the work.

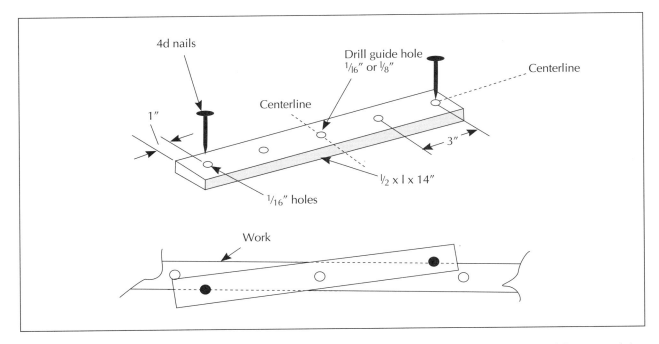

Illus. 1-32. This drilling jig accurately places holes in the center of board edges and also, if the size of the workpiece permits, in the center of the workpiece.

GEOMETRICAL CONSTRUCTIONS

Can you bisect any angle? Round off an inside or outside corner regardless of the angle of the converging lines? Draw parallel lines without measuring? Determine the center of any circle? These are just examples of steps needed when doing layout work that can be accomplished with geometrical constructions, and you don't have to be a math wizard to do them. Actually, if you can use a straightedge, a compass, and a sharp pencil, you can be proficient in this area. You can do the constructions on paper when planning a project, but they can also be valuable when you are doing full-size layouts directly on the wood.

Illus. 1-34–1-42 show geometrical nomenclature and some practical constructions that are useful at the drawing board or in the shop. Just follow the step-by-step information that is included with the drawings.

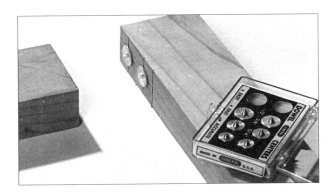

Illus. 1-33. Dowel centers, placed in one part, will mark the mating piece when the two parts are pressed together.

SEGMENTED FORMS

When a number of segments, or "staves," are bevel-cut along each edge at a particular angle,

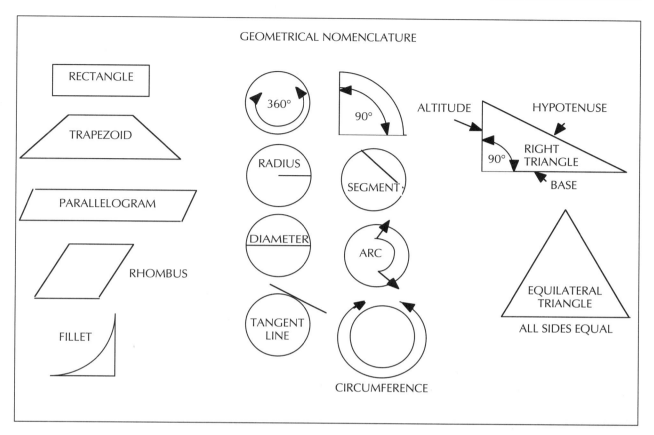

Illus. 1-34. Geometrical nomenclature.

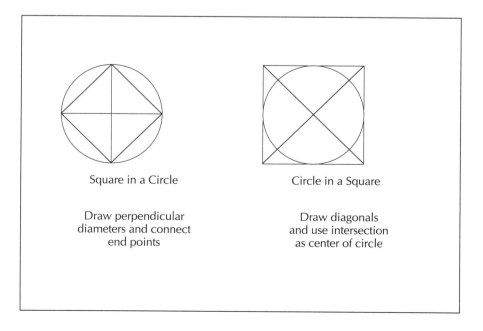

Illus. 1-35. How to form a square in a circle and a circle in a square.

LOCATE CENTER OF ANY CIRCLE

1. Draw arbitrary lines a-b & a-c from point a

2. Construct perpendicular bisectors for the two lines (e & d)

3. Intersection of perpendiculars (f) is center of circle

Illus. 1-36. Use this method to find the center of any circle.

FIND PERPENDICULAR BISECTOR

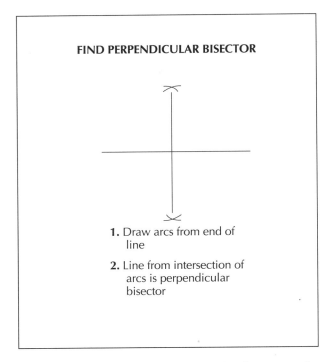

1. Draw arcs from end of line

2. Line from intersection of arcs is perpendicular bisector

Illus. 1-37. Drawing a line perpendicular to another line.

CONSTRUCTING CORNER RADII

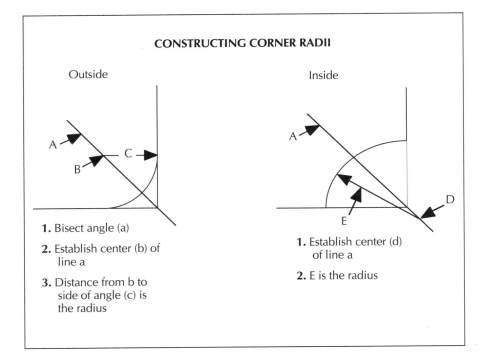

Outside

1. Bisect angle (a)

2. Establish center (b) of line a

3. Distance from b to side of angle (c) is the radius

Inside

1. Establish center (d) of line a

2. E is the radius

Illus. 1-38. Constructing inside and outside curved corners.

BISECTING ANY ANGLE

1. Use A as center to strike arcs B & C
2. From B & C strike arcs D & E
3. Line H is bisector

Illus. 1-39. How to bisect any angle.

the parts can be assembled to form a circle. This technique is needed for barrel-shaped projects like the storage seat shown in Illus. 1-43. The project will emerge closer to a true circle as you *increase* the number of staves and *decrease* their widths. Preparing the segments is not difficult, but neither their width or the angle of the bevel can be arbitrary, not if you want the parts to be assembled as a circle or the project to have a certain diameter.

Two essential angles are involved: the joint angle where segments meet, and the cutting, or bevel, angle that ensures they will meet correctly. To find the cutting angle, divide the 360 degrees of the circle by the number of segments, and then divide the result by 2 (Illus. 1-44). The width of the segments is immaterial if you follow the formula, but only if you are not designing a project of a particular size.

There are techniques to use if you are designing a project of a certain size and want to use a specific number of segments. One method is to make a full-size (or scaled) drawing of the project

Illus. 1-40. Drawing a line parallel to another line or to an edge.

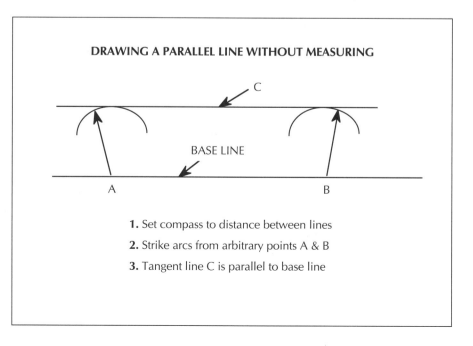

DRAWING A PARALLEL LINE WITHOUT MEASURING

BASE LINE

1. Set compass to distance between lines
2. Strike arcs from arbitrary points A & B
3. Tangent line C is parallel to base line

FORMING AN ELLIPSE USING FOLDED PAPER

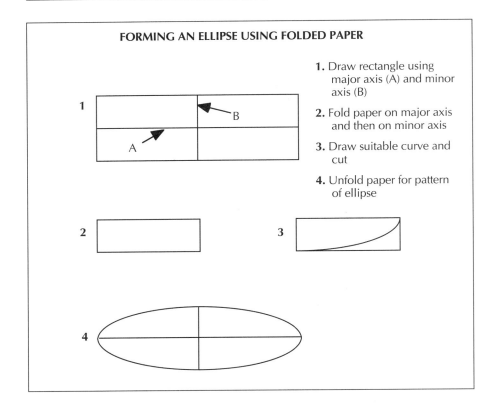

1. Draw rectangle using major axis (A) and minor axis (B)

2. Fold paper on major axis and then on minor axis

3. Draw suitable curve and cut

4. Unfold paper for pattern of ellipse

Illus. 1-41. How to form an "arbitrary" ellipse.

FORMING AN ELLIPSE WITH STRING

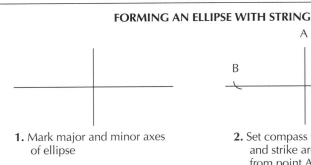

1. Mark major and minor axes of ellipse

2. Set compass to 1/2 major axis and strike arcs B and C from point A

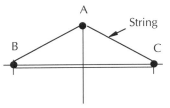

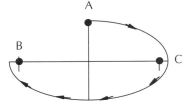

3. Use pushpins or brads at points A, B, and C. Tie string taut around the three points.

4. Substitute hard, sharp pencil for pin at A. Hold pencil vertically and tight against string as you follow it around to mark the ellipse.

Illus. 1-42. Using the string method to form a true ellipse.

Illus. 1-43. A typical project made by using segmented pieces, or "staves."

and then just measure the width of the staves. First, set a compass, or trammels, to equal the distance from the center to an outside corner of the project and draw a circle. Then, after constructing perpendicular diameters, use a protractor to mark divisions for the number of staves you want (Illus. 1-45). If, for example, 12 staves will be used, then the marks are made at 30- degree points: 360 degrees divided by 12 = 30 degrees.

Next, draw lines from the center of the circle through the division points, and measure the distance between them where they cross the circumference; this will tell you how wide the staves must be.

Another method to use when you want the project to be a specific size is to plan mathematically. First, determine the circumference of the project using the formula, diameter times 3.1416. Assuming a 34-inch diameter, multiply 34 x 3.1416; this equals 106.8144.

To determine *how many* staves are needed, divide the circumference by the *width* of the

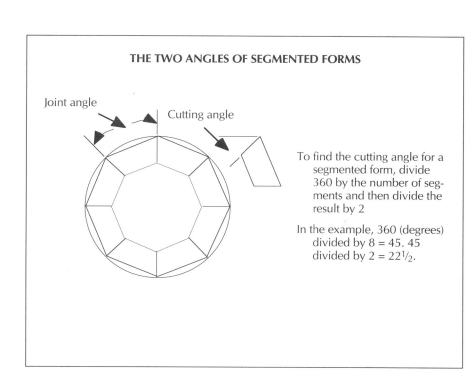

THE TWO ANGLES OF SEGMENTED FORMS

Joint angle

Cutting angle

To find the cutting angle for a segmented form, divide 360 by the number of segments and then divide the result by 2

In the example, 360 (degrees) divided by 8 = 45. 45 divided by 2 = 22½.

Illus. 1-44. How to determine the joint and cutting angles for segmented shapes.

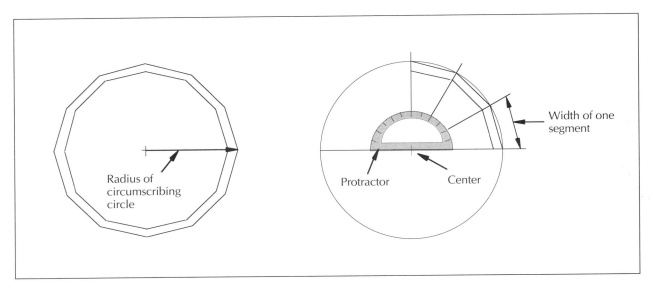

Illus. 1-45. Doing a full-size layout to determine the width of staves.

staves you plan to use (Illus. 1-46). If I decide to use staves with 3-inch widths, I would divide 106.8144 by 3; this equals 35.6048. Then divide the circumference by that number to determine the final stave width. These are a lot of staves to cut to a precise width, so my approach would be to cut all but one and check the width needed for this "key" stave directly on assembly (Illus. 1-47).

Regardless of the number of staves used and their widths, the perimeter of the project will always be a series of flats. However, when staves are narrow enough, it doesn't take much effort to bring the project to full round by removing the corners where the staves meet. This is done by using a portable belt sander or by working with a plane or spokeshaves and then sandpaper.

THE ART OF DUPLICATION

One of the phases of woodworking where we can really goof is when we need multiple

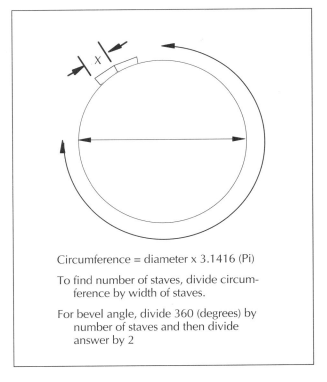

Circumference = diameter x 3.1416 (Pi)

To find number of staves, divide circumference by width of staves.

For bevel angle, divide 360 (degrees) by number of staves and then divide answer by 2

Illus. 1-46. How to discover how many pieces are needed when the width of the staves is known.

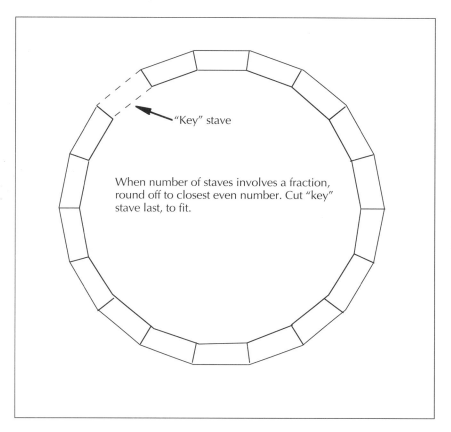

"Key" stave

When number of staves involves a fraction, round off to closest even number. Cut "key" stave last, to fit.

Illus. 1-46. Working this way can eliminate headaches. The width of the "key" stave is determined on assembly.

duplicate parts. The technique you should avoid is to make one part and then use it as a template so others can be produced individually by sawing and then sanding. Two methods that ensure duplication *and* save time are *resawing* and *pad sawing*.

Resawing is the operation done on a band saw to reduce the thickness of a board or to obtain thinner pieces from the board. Operational procedures do not change when producing component duplicates; it's just that the stock is first formed into the shape we need. Normally, the widest blades available are used for resawing, but since in this case we want to produce parts with as smooth a surface as possible and with minimum edge-feathering, it's okay to use a thinner blade with fine teeth so

long as it's in excellent condition and you don't feed the stock faster than the blade can handle it (Illus. 1-48–1-50).

Pad sawing is a matter of temporarily stacking together the number of pieces you require so they can be handled like a solid block of wood, and then sawing them. The pieces can be stacked together in several ways. You drive nails through waste areas, use double-sided carpet tape between layers, hold the parts together with plain tape, or even bond the pieces with dabs of glue placed strategically in areas that will fall away during sawing. Then, after drawing the profile of the part you need on the top layer, do the cutting as if the assembly were a single block (Illus. 1-51 and 1-52). Pad sawing can also be done

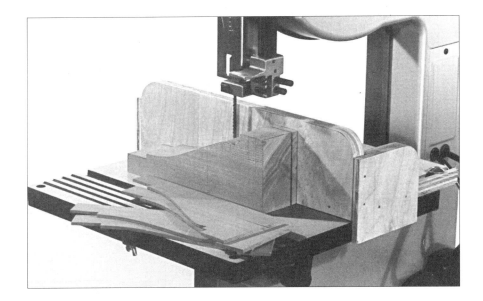

Illus. 1-48. Resawing to produce duplicate pieces from a preshaped block. A high fence is important.

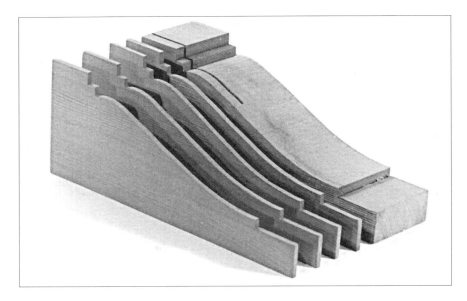

Illus. 1-49. Careful pre-shaping and resawing will result in duplicate parts that require little further attention.

on a scroll saw as long as the total thickness of the stacked pieces is within the capacity of the tool. This isn't too limiting, because the average scroll saw can cut 2-inch-thick stock.

Working on a router/shaper table is also practical, and you will be sure that edges are as smooth as need be. In this case, make a proto-type template, using something like ¼-inch-thick tempered hardboard. Trace the outline of the template on the workpieces and rough-cut them on a band saw or scroll saw. The template is attached to rough-cut pieces with small brads or double-faced tape. Next, place a flush-trimming bit in the router so its bearing rides against

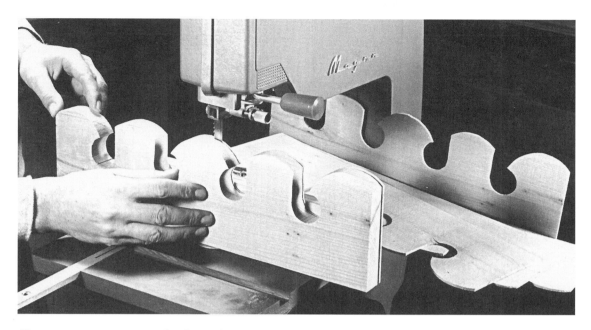

Illus. 1-50. Even intricately shaped pieces can be resawn. Here, a miter gauge is being used as a fence.

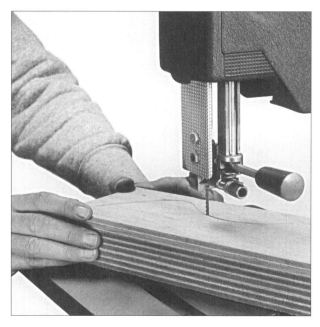

Illus. 1-51. In pad sawing, layers of pieces are stacked together in some fashion and sawed as a solid block of wood.

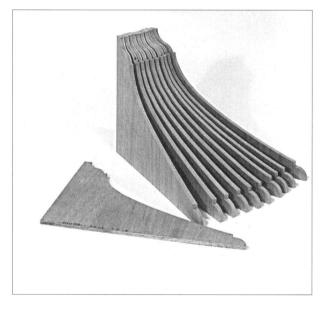

Illus. 1-52. The cutting capacity of a band saw makes it possible to produce a good number of duplicates. The layers that were stacked to make these parts were made of ¼-inch-thick plywood.

the edge of the template and its cutting edges extend a fraction above the edge of the workpiece (Illus. 1-53). Then do the cutting, moving the work, as you always should, *against* the rotation of the router bit.

Sometimes it's possible to make duplicate parts with minimum effort by working with ready-made products. We can't always work so, but, as an example, consider store-bought letters and numbers (Illus. 1-54).

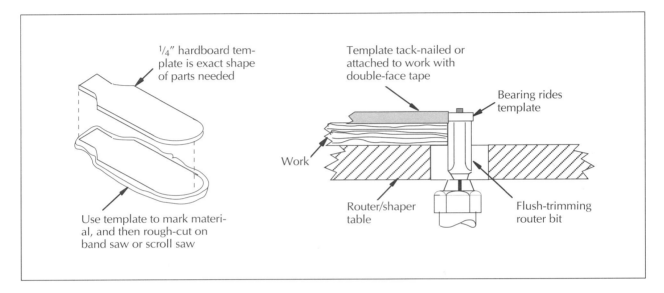

Illus. 1-53. How to cut duplicate parts on a router/shaper table. This system calls for a prototype template that is tack-nailed or held with double-face tape to rough-sawn workpieces.

Illus. 1-54. You can sometimes make duplicate parts easily by resawing ready-made products.

2

Joinery Facts and Construction Techniques

There is more to a piece of furniture, or any woodworking project, than meets the eye. We react individually to what we see, but the actual construction of the piece affects the quality and durability of the project and reflects the skill, or dedication, of the builder. All successful projects, regardless of function and viewer reaction, have a common characteristic: component connections that are meant to be long-lived.

There are choices as to what joints to use when building something, but, no matter whether you use simple or complex joints, there is no room for indifference and rarely room for compromise. A joint will either last indefinitely, which is the intent, or it will fail too quickly. Since we work with felled trees, we should face some facts about this material: how it reacts after it is sawed, dried, and made into the wood products we work with; and how it behaves during many years of use.

WOOD ALWAYS MOVES

We know that a tree starts from a seed, and that after the sapling gets started, it grows outward from its center, each year adding a roughly concentric ring of new wood; thus, the closer to the center of the tree, the older the wood (Illus. 2-1). The cells, or pores, of the "new" wood are more open than those at the center, so wood from that area is subject to greater shrinkage and expansion. The area of the tree from which lumber is cut also affects the natural distortions we call "warp" (Illus. 2-1 and 2-2). These facts are important because, after wood is "dried" and used to make furniture, it will continue to shrink or expand to a degree that depends on the dryness/dampness of the environment. "New" wood shrinks more as it dries and expands more when subjected to humidity.

To counteract varying degrees of wood movement when, for example, joining boards to

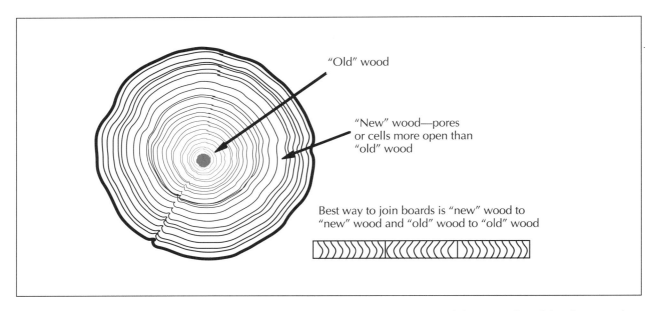

Illus. 2-1. A tree grows from its center outward. The closer to the center of the tree, the older the wood.

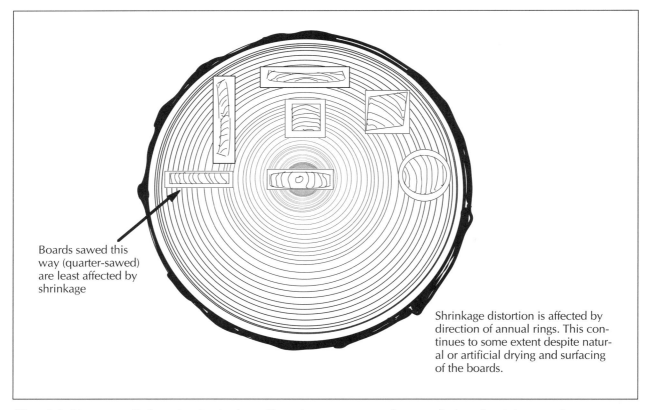

Illus. 2-2. How wood's location in the log affects its movement characteristics after it is sawed.

form a top for a table or dresser, it's good practice to choose and join boards by joining new wood to new wood, old wood to old wood. It's the most that can be done to guard against uneven joints caused by environmental changes.

CUPPED BOARDS

There are several points of view regarding minimizing the effect of "cupping"—warpage across the width of a board—when doing an edge-to-edge slab assembly. A common practice, with a single board, is to rip it into thirds and to rejoin the pieces after inverting the center one (Illus. 2-3). Whether this will be a solution can be determined by judging the degree of warp. If it is extreme, each of the pieces will have its own "cup" and the assembly will require considerable planing and sanding to bring it to acceptable flatness. My own procedure when faced with a board that is extremely cupped is to salvage it by storing it for when I need narrow strips.

Alternate boards (for a slab) are often inverted to compensate for the cupping caused by shrinkage (Illus. 2-3). This system can result in a washboard (rippled or wavy) surface that will be difficult to pin down. Also, it's likely that alternate pieces will contain a lot of sapwood; and because of cost and availability of pieces with sapwood, they should not be wasted.

When the boards are not alternated, the assembly will form a gentle arc that requires little surface treatment and that will actually be easier to hold down with a few screws (Illus. 2-3). Also, there is greater opportunity to place the boards for compatibility regarding color and grain pattern.

A factor that is often overlooked when cupped boards are ripped is that the sawed edges will not be square (Illus. 2-4). Before the parts can be rejoined, the edges that actually have slight bevels must be trued.

EDGE-TO-EDGE JOINTS

The strongest glue joint occurs when long grain connects with long grain. Thus, the vital consideration when joining boards is the condition of the mating edges. They must be square and flat,

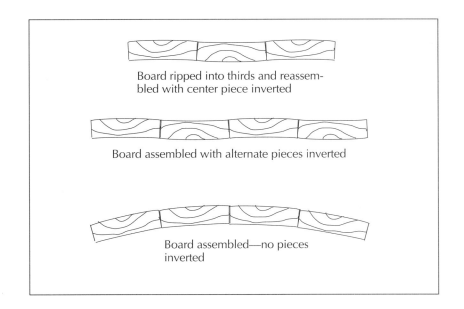

Board ripped into thirds and reassembled with center piece inverted

Board assembled with alternate pieces inverted

Board assembled—no pieces inverted

Illus. 2-3. Various ways that boards are assembled to form slabs.

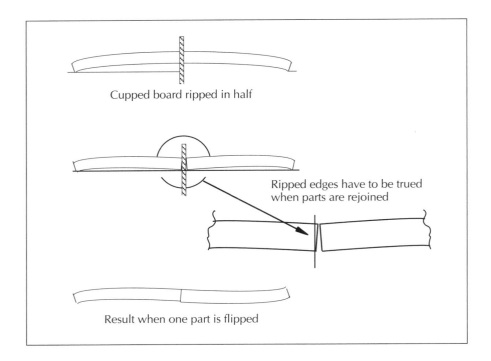

Cupped board ripped in half

Ripped edges have to be trued when parts are rejoined

Result when one part is flipped

Illus. 2-4. Factors that are often overlooked when a cupped board is ripped into separate pieces.

although the technique shown in Illus. 2-5 is often used. The idea is to work on a jointer or with a hand plane to create slightly concave edges before gluing the boards. This causes a slight pressure at the end of the boards. As the wood dries, giving off moisture at the ends first, the pressure is released and there will be no end splits.

If an assembly that is joined this way fails, it will not be the fault of the connection. Failure tests prove that breaks will occur somewhere in the field and that, should one happen in the joint, it would take wood from both edges. (In the field refers to an area of a board that is away from its edge.) This is proof enough that the joint is as strong as the material itself.

The test results are used as proof that dowels used in edge-to-edge boards are not effective and can actually do harm. For one thing, the dowels, having lengthwise grain, will remain fairly stable, but since the wood around them may not, there exists the possibility that the boards may split. When I use dowels in an edge-to-edge joint, I rely on them only for alignment of components—I don't glue them.

Other edge-to-edge joints are more effective than dowels. Tongue-and-groove, glue (formed by milling), and rabbet joints, for example, are long-grain to long-grain connections, and they do add some additional glue area (Illus. 2-5). The spline is not a strong joint because its grain direction must be across its small dimension, so there is cross-grain to long-grain contact.

A butt joint has an end-grain to long-grain connection, and is therefore a weak glue joint that requires reinforcement (Illus. 2-6). Even screws won't help much since the threaded portion of the screw will penetrate end grain where it will have little holding power. Glue blocks are a common addition, but a better way to provide strength is to insert a dowel into the long-grain piece so screws will have something to bite into (Illus. 2-7).

End-grain to end-grain joints are very weak, but dowels are effective here because they will

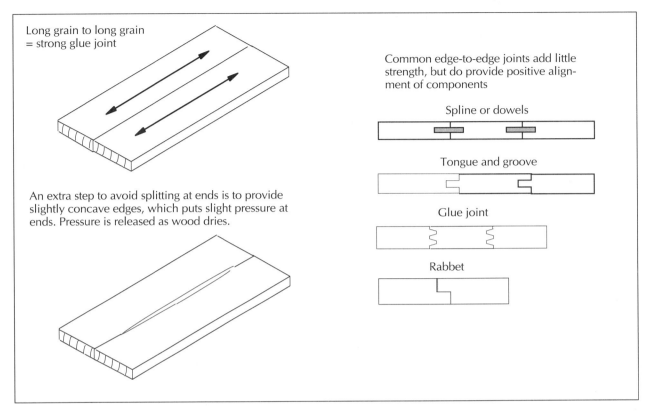

Long grain to long grain = strong glue joint

An extra step to avoid splitting at ends is to provide slightly concave edges, which puts slight pressure at ends. Pressure is released as wood dries.

Common edge-to-edge joints add little strength, but do provide positive alignment of components

Spline or dowels

Tongue and groove

Glue joint

Rabbet

Illus. 2-5. The professional way to join boards edge to edge. Other methods such as dowel, tongue-and-groove, glue, and rabbet joints may not add strength, but they do serve to align the components.

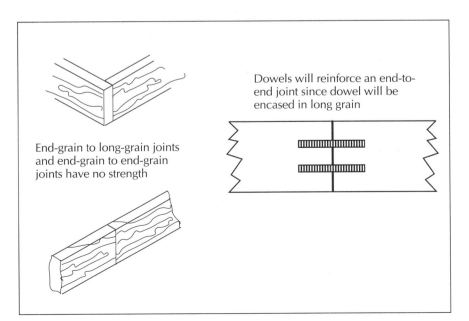

End-grain to long-grain joints and end-grain to end-grain joints have no strength

Dowels will reinforce an end-to-end joint since dowel will be encased in long grain

Illus. 2-6. A dowel joint is very acceptable when you are joining boards end to end.

Illus. 2-7. This is one way to add strength to a butt joint.

point of the slab pieces so they can "adjust" without stresses that can cause splits (Illus. 2-8). Another method is to plane the inside edge of the board so it will be very slightly concave. The ends will continue to exert pressure after the center areas have made contact.

There are other usable joints. A sliding dovetail is a more complex joint, as are individual mortise-and-tenon arrangements. On utilitarian projects where function is the major consideration, nails or screws can be used, but, as usual, the fasteners should be installed only at the center point of the slab parts. It's not unusual to see "old" pieces assembled this way, often with wrought-iron *cut* nails that add a decorative detail.

be entirely surrounded by long grain. Other ways that boards can be joined end to end include splices, plates, and types of scarf joints that will be shown later.

END BOARDS

End boards, often called "breadboard ends," are narrow boards that are secured at each end of a slab to help maintain the horizontal plane of the assembly. Their grain direction is always at right angles to that of the slab. End boards are worthwhile, but are often installed so they do more harm than good. A common attachment calls for forming a tongue on the end of the slab and a matching groove in the board. This design is okay, but using glue the full length of the connection locks all the parts together so the slab parts can't move; the board will maintain its length, but the center pieces will lack freedom to expand and contract due to seasonal changes.

The efficient way to join the components is to apply glue or to add pins at only the center

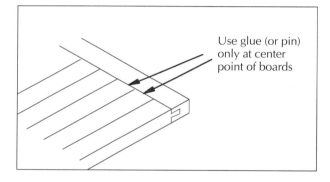

Use glue (or pin) only at center point of boards

Illus. 2-8. Don't glue end boards throughout their length. Glue only at the center point of the slab pieces.

DADOES

Dado Width

I've come to accept, as we all should, that the thickness of plywood, and even lumber, is often greater or less than indicated when you are buying it at the lumberyard. This becomes apparent, and frustrating, when you've formed a

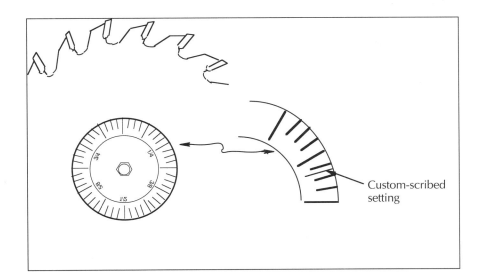

Illus. 2-9. Using a scriber to mark graduations when using a dado head on a table saw or radial arm saw.

½-inch dado or groove and discover that the panel is a bit thicker or thinner than the ½ inch you assumed it would be. The simple solutions are to check the thickness of the wood before cutting it and to make a test cut in scrap stock before cutting good material.

You can compensate for this discrepancy in thickness when using a dado head on a table or radial arm saw by using the paper or metal shims usually supplied with the head. Adjustable dado heads have a marked center hub that is rotated to widen or decrease their cutting widths. To help me work accurately and with minimum fuss, I identify the shims with a number so I can select the correct one for a particular cutting width. Also, since they are not vernier scales, I don't trust the settings on an adjustable dado head. Instead, I use a scriber to mark my own graduations when I'm sure the adjustments are correct (Illus. 2-9).

To avoid having to repeat test procedures, I keep a dado-width gauge like the one shown in Illus. 2-10. Each time I'm sure of a cut, I make one in the gauge and list the blades, chippers, and shims that I used, or note the graduation mark I scribed on an adjustable dado head. It

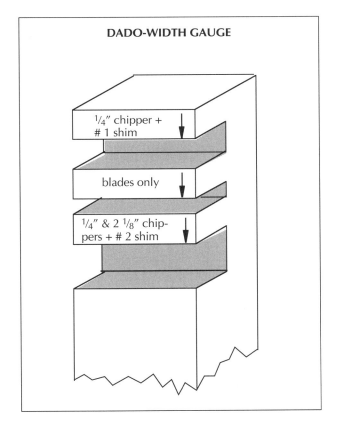

Illus. 2-10. A dado-width gauge provides the information that will help to eliminate the need to make repetitive test cuts.

eliminates trial and error and quickly helps me make the cut I want to make.

Making Back-to-Back Dadoes

Many projects require back-to-back dadoes. A typical example of such a project is a bookcase with intermediate partitions (partitions that are between the bookcase's sides). You can rely on careful layout to accomplish this task, but it's better to set up a mechanical means of ensuring the cuts will be truly aligned. The work can be guided along the rip fence, but tool capacity can limit the length of a piece you can work on. The jig that is detailed in Illus. 2-11 can be used to dado pieces of any length accurately.

The length of the jig parts is arbitrary,

although the distance between the bolts should be at least enough to accommodate a 12-inch board. The jig is secured along a line on the work that is marked with a square. Mating cuts are done simply by flipping the work and the jig as a unit.

Cutting Dadoes By Hand

The first step when hand-forming dadoes with a backsaw is to make a careful layout with a square, marking lines across the stock and down both edges. It's a good idea to mark one line with a square and then place the part that will be inserted on the line so it can be used as a guide for marking the second line. The two lines tell the exact width of cut that is needed, which is better than taking the thickness of the insert piece for granted.

Make the shoulder cuts first with the backsaw set up like the one being used in Illus. 2-12. The width of the strip of wood that is clamped

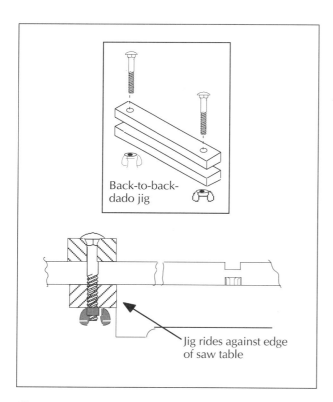

Back-to-back-dado jig

Jig rides against edge of saw table

Illus. 2-11. A jig you can make for accurately forming back-to-back dadoes.

Illus. 2-12. Using a backsaw to form the shoulders of a dado. The strip of wood that is clamped to the saw controls how deeply you can cut.

to the saw is determined by how deeply you want to cut. For example, if the width of the blade from the backsaw's spine to teeth is 3 inches and you need a dado ½ inch deep, then the strip of wood should be 2½ inches wide. The wood strip also aids in keeping the saw perpendicular to the work as sawing proceeds.

Use a chisel to remove the waste, cutting mostly toward the center of the board. Since the cutting action is cross-grain, the waste will be removed mostly in chunks rather than shavings (Illus. 2-13). Use the chisel almost horizontally, bevel side up, as you approach the bottom of the cut. Finish the joint with sandpaper wrapped around a suitable block of wood (Illus. 2-14), a block whose thickness equals the width of the dado. Use very fine sandpaper, since the idea is to smooth the dado, not widen it.

MORTISE-AND-TENON JOINT

The mortise-and-tenon joint (Illus. 2-15) is one of the classic wood joints. There are many variations, but the basic mortise-and-tenon joint is an integral projection (the tenon) on one part that slips into a square or rectangular cavity (the mortise) that is formed in the mating piece (Illus. 2-16).

The mortise-and-tenon joint is very strong and resists various types of stresses as long as vital factors are not overlooked, such as being sure there is enough wood around the tenon. A tenon that is too wide or thick, or a blind tenon that penetrates too deeply into the mortised part, can cause weak areas (Illus. 2-17).

Flaws can happen when forming a mortise near the end of a board, such as when attaching a rail or apron to a leg. It's wise to allow for some extra material at that point (sometimes called a "horn") to reinforce the area while the cavity is being made. The amount of extra material, which is removed later, isn't critical so long as it keeps the area from breaking as tools are applied. This preventive measure may not be so important when working with mortising bits and chisels, but it guards against breakage when you are chopping out a cavity with a mallet and chisels.

Illus. 2-13. Waste material between the shoulder cuts is removed with a chisel.

Illus. 2-14. The final cleaning of the dado is done with sandpaper wrapped around a suitable block of wood. Use very fine sandpaper to avoid widening the dado.

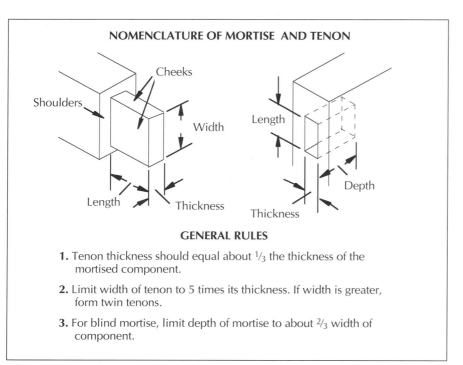

NOMENCLATURE OF MORTISE AND TENON

GENERAL RULES

1. Tenon thickness should equal about $1/3$ the thickness of the mortised component.

2. Limit width of tenon to 5 times its thickness. If width is greater, form twin tenons.

3. For blind mortise, limit depth of mortise to about $2/3$ width of component.

Illus. 2-15. Mortise-and-tenon-joint nomenclature.

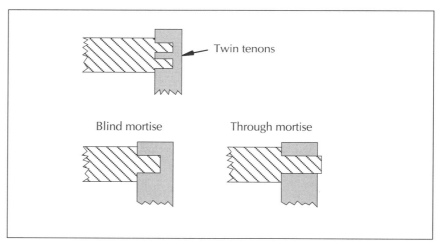

Illus. 2-16. Common types of mortise-and-tenon-joints.

When the parts are put together, the joint line is no more visible than if the components were simply butted together. To ensure that a hairline separation that might eventually happen will not be so obvious, the tenoned piece is often set back slightly. Another technique is to add a kerf (Illus. 2-18).

Always Make the Mortise First!

One rule to keep in mind when making mortise-and-tenon joints is to make the mortise first. There are woodworkers who feel this rule is too restrictive, but there are good reasons for following it. For one thing, redoing a mortise to fit a tenon is not an easy task, especially if

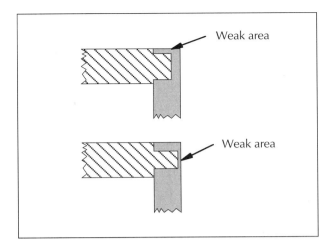

Illus. 2-17. Ignoring the rules that apply to sizes of tenons and mortises can result in weak areas. A tenon that is too wide or thick (top) or penetrates too deeply into the mortised part (bottom) can cause weak areas.

the cavity is too long or narrow. When cutting a mortise with a drill press (Illus. 2-19), the width of the cut is established, precisely, by the size of the square chisel that's used. In any event, it's more convenient, and easier, to adjust the size of tenons to suit the mortises, even if the latter are not exactly the size you planned.

Working on a drill press will produce flawless mortises if you avoid the possible blunders. For cutting efficiency and to avoid burn marks on the cutters and the work, the bit must be installed so there is a gap of $1/16$–$1/8$ inch between the end of the bit and the corners of the chisel. The angle between the side of the chisel and the fence must be 90 degrees. Signs that this has not been established are serrated edges and slanted ends on the mortise. Use the hold-down, and the hold-in if there is one, to keep the work firm while cutting.

It's good practice to make end cuts first and then remove the waste between them with a series of overlapping cuts (Illus. 2-20). Ideally the cuts should overlap from one half to one third of the chisel's width. This isn't always feasible, but stay as close as possible to these guidelines. The purpose of overlapping cuts is to prevent the chisel from slanting toward a cavity that's already formed.

Don't leave narrow shoulders if the mortise you need is wider than the largest chisel available. It's better to use a smaller chisel so overlapping can be done across the cut as well as along its length.

Illus. 2-18. Examples of mortise-and-tenon joints that are used when attaching rails or aprons to legs.

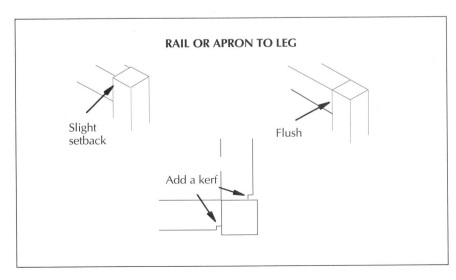

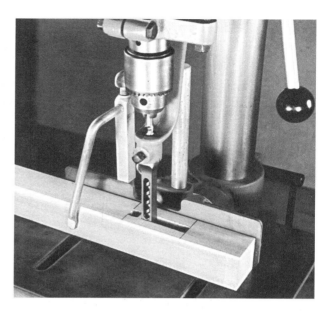

Illus. 2-20. Good practice calls for making end cuts first, and then cleaning out the waste by making a series of overlapping cuts.

Illus. 2-19. Standard drill-press mortising accessories. The width of the cut is determined by the square chisel that is used.

Always use a backup between the work and the fence when forming a side mortise so the chisel won't wander from where it should be (Illus. 2-21). When the width of the mortise is less than the size of the chisel, you can cut into the backup as well as the work.

Tenons

Forming tenons is usually a chore done on a table saw with a special jig that provides accuracy as well as safety. Often overlooked is that they can also be produced with a portable router.

Illus. 2-21. Use a backup between the work and the fence when forming side mortises. You can cut into both the work and the backup when necessary.

Since duplicate ones are often needed for a project (for example, rails and stretchers for a table or chair), I set up to form them in the "mass-production" fashion that is shown step-by-step in Illus. 2-22. It's one way to avoid the errors that can occur when parts are sawed individually.

Start with a piece of stock that is wide enough to accommodate the number of parts you need and cut it to correct length. If, for example, four parts that are 2 inches wide are needed, then the stock should be about 9 inches wide to allow for the saw cuts that will be made to separate the parent piece into individual parts.

The next step is demonstrated in Illus. 2-23. Equip the router with the largest straight bit on hand and guide it with a straightedge that is clamped to the work. The depth of the cut, which is made on both sides of the work, should leave a projection that provides the correct tenon thickness. In the example shown in Illus. 2-23, 1½-inch-thick material is being cut, and the cutting depth is ½ inch, so the thickness of the tenon will be ½ inch. Mark layout lines carefully on both surfaces so the straightedge will be positioned accurately for the back-to-back cuts.

When this phase of the routing is finished, the stock is sawed into correct-width components. If the tenon is for an open mortise-and-tenon joint, then the job is done. If a full tenon

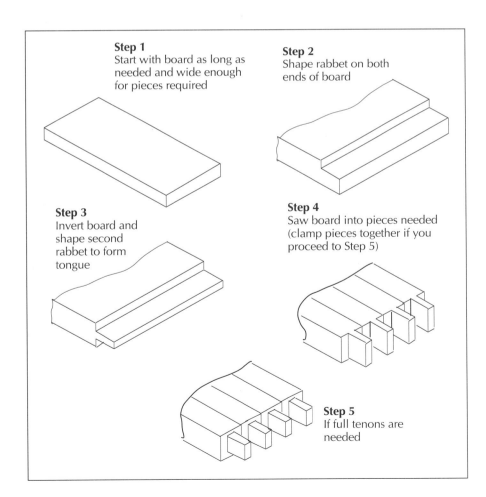

Step 1
Start with board as long as needed and wide enough for pieces required

Step 2
Shape rabbet on both ends of board

Step 3
Invert board and shape second rabbet to form tongue

Step 4
Saw board into pieces needed (clamp pieces together if you proceed to Step 5)

Step 5
If full tenons are needed

Illus. 2-22. The procedure to follow when forming multiple, similar tenons with a portable router.

Illus. 2-23. The first step is like forming back-to-back rabbets. Use the largest straight router bit that you own. Repeat passes are usually needed.

with four shoulders is intended, then the additional step shown in Illus. 2-24 must be taken. This is similar to the first phase of the operation. The separate pieces are clamped together or secured in a vise, and the routing is done as if the assembly were a solid piece of wood.

Illus. 2-24. This is the final step when full tenons are needed. Be careful when aligning and clamping the parts.

Like many other woodworking techniques, this system isn't foolproof. Success depends on careful work—placing the straightedge accurately for each cut, being sure of the router-bit projection, etc.

Saving Tenons

A tenon that is oversize in length, width, or thickness is easily saved by shaving or sawing off the offending material. If it is undersize in length, width, or thickness, it can be salvaged by gluing on thin veneer or patches cut from a scrap piece of similar material (Illus. 2-25). This works best when the grain direction of the additional pieces matches that of the tenon.

Using Wedges and Tusks

Wedges can be used to lock a tenon, but only if it's understood that they create a stress by spreading the tenon so it is forced against the ends of the mortise. This may not be so critical when the joint is at some midpoint so there is

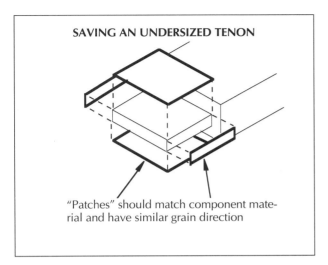

SAVING AN UNDERSIZED TENON

"Patches" should match component material and have similar grain direction

Illus. 2-25. Undersize tenons can often be saved by widening or thickening them with patches cut from scrap wood.

plenty of wood to back it up, but it can be damaging when the joint is at an end point (Illus. 2-26). Therefore, wedges must be sized to provide the locking feature without having to be muscled into place, and their width must match that of the tenon.

Tusks—whether wedge-shaped, round, or round with a flat surface—are often used as

shown in Illus. 2-27. If they are installed only as decorative details (that is, the joint is functional without them) and they just slip into place, there probably won't be a problem. But if they are used, as they often are, to pull the joint parts together, then the projecting part of the tenon must be strong and large enough to withstand the stresses. It's obvious that breakage will occur if a wedge is driven through a tenon that has very little material at its end.

A Dowel Lock

One way to lock a mortise-and-tenon joint without causing problems is to drill through it after it has been glued and held under clamp pressure and then tap a dowel through the hole. A second method, one that will pull the parts together, is shown in Illus. 2-28. Here, the holes for the dowel are drilled in each piece before the parts are joined, with one of the holes offset about $1/32$ inch. When the dowel is tapped into place, it will pull one part tightly against the other. Round off one end of the dowel so it will be easier to drive through the misaligned holes. In both cases, use a dowel that is slightly longer than needed so it can be sanded flush after the glue dries.

Illus. 2-26. Oversize wedges can add stresses the joint doesn't need.

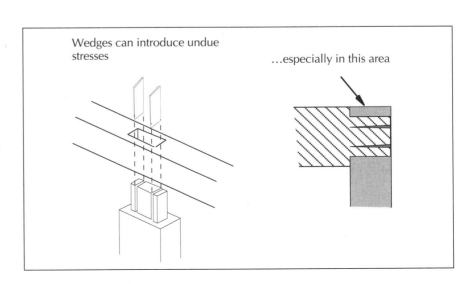

Wedges can introduce undue stresses

...especially in this area

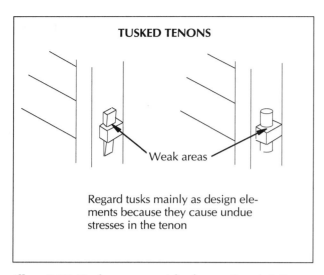

TUSKED TENONS

Weak areas

Regard tusks mainly as design elements because they cause undue stresses in the tenon

Illus. 2-27. Tusks can provide decorative details on particular projects, but they can also cause stress.

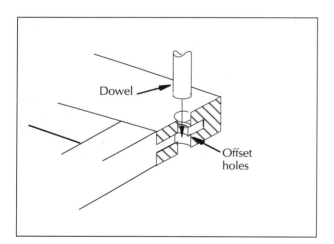

Dowel

Offset holes

Illus. 2-28. Locking a mortise-and-tenon joint with a dowel. The offset holes cause the dowel to pull one part tightly against the other.

Integral Round Tenons

Integral round tenons, which can be formed on round or square stock, make a stronger connection than a routine dowel joint. On square stock, first decide the length of the tenon and its diameter. Then form the shoulders of the tenon by making saw cuts on each side of the stock. The height of the saw blade is set so the cut is tangent to what will be the circumference of the tenon. The next step is to set up a drill press so a plug cutter can be used to form the cylinder (Illus. 2-29). If the piece's length allows, it can be set directly on the table and held securely, possibly with a hand-screw clamp that is, in turn, clamped to the table. When this can't be done, tilt the table 90 degrees so the piece can be clamped vertically.

If you have worked carefully, the waste part will be easy to remove to reveal the tenon (Illus.

Illus. 2-29. Using a plug cutter to form an integral, round tenon. Make sure the work is centered under the spindle and that it is securely clamped.

2-30). The plug cutters that are generally available will allow you to form tenons up to ½ inch in diameter and as long as 2 inches.

The same technique can be used to form integral tenons on dowels and rounds. In this case, it's best to make a jig that will hold the

Illus. 2-30. If the job is done correctly, the waste can be removed with little fuss.

cylinders snugly while the cutting is being done (Illus. 2-31). How long the work can be will depend on the capacity of the drill press, but you can improvise somewhat if you swing the table aside and use the base of the tool as a table. You can remove waste not removed by the plug cutter with a knife or chisel. Construction details for the jig are shown in Illus. 2-32.

Fixing a Round Tenon

When a round tenon is oversize, you can reduce its diameter by stroking it with a narrow strip of sandpaper; use the sandpaper like the shoe-polish rag. If it's undersize, it can be saved by wrapping thin veneer around it. Thin veneer can also be used to thicken a common tenon (Illus. 2-33).

Fitting a Square Part into a Round Part

How do you tailor the end of a square or rectangular component like a rail or stretcher to fit the contour of, say, a round leg? The shape can be rough-sawn on a band saw or scroll saw

Illus. 2-31. This jig is used to form integral tenons on dowels and larger rounds.

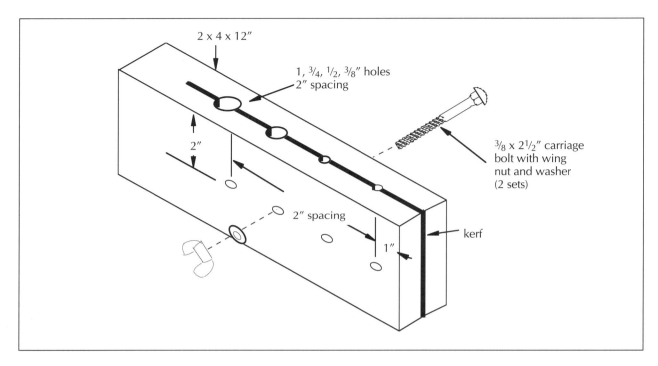

Illus. 2-32. Construction details for the jig shown in Illus. 2-31.

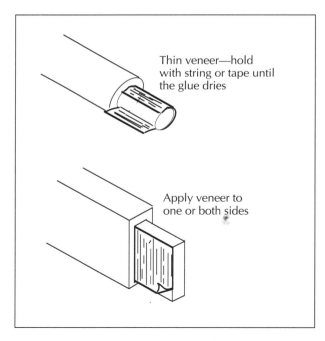

Illus. 2-33. Simple ways to salvage undersize tenons.

and then finished with files or rasps and sandpaper, but I do it in other ways that help me work faster and more accurately.

Assuming the leg to which I need to join the rail is 2 inches in diameter, I cut the rail a bit longer than needed and then use a two-inch hole saw to shape its ends (Illus. 2-34). This technique does waste some material, but not as much as some other methods that allow more room for error, and the connection between leg and rail needs very little trimming. The job must be done on a drill press with the work firmly clamped so its centerline is perfectly aligned with the saw's pilot drill.

I also do such work with Forstner bits, those great boring tools that can make partial cuts even when the center point is not contacting the work. Actually, Forstner bits allow more flexibility than hole saws since the arch that is formed can be varied depending on how the

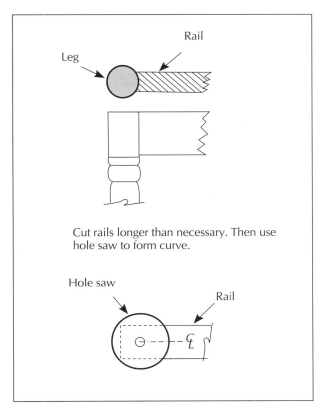

Cut rails longer than necessary. Then use hole saw to form curve.

Illus. 2-34. A hole saw can be used to form an arch that will fit against a round leg.

work is placed in relation to the bit (Illus. 2-35). Here, too, it is important that the work is placed for correct alignment with the cutter and is clamped firmly to the drill-press table. Incidentally, there are occasions when an off-center arch is suitable. Forstner bits, and sometimes hole saws, make it possible to cut an off-center arch with minimum fuss.

Any touch-up that is needed is quickly accomplished by working on an oscillating drum sander or simply by wrapping sandpaper around a suitably sized dowel.

Mortising "In the Round"

Sometimes mortises are required in round components. The operation does present some problems, and often a flat is formed on the leg in the area where the mortise must be cut. But many times using a flat may not be ideal for the design of the project. Actually, there's no reason why mortising can't be done in round stock in a straightforward manner and with accurate results. What is needed, and what I use, is a jig like the

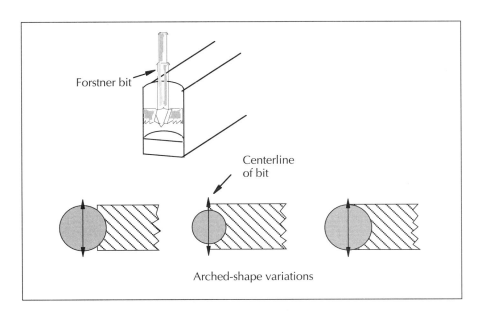

Arched-shape variations

Illus. 2-35. Forstner bits are ideal for forming arched shapes.

one that is shown set up in Illus. 2-36 and is detailed in Illus. 2-37.

The jig shown in Illus. 2-36 is on a stand that supports a hollow chisel mortiser, one of the tools that have recently become available at a price that makes them attractive to home woodworkers. While mine is bolted to the stand, there's no reason why the jig can't be treated as an independent unit and clamped to the table of a drill press where it can substitute for the regular mortising attachments.

There is an alternate way to make this V-block jig. Instead of forming a V down the center of a board, saw down the board's center with the saw blade set at 45 degrees. Then, flip one piece and attach both pieces to the base with glue and flathead screws. If nothing else, this method will result in a deeper V shape (Illus. 2-38).

To be sure that I set up the jig accurately, I made the gauge shown in Illus. 2-39. After I've determined, in the usual manner, that the chisel is square to the fence (by using a square to check the angle between the side of the chisel and the fence), I remove the fence and place the jig so the gauge is snug in the V while it "embraces" the chisel. This ensures that the chisel is square to an imaginary line across the V and that the bit is correctly positioned.

Operational procedures do not change if you use the alternate approach. The purpose of the jig is to act as a holding device so cylinders can be held securely and positioned correctly during the mortising operation (Illus. 2-40).

Another jig for gripping cylinders that is more like a portable vise is detailed in Illus. 2-41. This jig is practical to use with conventional drill-press mortising accessories, and it can serve other purposes. Guide it with a fence clamped to the drill-press table; you can drill through cylinders any number of holes that must be on a common centerline.

TO SPLINE OR NOT TO SPLINE

Splines are slim strips of wood set into matching grooves that are cut in the edges of pieces that will be joined together (Illus. 2-42). There is a

Illus. 2-36. A close-up of the jig I use to form mortises in round components.

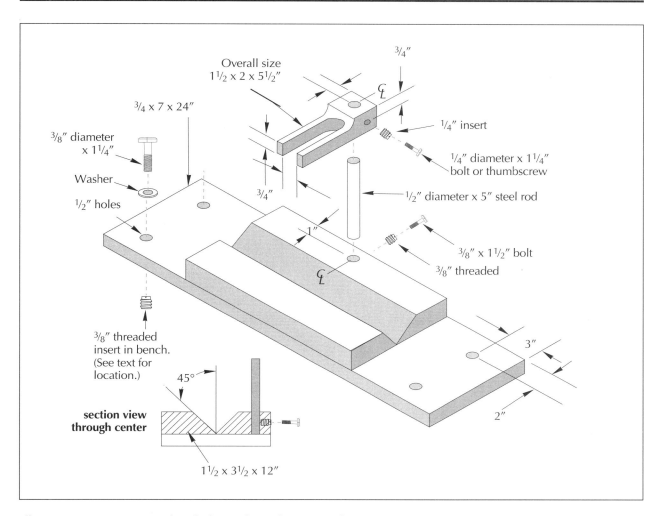

Illus. 2-37. Construction details for making the jig used to mortise in round stock.

great deal of debate as to whether splines provide reinforcement, and even as to whether they are more harmful than helpful. This mostly has to do with how the strength of a glue joint is affected by the grain direction of the parts being joined.

Since wood splits more easily along the grain than across it, a spline is strongest when the grain runs across its width. When used as such in a long-grain-to-long-grain edge joint, there is cross-grain-to-long-grain joining, which doesn't lead to an ideal connection and can contribute to

stresses since the joined parts will expand and contract at different rates. However, if the spline's grain is lengthwise, it will be compatible with that of the joined parts. The spline itself may not be very strong, but at least the joined parts will expand and contract at the same rate.

Whether the spline adds strength is questioned because it is argued that the additional piece is merely a filler for the grooves that were cut for it. We've already established that joining two edges that have been properly prepared and

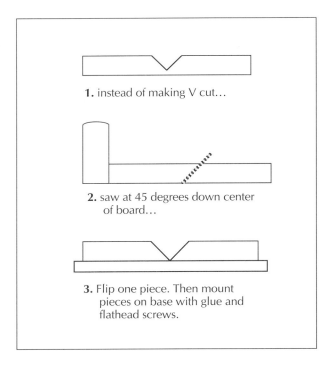

1. instead of making V cut…

2. saw at 45 degrees down center of board…

3. Flip one piece. Then mount pieces on base with glue and flathead screws.

Illus. 2-38. The V-block can be one piece, but it's easier to produce and will have a deeper V if it's made as shown here.

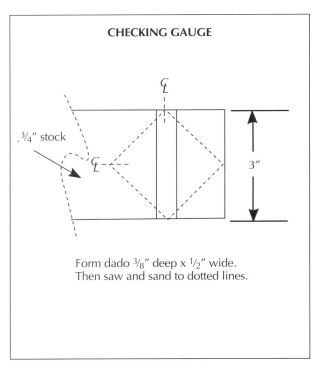

CHECKING GAUGE

3/4″ stock

3″

Form dado 3/8″ deep x 1/2″ wide. Then saw and sand to dotted lines.

Illus. 2-39. Construction details for the gauge I use to check the setup of the jig.

Illus. 2-40. The jig positions the work accurately; the hold-down keeps it steady. A strip of wood, tack-nailed across the V block, acts as a stop to gauge the length of the mortise.

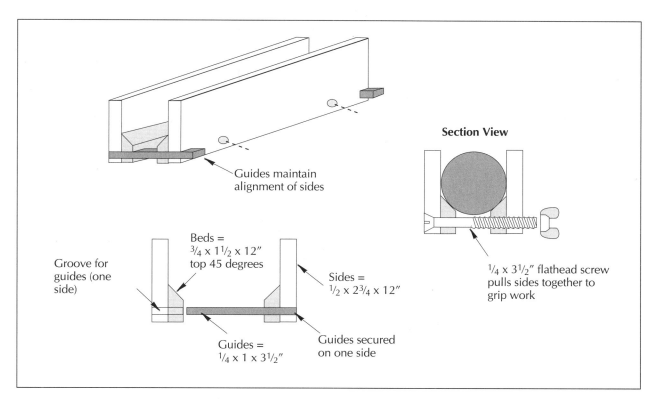

Section View

Guides maintain
alignment of sides

$^{1}/_{4}$ x $3^{1}/_{2}$″ flathead screw
pulls sides together to
grip work

Groove for
guides (one
side)

Beds =
$^{3}/_{4}$ x $1^{1}/_{2}$ x 12″
top 45 degrees

Sides =
$^{1}/_{2}$ x $2^{3}/_{4}$ x 12″

Guides =
$^{1}/_{4}$ x 1 x $3^{1}/_{2}$″

Guides secured
on one side

Illus. 2-41. Another type of jig that will secure round pieces. It works like a portable vise.

glued will result in a long-lived connection *without* reinforcement. It is contended by others, however, that the spline won't do harm if correctly installed and *will* provide positive alignment of components.

To minimize the problem of grain direction, splines are often cut from thin plywood or hardboard; plywood has multiple grain directions, and hardboard has no grain direction. These materials should not be used when joining boards end to end. In this, and similar cases, a cross-grain spline, preferably cut from the same material as the project, is, like dowels, perfectly acceptable.

It is also important that the spline slip nicely into the grooves cut for it. If it's too thin, it will be useless. If its too thick and must be forced into place, it immediately imposes stresses that

will cause problems. If it's too wide, the joint components won't come together. If they are forced together with clamp pressure, unnatural stresses are again created. It's also important that the grooves cut for splines be at right angles to the edge the spline will enter.

In the final analysis, two indisputable pluses for splines are that they help when assembling components, especially joints involving miters or bevels, and that they often solve alignment problems.

SECURING TOP SURFACES

A common mistake when fastening, say, a tabletop of solid lumber to the substructure, is to glue it in place or secure it around its perimeter with nails or screws. Forgetting that wood

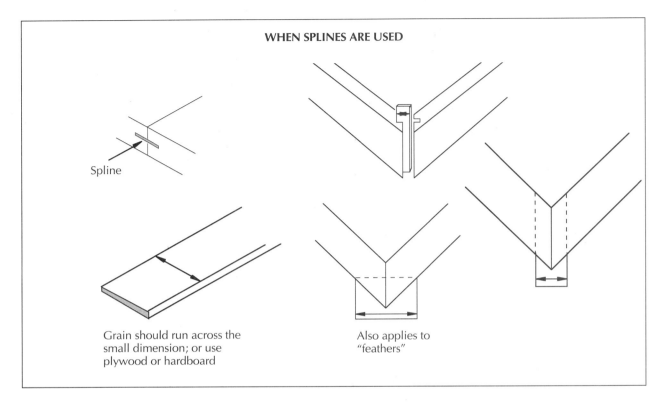

WHEN SPLINES ARE USED

Spline

Grain should run across the
small dimension; or use
plywood or hardboard

Also applies to
"feathers"

Illus. 2-42. Examples of how splines are used.

always moves and not allowing for its
inevitable expansion and contraction can result
in buckling and joint separation. For this reason,
the attachment methods shown in Illus. 2-43
should be followed.

Metal clips that are made for the purpose
are the easiest to install. A groove that receives
the bent end of the clip is cut around the inside
surface of the rails. The clips, spaced about 12
inches apart, are attached to the top with screws.

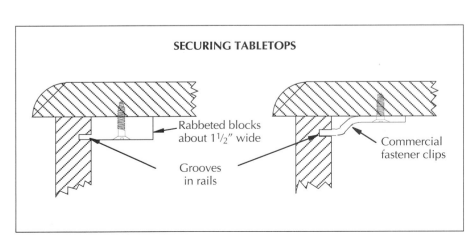

SECURING TABLETOPS

Rabbeted blocks
about 1½″ wide

Grooves
in rails

Commercial
fastener clips

Illus. 2-43. The tops of projects should be installed so
they can move.

Rabbeted blocks can substitute for the clips. Make them by forming the rabbet on a long strip of hardwood and then cutting off pieces about 1½ inches wide. The blocks can be square, but often, their front end is rounded so they can be rotated, and the top removed without having to remove the screws.

The same idea applies when securing a top to a case with a web frame, although it may be necessary to add strips of wood so the fastener can be seated securely (Illus. 2-44).

NO-MISTAKE MITERS

It is important that you use the correct miter angle when joining parts that are dissimilar in width. The method that establishes the cutting line can be seen in Illus. 2-45. Mark the width of the narrow piece across the end of the mating part. The first cut, on the wide piece, is made on a diagonal line that bisects the marked rectangle. The part is then used to mark a complementary cutting line on the narrow piece. When work like

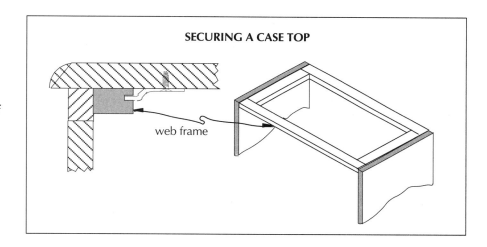

SECURING A CASE TOP

web frame

Illus. 2-44. One method of securing a top to a case.

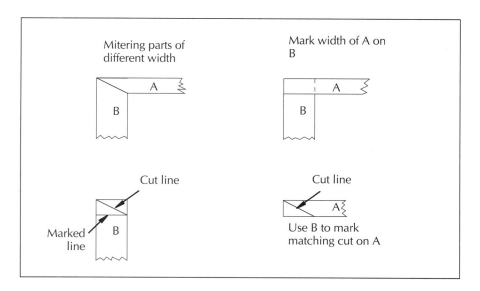

Mitering parts of different width

A

B

Mark width of A on B

A

B

Cut line

Marked line

B

Cut line

A

Use B to mark matching cut on A

Illus. 2-45. How to form an accurate miter when joining pieces of different widths.

this is done by hand or on a band saw or scroll saw, it's a good idea to cut slightly outside the line and trim the work on a belt or disc sander.

DOVETAILS

Ensuring Dovetail Accuracy

You can lay out the cutting lines for dovetails with a square and bevel, but working so increases the chances for error. It's better to make a marking template that can be used, instead of doing individual dovetail layouts. The one shown in Illus. 2-46 is just a rabbeted piece with slanted sides that suit the design of the dovetail. Although it is a specific size, there are still options since the spacing between layouts with the template can be variable.

The L-shaped template shown in Illus. 2-47 does more than help you saw accurately. When designed correctly, it will also serve as a cut-depth gauge, since the spine on the dovetail saw will act as a stop when it hits the top edge of the template.

A Dovetail Repair

It is not uncommon to make mistakes when hand-sawing dovetails, but it isn't always necessary to discard the wood unless the flaws are so extreme that salvaging isn't feasible. If the dovetail is a little less than perfect, glue it up anyway. When the glue is dry, use a dovetail saw or fine-tooth backsaw to cut a kerf along the botched area (Illus. 2-48). The kerf will be a uniform gap that you then fill by gluing in an oversize piece of thin veneer or wood. Allow the glue to dry before trimming and sanding the repair piece. Since the added part will show end grain and therefore be practically invisible, only a persnickety critic will point out the repair.

A BETTER PROCEDURE FOR STRAIGHT INLAYS

I became aware of a better way for making straight inlays while visiting a fellow wood-

Illus. 2-47. This type of template is also a guide for the saw when you are cutting dovetails. It can be made so it also acts as a stop to control the depth of the cut.

Illus. 2-46. Working with a template makes it easy to mark cutting lines for dovetail joints.

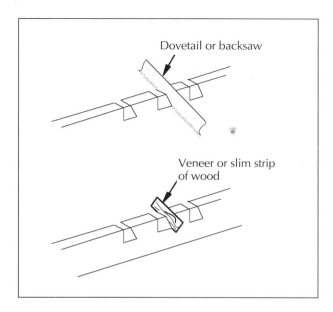

Illus. 2-48. An easy way to salvage less-than-perfect dovetail joints.

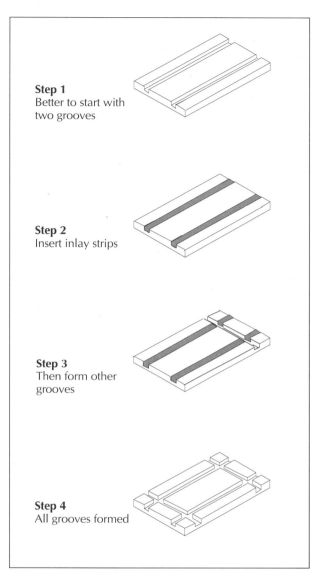

Illus. 2-49. A better way to form grooves for inlay strips.

worker who was forming grooves for inlay strips with a portable router. Using a router is fine, but, as I pointed out, making all four of the grooves first is wrong. Why? Because after the first long strips are put in place, the strips that cross them have to be custom-sized perfectly, a precision-cutting that isn't necessary.

An efficient procedure that guarantees accuracy with minimum fuss is to first form only two sets of grooves and, then, after they have been filled, do the final ones (Illus. 2-49 and 2-50). Now, the finishing inlays can be placed as long strips; they do not have to be cut to size, and the cross-point connections will be perfect.

GENERAL JOINT INFORMATION

Stresses on Joints

All joints are subject to stresses that tend to cause failure or separation (Illus. 2-51). Some joints fight stress from one direction, and others from various directions. Therefore, it's wise to have some idea about stress and joints, so you can determine not just what is the best joint to use, but also what is the easiest joint to make that will be adequate. Let's face it: Dovetail joints would be pretentious when you are making utilitarian storage units, say, for the garage,

Illus. 2-50. The final grooves are formed after the first ones are filled. Then, the last inlay strips can be installed as full pieces.

and simple butt joints won't be adequate when you are producing fine furniture.

It isn't difficult to understand the directions of stress if you view the project as a whole and accept its function. Let's consider the example of a drawer. Because a drawer is opened and closed countless times, there is much stress where the front is connected to the sides. The heavier the contents of the drawer, the larger the drawer is, and the greater the stress. That's why the dovetail joint is a prime candidate for the drawer front-to-sides connection. The sockets and tails of the joint form an interlock that holds components together and will continue to do so even if the glue should fail.

Drawer bottoms will fail if they are not installed to support what the drawer will con-

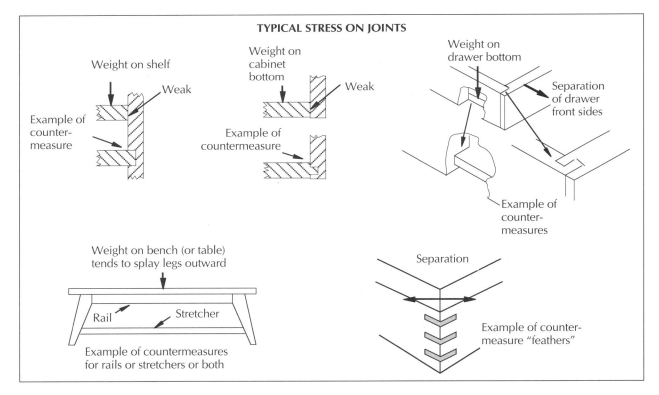

Illus. 2-51. Anticipating in which direction stress will be applied to joints will help you choose the best joint for a project.

tain. Inserting them in grooves cut into the sides and front (not necessarily the back) is a standard procedure that adds strength. The back of the drawer has to do more than stabilize the position of the sides; it must also withstand the stress exerted when the contents of the drawer slide to the rear. The butt joint that is frequently found in the back of the drawer is *not* the best joint to use. It is better to let the back into dadoes cut in the sides.

Why use complex joinery on a drawer with lightweight contents such as stamps or pencils? Obviously, stress will be minimal, not at all like what happens with a shop drawer that holds tools. One reason is because the builder desired such a joint. Another is the material being used. We can easily tolerate simple joints, reinforced with mechanical fasteners, when they are applied to shop-grade plywood, but we would be shocked if the same methods were used with species such as rosewood, walnut, or Honduras mahogany.

The major stress on a trestle-type project such as a sawhorse occurs when the project has to hold up weight. Even though there is an ample, sturdy connection between the beam and the legs, usually with bolts or lag screws, there is always the tendency for the legs to splay outward. The possibility of failure increases with use. A simple brace placed across the legs is an obvious countermeasure. To make the brace even more effective, it can be let into wide dadoes cut in the legs.

To some extent, this principle also applies to projects like tables and benches. Connections are least likely to fail if the legs are vertical, but stresses increase if the legs slant in any direction, so it's possible for joints to eventually loosen, especially if the project is a bench or a low table that people are apt to sit on. Countermeasures include rails (or aprons) and stretchers. If only rails

are used, it's preferable to install four of them so a top view of the leg-rail assembly would show a closed frame. Regardless of the design, consider the substructure as an individual project that will stand rigidly on its own. See the top as a platform, not as reinforcement. As we have indicated, tops should be attached to allow movement that can be caused by environmental changes.

In the final analysis, we invite joint failure when we don't consider what the component must do; for example, bear weight. A shelf that is simply butted against the side of a cabinet isn't likely to stay there too long. Insert the shelf in a dado cut into the side, and you can be reasonably sure it will stay put. If you attach the bottom of the cabinet by butting it against the sides or the bottom end of the sides, the joint there too will fail. Taking the time to use a tongue-and-groove joint in this location will prove to be wise insurance.

Joint Components Must Fit Together Tightly

Joint components that do not make maximum contact with each other will not result in strong bonds. No amount or type of glue can compensate for a sloppy fit. Carefully look over the contact areas of even a butt joint before assembling the joint. If you hold the parts together with a light in back of them and see slivers of light shining through the joint, one or both of the pieces requires further attention.

Joint components that do not fit together strongly without excessive clamp pressure or blows from a mallet can cause serious problems. An oversize tenon or tail in a dovetail joint subjects mating parts to unnecessary strain, which merely adds to stresses the joint must withstand. A dowel that fits too tightly and is not designed to allow air and excess glue to escape can cause splitting. It's not strange for excess glue, unable to escape as it should, to find its way through pores of the wood and to emerge on a surface where it forms a glaze that causes blemishes in the finish.

It's frustrating and discouraging to coat parts with glue and then discover they will not mate nicely even under clamp pressure. The simple answer is to work carefully so cuts will be accurate. Doing a dry run before final assembly isn't a bad idea, either. A dry run consists of assembling components without glue and with only hand pressure so you can check how they fit before assembling them permanently.

3

Power-Tool Alignment

You wouldn't drive an automobile whose front wheels choose to go in opposite directions, so why would you want to use power tools with misaligned parts? To get precise cuts from a machine, and to use it safely, it is critical to ensure that the relation between components is correct to start with and that this relation remains correct over time.

Instructions for power-tool alignments are often casually obeyed, because we're so eager to start using the tool, especially when it's new, just out of the box. There really can't be anything wrong with a tool that just arrived from the factory, we assume. We have to understand that ensuring that power tools are correctly aligned is essential for the economical use of wood, mistake-free woodworking, and quality production.

Following are alignment techniques for table saws, radial arm saws, jointers, band saws, and drill presses. Before proceeding with this information, please note that the Appendix on pages 197–213 contains troubleshooting charts for using table saws, jointers, radial arm saws, band saws, scroll saws, drill presses, shapers, lathes, and sanders.

TABLE SAW

The correct relationships between the components of a table saw are indicated in Illus. 3-1. These components are either correctly aligned, which is necessary for accuracy, or not, as you will discover when checking sawed pieces or assembling parts of a joint. The correct alignment of all these parts is based on the installation of the saw blade. *Remember, check any settings with the machine unplugged!*

The first step is to determine whether the miter-gauge slots in the table are parallel to the saw blade. A time-proven and easy way to do this is demonstrated in Illus. 3-2 and 3-3. Use the hole and the setscrew that are in the miter gauge to secure stop rods to grip a short length of steel rod. If this isn't feasible, just lock a length of rod to the miter gauge with a small clamp. Then, with the blade raised to its highest projection, position the rod so it barely touches a tooth at the forward edge of the blade. Rotate the blade so that the *same tooth* is at the rear of the machine, and move the miter gauge forward to see how the rod relates to the tooth in its new position. If the contact isn't exactly the same as

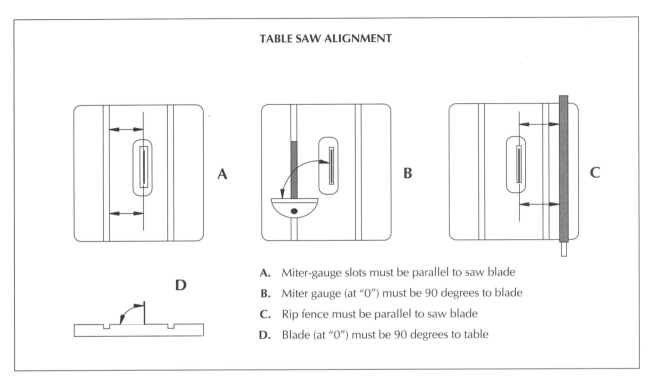

TABLE SAW ALIGNMENT

A. Miter-gauge slots must be parallel to saw blade

B. Miter gauge (at "0") must be 90 degrees to blade

C. Rip fence must be parallel to saw blade

D. Blade (at "0") must be 90 degrees to table

Illus. 3-1. Essential alignment factors that apply to the table saw.

Illus. 3-2. Shown here is the first step when checking that a table-saw blade is parallel to the miter-gauge slots. The rod should just barely touch a tooth at the front of the blade.

Illus. 3-3. The second step consists of rotating the blade by hand so the same tooth is at the back. Advance the miter gauge and see if the rod touches the tooth the same way it did in the first step.

it was at first, or if there is a space between the tooth and rod, the table needs to be adjusted slightly to bring it into correct position.

How you adjust the table will depend on the design of the machine, so check the owner's manual for the instructions. On my Delta Unisaw, the table is secured to the cabinet with a cap screw in each corner. By loosening them, I'm able to nudge the table one way or another until I'm certain that the blade is parallel to the miter-gauge slots (Illus. 3-4). At this stage, you can also make sure that the blade is in the center of the insert's slot and adjust the table if it is not.

The second alignment step consists of determining that the rip fence is parallel to the miter-gauge slots. When this is so, it will also be parallel to the saw blade. One way to adjust it is to place the fence close to a slot and then run the tips of your fingers along the bottom edge of the fence and the top of the slot, but this isn't reliable. A better way is to place one edge of a board with parallel sides against the saw blade and then bring the fence to bear against the opposite edge of the board. An easier way that is just as good is to place a strip of wood in the slot, and then move the fence against it (Illus. 3-5).

The rule of parallelism between fence and blade is often disregarded by some craftsmen who feel that it's good practice to have an offset at the rear of the blade so the "back" teeth of the blade will not scrape the wood after the "front" teeth have cut it. This offset, which must be fractions of an inch, can help to reduce roughness in the cut and minimize feathering, which is the slight lifting of surface fibers. This technique may apply when doing ripping opera-

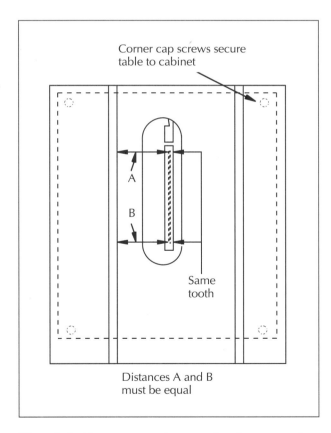

Corner cap screws secure table to cabinet

A

B

Same tooth

Distances A and B must be equal

Illus. 3-4. If necessary, loosen the fasteners that secure the table to the cabinet so the table can be nudged one way or the other until the blade and the miter-gauge slots are parallel to each other.

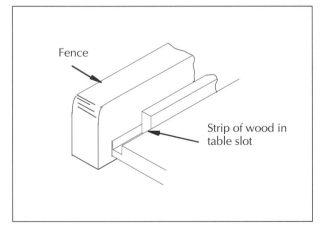

Fence

Strip of wood in table slot

Illus. 3-5. A simple way to set the rip fence so it is parallel to the miter-gauge slots. The wood must be as long as the fence and straight, but it does not have to be sized to precisely fit the slot.

tions, but it's not a good way to work when you are making a shoulder cut for a rabbet or forming a groove with a dadoing tool.

What you must be certain of, always, is that the distance between the back teeth and the fence is not *less* than that between the front teeth and the fence. This can cause the work to bind between the blade and the fence so it can be thrown back toward the operator (kickback).

The third alignment step consists of making sure the angle between the side of the saw blade and the table is 90 degrees before you do routine crosscutting, mitering, and ripping. If it isn't, cut edges will not be square to adjacent surfaces. A simple way to determine that the blade and table are at the correct angle is to raise the blade to its highest point and then use a square to check the angle. But, often, the blade's teeth prevent you from placing the blade of the square flush against the side of the blade. Often, it's necessary to provide some light in the background so you can make sure the parts are flush by using your eyes.

Illus. 3-6 shows a gauge that can be a standby checking tool. It must be carefully made with wood such as hard maple or birch that will withstand use. It has a notch at the top that allows the bearing edge of the gauge to bear fully against the blade without interference from the teeth.

Illus. 3-7 shows my own gauge based on the one just described. Its long base provides stability, and the open area between contact points provides good visibility. Construction details for this tool are shown in Illus. 3-8. It is important that the nails on this gauge fit snugly and project an equal distance.

The fourth alignment step when preparing for normal crosscutting is to ensure that the angle between the head of the miter gauge and the side of the saw blade is 90 degrees. If it isn't, the cut edge will not be square to the work's edges. Checking is often done with a square, but, again, the blade's teeth can interfere when you try to set the square's blade flush against the saw blade. Illus. 3-9 offers a practi-

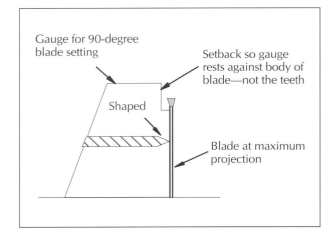

Illus. 3-6. A shop-made gauge can be used to check the angle between the table's surface and the side of the blade. Making it as shown prevents interference from the blade's teeth.

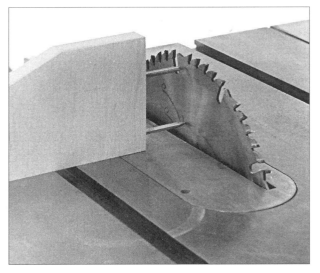

Illus. 3-7. A gauge like this is easy to use because the contact points are easily seen.

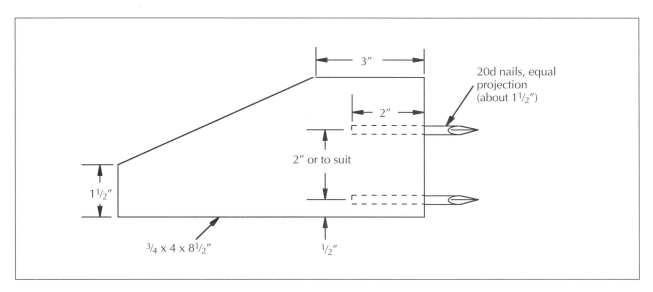

Illus. 3-8. Construction details for making the gauge shown in the previous illustration. Seat the nails snugly, and be certain they project the same distance.

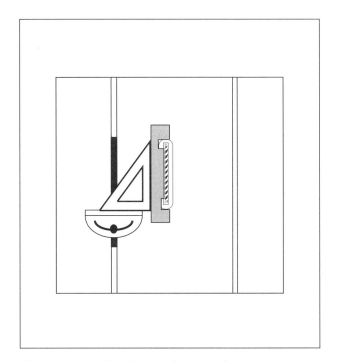

Illus. 3-9. Checking the 90-degree settings between a miter gauge and a saw blade. A strip of wood, made and used as shown, prevents interference from the blade's teeth.

cal solution. Prepare a piece of hardwood so it has parallel sides and then modify it as shown so it will fit snugly against the side of the blade without hitting the teeth. Then, use a square or a draftsman's triangle to adjust the head of the miter gauge.

Making an occasional check on the work itself as you go is good practice. After you make a crosscut, flip the cutoff and hold it against the parent piece. If the parts don't mate, you'll know the miter-gauge setting needs attention (Illus. 3-10). It's also wise when crosscutting to use a square to mark the cutting line. If the blade doesn't follow the line as you cut, it's probably the setting of the miter gauge that requires attention.

Cutting Miters

There are no two ways about it: miter cutting can be one of the more frustrating woodworking chores. There's no problem with the actual sawing, but the cuts must be precise.

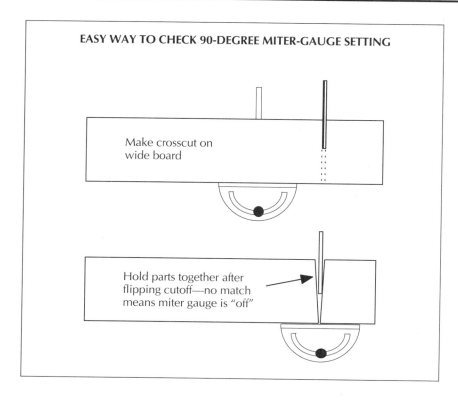

EASY WAY TO CHECK 90-DEGREE MITER-GAUGE SETTING

Make crosscut on wide board

Hold parts together after flipping cutoff—no match means miter gauge is "off"

Illus. 3-10. An easy way to check crosscuts as you make them.

Otherwise, you will waste wood or have to resort to patching when joining the parts. If you are the least bit off when making the cut, the cut edges will come together nicely, but they will not form, say, the 90-degree corner that is the goal. Multiply the error by eight and you can preview what results on assembly when trying to join four frame parts, each of which was inaccurately cut at each end. This can be discouraging and frustrating on constructions that range from picture frames to case goods to face frames. The solution is simple: know the pitfalls and work with precision to avoid them.

Cuts other than those made at 90 degrees are accomplished by rotating the head of the miter gauge and locking it at a particular angle setting. It's a mistake to rely solely on the graduations of the semicircular scale, or even on the stops that might be part of the miter gauge's design. A bevel can be used to set the gauge for not-so-com-mon angles, and then used again to check the cut. For more commonly needed angles like 30, 45, and 60 degrees, draftsman's triangles, equipped as shown in Illus. 3-11, can be used. The idea is to form a kerf in a strip of wood that will provide a snug fit for the triangle, and then to size the strip so it fits snugly in the table slots. This allows the triangles to be flipped, and adapts them for use on either side of the saw blade.

There is another insidious problem that we call "creep" that can interfere with accuracy when sawing miters. The blade, in effect, opposes the forward movement of the work-piece and miter gauge and tends to move the work along the face of the miter gauge. Additionally, there can be a pivoting action at the point where the work meets the inside edge of the gauge. Therefore, it is mandatory that you hold the work firmly against the head of the miter gauge throughout the pass.

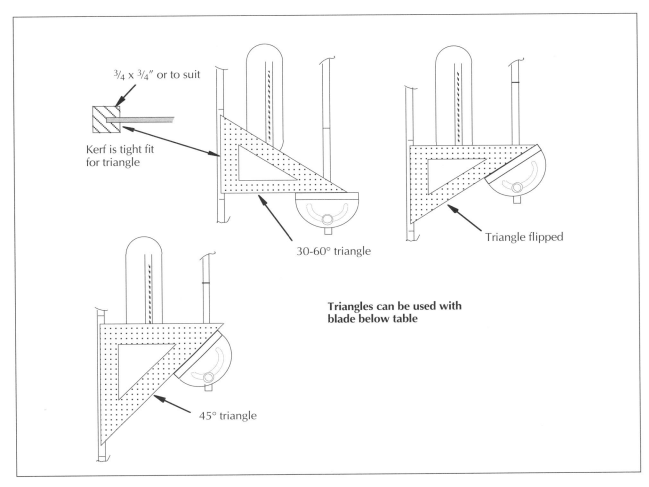

³/₄ x ³/₄″ or to suit

Kerf is tight fit
for triangle

30-60° triangle

Triangle flipped

**Triangles can be used with
blade below table**

45° triangle

Illus. 3-11. Using draftsman's triangles to check miter-gauge settings. The triangle is held tightly in a strip of wood that fits the table slot.

A countermeasure that is easy to provide is an extension that is secured to the miter gauge so there will be considerably more bearing surface for the work. Holes are provided in the head of the gauge so screws can be used for just such a purpose. Attaching medium-grit sandpaper to the face of the miter-gauge extension will provide an additional advantage (Illus. 3-12).

Always mark the cutting line on the work so you can judge accuracy as you cut. Illus. 3-13 suggests a way to check the miter-gauge setting as you make the cut. Flip the cutoff, or compo-nent if you are sawing consecutively along a length of stock, and determine if the pieces form the angular corner you need.

There are other ways to ensure accuracy of miter cuts, but we will talk about them in another section.

Setup Gauges

Many craftsmen make permanent gauges that provide accuracy with minimum fuss when they are used to establish the angular relation-

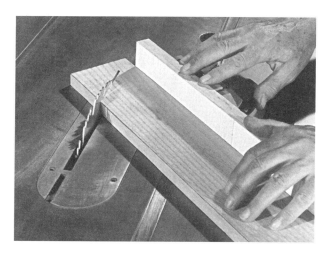

Illus. 3-12. A miter-gauge extension with sandpaper attached to its face can ensure accurate miter sawing. Keep the work snug against the extension through the entire cut.

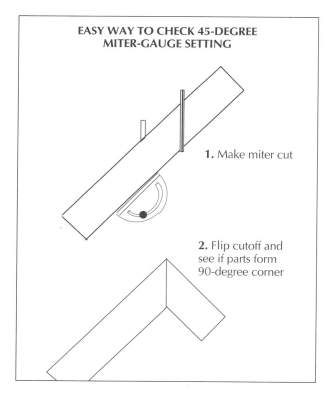

EASY WAY TO CHECK 45-DEGREE MITER-GAUGE SETTING

1. Make miter cut

2. Flip cutoff and see if parts form 90-degree corner

Illus. 3-13. How to check the accuracy of a 45-degree miter cut as you make the cut.

ship between saw blade and miter gauge (Illus. 3-14 and 3-15). Needless to say, the gauges will be used successfully only if they are carefully made of durable hardwood and maintained as precision instruments. It is also important that the blade that will be used for mitering is the one used for forming the control kerfs. The gauges will not be accurate if a blade that forms a thinner or thicker kerf is substituted. In use, the gauge is placed so the saw blade is in the correct kerf, and then the miter gauge is adjusted against the bearing edge of the setup gauge.

Kerf

The kerf is the slot that is formed by the saw blade. It's width is determined by the "spread" of the blade's teeth, and must be greater than the gauge of the disc on whose perimeter teeth are attached or formed (Illus. 3-16). Actually, only the teeth touch the wood. The kerf provides relief for the disc, eliminating friction that can cause burn marks on the workpiece or blade, and making it easier to feed stock without forcing it.

To ensure cutting accuracy and prevent dangerous kickbacks, the kerf must be kept open *after* the work has passed the saw blade. *Splitters* keep the work open. Most times, they are part of the guard that is supplied with the table saw, but too often they are flimsy and difficult to keep aligned with the saw blade. There are some operations in which it is necessary to work without the guard. In these cases, the splitter is obviously also not available for use. However, there are solutions, like making a special one. Never work without a splitter.

The splitter I made for my table saw is shown mounted to the saw in Illus. 3-17. It works nicely because its rigidity is maintained by bolts inside and outside the saw. The design may not be right for you, but if you check the details in Illus. 3-18, you may find it can be

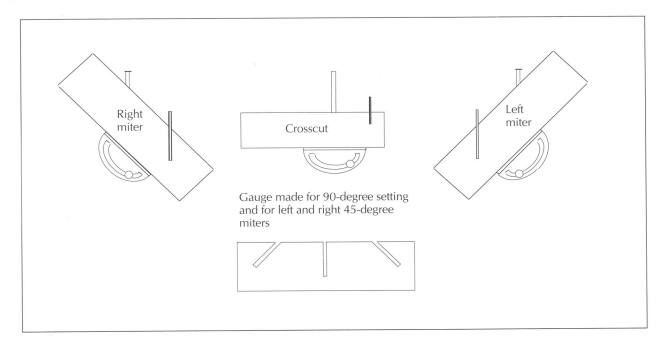

Illus. 3-14. Typical gauges used to establish miter-gauge settings.

modified to suit the machine you work on.

Another option is to provide a special table insert with an integral splitter to use in place of the standard insert (Illus. 3-19). Use the standard insert to mark a piece of hardwood or hardboard whose width and thickness matches

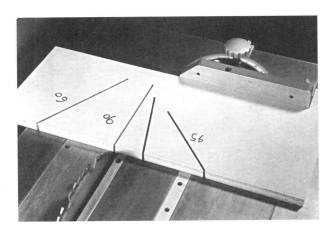

Illus. 3-15. Setup gauges must be made precisely. Note that this one has an L-shaped notch to fit the miter gauge. This is done before the guide kerfs are cut.

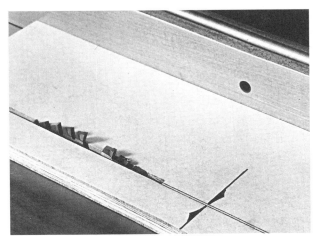

Illus. 3-16. The kerf that is formed by the blade. Its width is determined by the teeth, not the gauge of the blade.

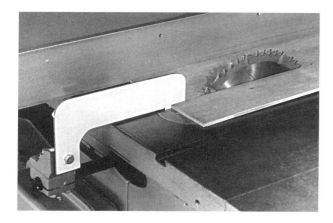

Illus. 3-17. A splitter, like this shop-made one, keeps the kerf open as the wood passes the blade.

as the splitter. It's important for the new insert to fit snugly in the table opening. Imitate the method of installation for the regular insert if it is held with screws.

The thickness of the splitter, must match the width of the kerf made by the saw blade. Round off or taper its forward edge a bit so the sawed wood can easily get by. Also, keep the splitter smooth. Achieve this by first brushing or wiping on several coats of sanding sealer, with a light sanding between coats and after the final one. Then, apply paste wax generously and rub it to a polish.

Hold-Downs and Other Cutting Aids

Inaccurate cuts and sawed edges that are less than perfect can happen even when the table saw is properly aligned. There are reasons for this. A slight distortion in the wood can cause it to move away from the rip fence, thin material can "chatter" as it is moved past the blade, the

that of the insert. Illus. 3-19 shows the piece as longer than the regular insert, but that's only so you can form the kerf without getting your fingers close to the blade. After shaping the new insert, glue a length of hardwood into it to serve

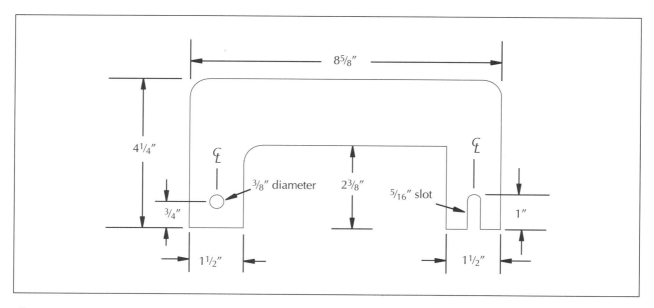

Illus. 3-18. The construction details for a custom-made splitter. This one fits a Unisaw, but it can be modified to suit other machines.

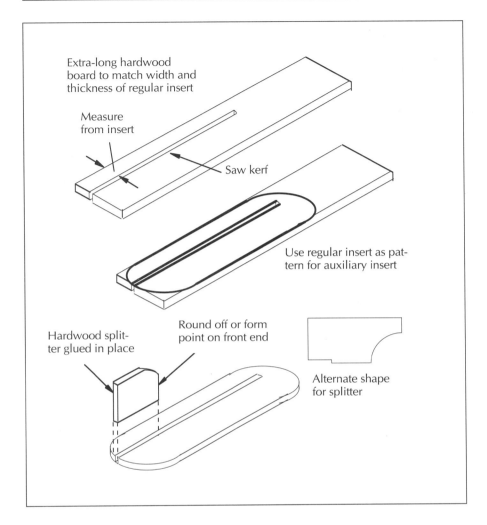

Extra-long hardwood board to match width and thickness of regular insert

Measure from insert

Saw kerf

Use regular insert as pattern for auxiliary insert

Hardwood splitter glued in place

Round off or form point on front end

Alternate shape for splitter

Illus. 3-19. Another way to provide a splitter. This splitter is an integral part of an insert that is used in place of the one supplied with the tool.

bottom of a dado or groove can be uneven because the dadoing blade has lifted the work, or perhaps the work was not kept in the correct position while the cut was being made. The use of accessories that act as extra hands is the way to avoid such errors.

The miter gauge hold-down shown in Illus. 3-20 and the spring-type unit shown in Illus. 3-21 are examples of what is available commercially. There are many other hold-downs with different designs. Some are easy to mount and use, others require setup time that becomes a nuisance. Most workshops have shop-made miter gauge hold-downs that aren't difficult to make. One of the mainstays for my ripping operations is a semicircular, hardwood hold-down that is bolted in place through holes in the rip fence (Illus. 3-22). If this type of mounting is not feasible, the hold-down can be set on an arm that is clamped to the fence (Illus. 3-23). A carriage bolt is used when the hold-down attaches directly to the fence; a flathead bolt is needed when the unit is secured to a clamp arm (Illus. 3-24).

As often happens, an accessory made for one purpose also serves another. In this case, if the

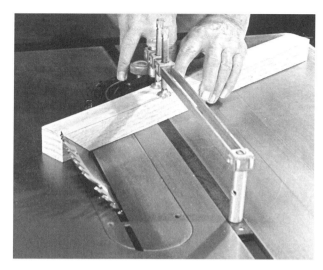

Illus. 3-20. A commercial miter gauge hold-down. This one will grip wide and narrow stock. There are other designs.

Illus. 3-22. This semicircular hold-down is slotted so it can be adjusted to suit the thickness of the stock.

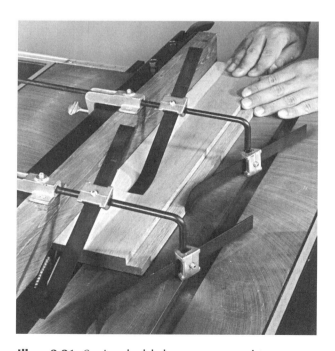

Illus. 3-21. Spring hold-downs are used to secure stock when ripping, and for other cuts that require guidance from the fence. Note that in this case the hold-downs are secured to a wood facing that is clamped to the rip fence.

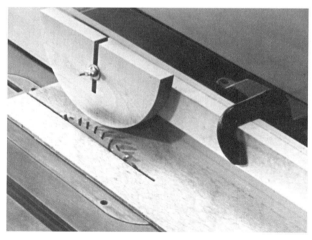

Illus. 3-23. If the rip fence lacks holes, the hold-down can be secured to a wooden bar that is clamped to the fence.

hold-down is placed as demonstrated in Illus. 3-25, it serves as a stop to gauge length when multiple, similar parts are required. The dimension for the parts is established between the blade and the surface of the stop. Since this is less than the

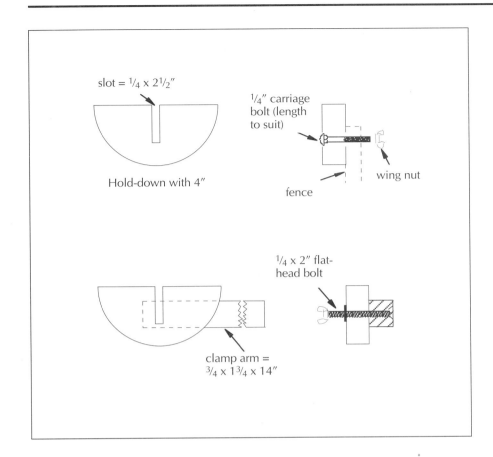

slot = ¼ × 2½″

Hold-down with 4″

¼″ carriage bolt (length to suit)

fence

wing nut

¼ × 2″ flat-head bolt

clamp arm = ¾ × 1¾ × 14″

Illus. 3-24. How to make the hold-down shown in Illus. 3-22 and 3-23. It may be attached to the fence or to a clamp arm.

distance between the blade and rip fence, the cut-offs will be free when they pass the blade, which is an essential safety factor!

The items that are detailed in Illus. 3-26 have various names—push sticks, spring sticks, fingerboards, feather boards—but their names are immaterial. What is important is the job they do as hold-downs, depending on how they are positioned and clamped. Actually, the sizes and shapes shown in the drawing are just examples of how these accessories can be made. They can be wide or narrow, long or short, and made of soft or hard wood. Often, it is the size of the tool they will be used on that affects how long they should be. The important detail is that the fingers are narrow and long enough, and spaced so they provide some spring action.

Illus. 3-25. The hold-down can also be used as a stop for gauging the length of multiple, similar pieces. Always place it well in front of the saw blade.

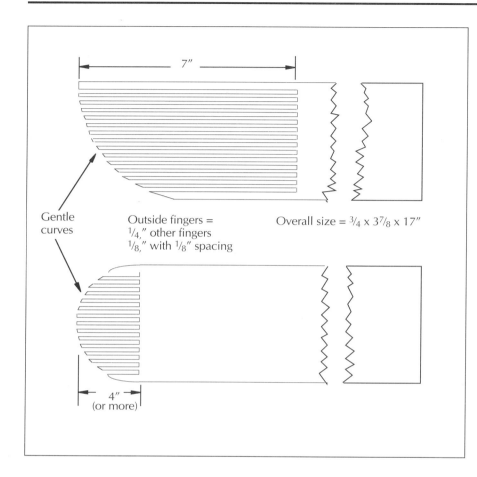

Gentle curves

Outside fingers = $1/4$," other fingers $1/8$," with $1/8$" spacing

Overall size = $3/4$ x $37/8$ x 17"

7"

4" (or more)

Illus. 3-26. Typical spring sticks. Their length is arbitrary. Often, their length can be determined by the size of the machine they will be used on, and what they will be used for.

A typical application of such an accessory can be viewed in Illus. 3-27, where one is used to provide pressure that keeps the work against the fence during a rip cut. The setup, which also includes a hold-down and splitter, may seem a bit much, but that length of plywood, being held *down* on the table, snug *against* the fence, and with the kerf held *open,* will be cut exactly the way I want it to be.

Illus. 3-28 and 3-29 show other practical uses for spring sticks. In all cases, the accessory is positioned to bear against the work at the front of the saw blade or other cutting tool being used. Do not put pressure against the side of the blade except when the workpiece is long and a spring stick is used as a hold-down. In

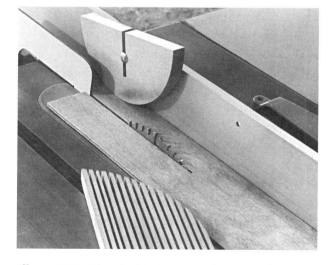

Illus. 3-27. The hold-down, splitter, and spring stick all contribute to a perfect rip cut.

Illus. 3-28. This spring stick is serving as a hold-in to keep the work against the fence as the cut is made.

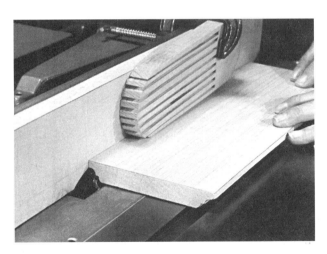

Illus. 3-29. A spring stick being used as a hold-down.

that case, spring pressure, being just downward on the table, is not going to interfere with the action of the cutting tool.

Often, it's wise to make a special setup to be sure that workpieces are held securely and will be cut accurately. To describe all possible situations would alone require a good-size book, but here's one example. I needed numerous pieces of slim molding and chose not to go through the procedure of molding the shape on the edge of a wide board, ripping off the part I needed, and then repeating the steps the number of times required—a tedious process and prone to errors. Instead, I cut strips to size and fed them through the jig that is shown set up in Illus. 3-30. The front piece, rabbet-cut to provide the correct opening, and a backup piece are clamped to the fence. They supply all the holding action that is needed and encase the cutting tool so there's no danger. The precut pieces are fed in one end and pulled out the other. Similar setups are usable for jobs such as resawing or forming grooves in slim pieces of wood.

Cutter Height

The projection of the saw blade above the table is not important when you are doing routine sawing just as long as it is above the work, but

Illus. 3-30. The jig I made so I can shape precut strips accurately and safely. Individual strips can be cut to the correct lengths, or a long strip can be shaped and then cut into individual pieces.

when you are forming grooves or dadoes or making shoulder cuts for rabbets and tenons, the height of the cutting tool must be exact. Using a measuring tape or even a square can lead to errors since it isn't easy to align the tip of a saw tooth with the correct graduation mark. Using a gauge is a more professional way to work.

A plan for a gauge that is easy to make and can provide accuracy is offered in Illus. 3-31. One-eighth-inch-thick tempered hardboard, smooth on both surfaces, is a good material to use. Start with the top layer, making it long enough to provide ample span across the table's insert. The length of the first piece dictates how the other layers must be cut. Illus. 3-31 suggests a setback of $\frac{1}{4}$ inch, but there is no reason why it can't be increased to $\frac{3}{8}$ or $\frac{1}{2}$ inch. The layers can be assembled with glue, but be very careful, since adding thickness between layers destroys the purpose of the

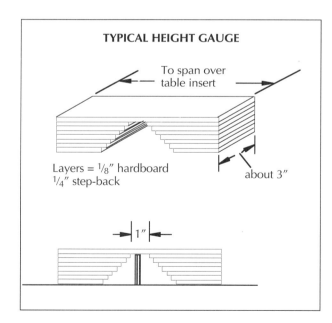

Illus. 3-31. An easy-to-make height gauge. The one-inch spacing is needed so the gauge can be used with dadoing tools as well as saw blades.

gauge. Tiny brads or a spray adhesive that supplies a fine film will work nicely.

If you would prefer a more sophisticated height gauge, refer to the gauge shown in Illus. 3-32 and 3-33. If you make this version, start by cutting the body to precise size, and then form the $\frac{1}{4}$-inch-wide by $\frac{3}{8}$-inch-deep dado at each end. The top block and the base have tongues to fit the dadoes. These are small pieces, so it's best to form the tongues on a piece of stock that is long enough for safe handling and then saw off what is needed.

The opening in the top block that the beam passes through can be formed with mortising equipment, but if that equipment is not available, drill a $\frac{1}{2}$-inch hole and then square the corners with a file or chisel. Attach the top block and the base to the body with glue. Prepare the beam, which should fit snug in the square hole, and the spacer, and put them together with glue.

Cut the sheet-metal pointer and, after smoothing its edges, attach it to the beam with epoxy glue. Thin, rigid plastic instead of metal can be used for the pointer. An easy way to supply the graduations for the beam is to cut a 6-inch strip from a length of self-adhesive measuring tape. A piece cut from a thin, plastic rule will also do.

Gauges For Making Joints

Many shop-made gauges will help make consistently accurate cuts for joints. For example, when making tenon and rabbet cuts, you can do the following: Set the height of the saw blade and its distance from the fence for the shoulder cuts. Then, after doing a test cut to ensure accuracy, make the cut in a piece of hardwood and save it for future use. Such gauges can be made to set the tilt angle of the saw blade as well as its height (Illus. 3-34).

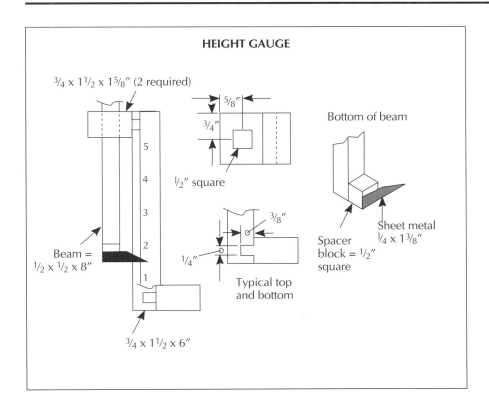

HEIGHT GAUGE

³/₄ x 1¹/₂ x 1⁵/₈" (2 required)

5/₈"

³/₄"

¹/₂" square

Bottom of beam

5

4

3

2

1

Beam =
¹/₂ x ¹/₂ x 8"

³/₈"

¹/₄"

Spacer
block = ¹/₂"
square

Sheet metal
¹/₄ x 1³/₈"

Typical top
and bottom

³/₄ x 1¹/₂ x 6"

Illus. 3-32. A more-sophisticated height gauge. Size the beam so it will slide through the square hole without wobbling.

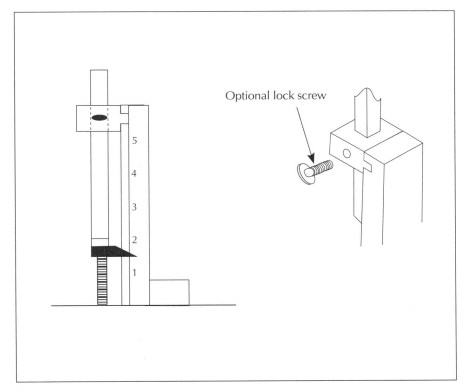

Optional lock screw

5

4

3

2

1

Illus. 3-33. Place the gauge in position, and then raise the cutting tool until the pointer indicates the correct graduation. A lock screw can be added by using it as a tap to form threads in an undersized hole drilled in the block.

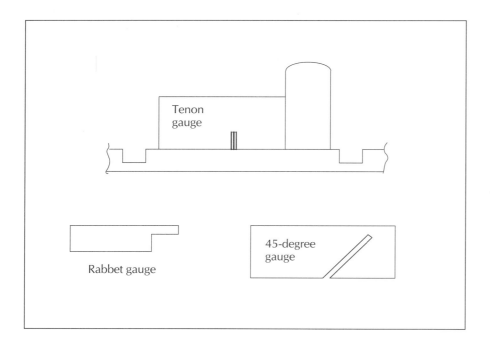

Tenon gauge

Rabbet gauge

45-degree gauge

Illus. 3-34. Gauges like this make it easy to set up for repetitive cuts. Store them for possible future use even if you made them especially for the project you are working on.

Preventing Mental Mistakes When Using a Table Saw

Mental mistakes are the easiest to avoid, yet they occur too often. No amount of learning or increase in expertise can compensate for neglecting to give proper attention to the chore on hand. Sawing on the wrong side of a line, and similar mistakes, are caused because you were thinking of how you almost broke par or the size of the last fish you caught. A crosscut line may be correct, but if you line it up with the *outside* of the blade, the board will be shorter by the width of the kerf. Measure from the outside of the blade to the rip fence and the board will be narrower than it should be.

Being preoccupied can cause errors even when dimensions have been checked and rechecked, and it can interfere with working safely. Actually, some of the rules established for safe woodworking also apply for doing accurate woodworking. Always be alert. Pay maximum attention to the work you are doing and the tool you are using. Don't work in the shop when you are tired or after you have taken medication or an alcoholic drink. The workshop is not a place for socializing. Using tools and entertaining visitors is a bad combination.

RADIAL ARM SAW

Alignment procedures for radial arm saws differ somewhat from those for table saws because the radial arm saw is designed differently. The blade on the radial arm saw is above the table instead of under it, and there are no table slots, miter gauge, or rip fence. On a radial arm saw, you have to check the swing and elevation of the arm, the vertical and horizontal pivoting action of the motor on whose arbor the saw blade is mounted, and the travel of the motor along the arm, to name a few procedures. How adjustments are made and secured varies from radial arm saw to radial arm saw, so it is important to obey the advice in the owner's manual. As always, verify the correct relationships of the parts the first time you use the tool and periodically thereafter. Also, check the alignment of certain parts as you undergo the pertinent woodworking procedure, as suggested when using a table saw.

A first step when checking the alignment of any radial arm saw is to be sure the surface of the table is parallel with the horizontal plane of the arm (Illus. 3-35). A procedure that applies to all saws is as follows: Raise the arm to a high point and then tilt the motor (without guard or blade) until the arbor is 90 degrees to the table. Place a small block of wood on the table and lower the arm until the arbor barely touches the block. Then, swing the arm and move the motor to and fro while using the test block at various points on the table to see if there is any variation in the height of the arbor above the table. If the block is forced against the table, or there is obvious clearance between the arbor and the block, the table must be adjusted. Usually, this a matter of resetting screws or bolts that secure the table to the subbase. A good way to work is

to find the table's highest point as close to an adjustment screw as possible and to use that area as a benchmark for the rest of the table.

An important safety factor when setting up the machine is to be sure the table is either level or tilts toward the back a degree or two. If it tilts to the front, the motor and blade might travel toward the operator.

Saw-Blade Travel

The path of the blade when it makes crosscuts must be 90 degrees to the guide fence. An easy, practical method for checking it is shown in Illus. 3-36. Place one leg of a square, prefer-

Illus. 3-36. Using a square to check the crosscut travel of the blade on a radial arm saw.

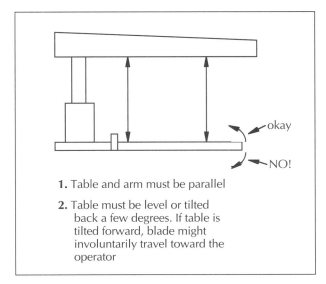

1. Table and arm must be parallel

2. Table must be level or tilted back a few degrees. If table is tilted forward, blade might involuntarily travel toward the operator

Illus. 3-35. The arm and table surface of a radial arm saw must be parallel to each other. Be certain the machine does not have a forward tilt.

ably a large one, snugly against the guide fence and positioned so the other leg is in line with the saw cut in the fence. Pull the blade through its full crosscut travel and judge whether its movement is parallel to the square. Corrective measures, as will be explained in the owner's manual, are in order if the blade scrapes unduly against the square or moves it.

Eliminating "Heeling"

"Heeling" is a term used to identify what happens when the "back" teeth of the saw blade do not follow the path of the "front" teeth (Illus. 3-37). If the misalignment were exaggerated and a slight cut were made into the surface of a piece of stock, the result would be a cove instead of a true kerf. To check for heeling, place a piece of wood that is 2 inches thick or thicker against the guide fence on the right side of the blade and make a crosscut that just trims the end of the stock. Don't, however, move the blade completely past the wood. Move the wood away from the blade and check the area indicated by the arrow in Illus. 3-38 for pronounced radial marks, which are scored arcs that travel from the bottom to the top edge of the test block. If the marks are pronounced, check the owner's manual to learn what correction is needed.

Heeling is often indicated by a drag on the blade as a cut is made, or if the cuts are rough or sawed edges have excessive feathering.

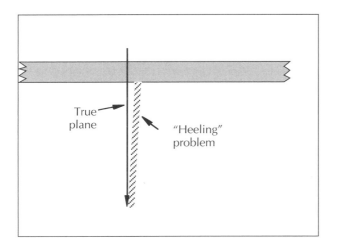

Illus. 3-37. Heeling happens when the "back" teeth of the saw blade do not follow the line of the "front" teeth.

Illus. 3-38 The arced score marks that appear on this thick test block that has been end-trimmed reveal heeling. Don't pull the blade completely through the block of wood when testing it for end-trimming.

Blade Setting

The normal perpendicular setting of the saw blade is easily checked with a square. To check common angular settings, such as 60, 45, and 30 degrees, I find, because the blade is above the table, that draftsman triangular templates work nicely (Illus. 3-39). For "in-between" angles, I use a preset bevel. As usual, I do not blindly accept the reliability of auto-stops or graduations on the machine's scales. I assume they are approximately right and proceed accordingly. And I don't shun test cuts that will prove whether *I'm* right.

The procedures you use while the work is in progress, as discussed in the section on table saws, are fairly routine. One procedure consists of simply using a combination square to draw the cutting lines on the work and then observing whether the saw blade follows the lines (Illus. 3-40 and 3-41).

Illus. 3-39. A draftsman's triangular template is a good tool for checking the setting of a blade when the blade must be tilted to common angles such as 30, 45, or 60 degrees. In-between angles can be checked by using a preset bevel.

Illus. 3-41. The same concept applied in Illus. 3-40 applies to miters and, for that matter, other angular cuts. Make this check even if you've been extremely careful when going through adjustment procedures.

Illus. 3-40. It's wise to occasionally mark a crosscut so you can see if the blade is following it correctly.

Using Stop Blocks

Stop blocks can be clamped to the radial arm saw fence to gauge part length when multiple, similar pieces are needed. However, enough sawdust can accumulate against the end of the stop to spoil accuracy. To avoid this problem, bevel the end of the stop block (Illus. 3-42). Even if it does not prevent sawdust from accumulating, at least it makes it easier to brush away waste material.

JOINTER

Accurate work on a jointer depends on two vital factors: how the horizontal plane of the tables relates to the cutting circle of the knives in the cutterhead; and how the fence is set for square or bevel cuts. The tables-to-knives adjustment is accomplished, depending on the design of the

Illus. 3-42. Sawdust can accumulate at the end of a stop block that is used to gauge the length of many duplicate pieces. A bevel will eliminate the problem or, at least, make it easy to brush away waste.

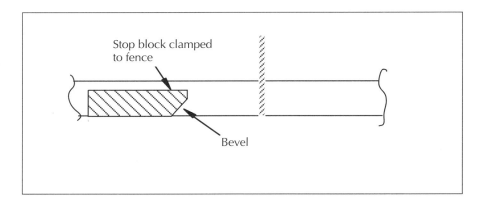

machine, either by adjusting the height of the knives so they are even with the out-feed table, or vice versa.

Checking the alignment of the table and knives is pretty straightforward. Place a straightedge on the surface of the out-feed table so it juts out over the cutterhead and then rotate the cutterhead carefully by hand. Each knife should barely touch the straightedge (Illus. 3-43). Do the testing at each end of each knife. If the knives don't touch at all, or if the straightedge is lifted, check the owner's manual for the adjustment procedure. Warning signals of misalignment are: the work hits the front edge of the out-feed table after passing the knives (which indicates the table is too high); the work drops at some point during the pass so it is gouged by the cutterhead; or a tapered edge is

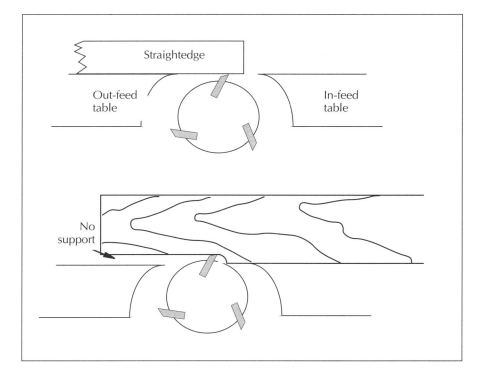

Illus. 3-43. The horizontal plane of a jointer's out-feed table must be level with the cutting circle of the knives. If the table is too low, the work will not be supported after it passes the cutterhead. If the table is too high, the work will butt against its edge.

produced (which indicates the table is too low).

It's also important to check the lateral position of the knives. They should project beyond the side of the out-feed table by $\frac{1}{32}$ to $\frac{1}{16}$ inch. This is necessary so that work being rabbeted won't butt against the out-feed table after passing the knives.

The in-feed table is adjustable vertically for depth-of-cut settings. When it is in neutral position, its surface should be on the plane of the out-feed table. Checking for this alignment can also be done with a straightedge. When it is correct, set the pointer on the machine's depth scale to read "0." Since we're leery of scales, always make a partial jointing cut on a piece of scrap and measure it before trusting the setting.

The angle between the tables and the fence when it is in normal position must be 90 degrees. If this isn't so, jointed edges will not be square to adjacent surfaces. The check to prove correct alignment is simple; just use a square as shown in Illus. 3-44. The tool will surely have an auto-stop, and now is the time to set it so the

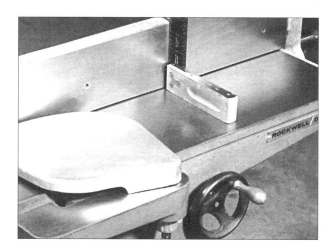

Illus. 3-44. When the jointer's fence is in neutral position, the angle between it and the tables must be 90 degrees. If it isn't, jointed edges will show a slight bevel.

fence can be returned to normal position after it has been tilted for some reason. The tool will have other auto-stops, usually for 45-degree left and right positions. Set them now after positioning the fence with a bevel, the head of a combination square, or a triangular template. Later, when doing some beveling work, you can reset the stops if you have checked the beveled edge with a protractor and determined that an adjustment is necessary.

Beveling is an area of jointer work where things can really go wrong. Frankly, I'm not at all fond of working with the fence set at an open angle. There is too much opportunity for the work to slip, which means bad edges and a possibly dangerous situation. I much prefer a closed angle, and using a clamped block to keep the work secure (Illus. 3-45 and 3-46). Beveling, unless you're planning just a slight chamfer, should also be accomplished by making repeat passes. Even if the jointer has an impressive depth of cut, making several shaving cuts instead of a full cut will result in more accurate, smoother edges.

When you are jointing end grain or plywood, the knives will inevitably split off a portion of wood at the end of the pass. One way to minimize fractures is to use slight, repeat passes. Another common technique is to pass the work over the knives for about an inch or so (Illus. 3-47), and then turn the work end for end to complete the cut. The work will be more accurate and cuts will be smoother when you are jointing all edges of a component if you make end-grain cuts first. The final passes, made with the grain, will remove the imperfections left by the first two cuts. This procedure does *not* apply to plywood.

The jointer is an excellent machine for forming accurate rabbets if its maximum depth of cut is adequate and you plan the layout so the shape of the rabbet will be uniform throughout

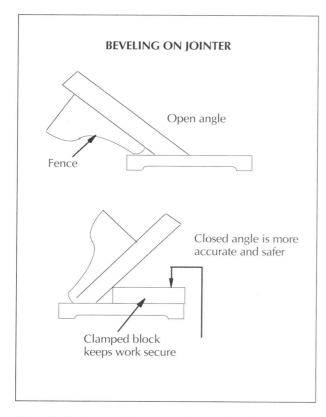

BEVELING ON JOINTER

Open angle

Fence

Closed angle is more accurate and safer

Clamped block keeps work secure

Illus. 3-45. I don't like to work with the fence set at an open angle when making bevel cuts on a jointer. It's too easy for the work to slip.

the length of the board. The major consideration is to keep the board down on the table and rabbeting ledge and against the fence for the entire cut. Helpers in this area consist of hold-downs or hold-ins. Whether the workpiece is held on edge or flat on the rabbeting ledge, guide blocks, clamped in place as shown in Illus. 3-48, will serve as extra hands to keep the board in position as you move it.

Surfacing

Surfacing is a feasible jointer application as long as the width of the stock isn't more than the length of the knives. It's sometimes suggested that wider boards can be surfaced by turning the stock end-for-end after the first pass and then making a second one. However, one of the passes will be against the grain of the wood, which never contributes to smoothness, and the likelihood that the board's surface will emerge uniformly is remote.

Anyway, for surfacing to be successful, free of tapers, gouges, and other unsatisfactory results, the knives must be in uniform contact

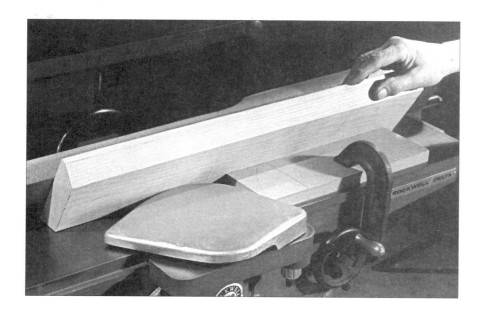

Illus. 3-46. Even when working with a closed angle, it's a good idea to use a clamped block as a hold-in, if only for the sake of accuracy.

Illus. 3-47. Splintering at the end of the pass is inevitable when you are jointing plywood or across end grain. To eliminate this problem, start the job by making a cut an inch or so long. Then turn the stock end-for-end and make a second pass.

with the work for the entire pass. Evidence that you are not working efficiently or that you are asking too much of the tool is work chatter and an obvious decrease in the cutterhead's RPM. When these factors appear, it's likely that you are cutting too deeply or moving the work too fast. Work with a minimum depth of cut; just a light shaving will often get the job done satisfactorily. If not, just make a second pass; quality is more important that speed.

Surfacing should be done with a tool that is a combination pusher/hold-down. This accessory, which you can make, and which is shown in Illus. 3-49 and 3-50, does much more than help do a good job. It provides an extra degree of safety because it automatically positions your hands so they are away from the cutting area.

Incidentally, pusher/hold-downs are not exclusively for jointer applications, nor do they have to be to a particular length or width. For

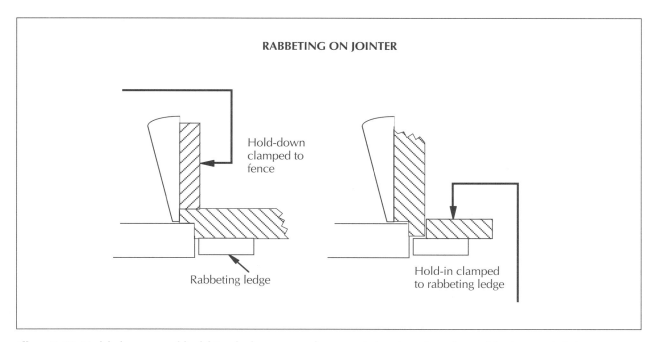

Illus. 3-48. Hold-downs and hold-ins help you work accurately when forming rabbets on a jointer.

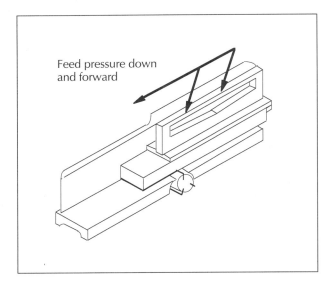

Illus. 3-49. A combination pusher/hold-down is the tool to use when doing surfacing on a jointer. It supplies downward and forward pressure at the same time.

example, they can help you work more accurately and with greater safety on many table saw operations (Illus. 3-51).

BAND SAW

Band-saw blades have to be flexible enough to conform to the circumference of the wheels that drive them, so it is possible for them to bend and twist and follow a cutting path of their own unless they are properly supervised. For error-less sawing and high-quality cuts, it is critical that alignment procedures be attended to step-by-step and very carefully.

The first two alignment procedures consist of *tracking* and *tensioning* the blade. Tracking, the first step, consists of centering the blade on the wheels (Illus. 3-52). Tensioning consists of making the blade taut in relation to its width so

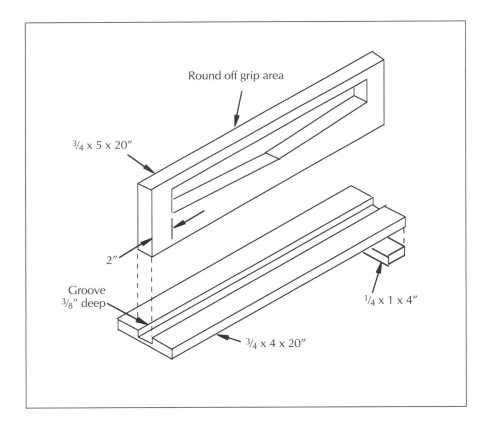

Illus. 3-50. Construction details for a combination pusher/hold-down that you can make.

Illus. 3-51. Pusher/hold-downs are not limited to any particular size and shape, and they are practical tools that aid accuracy and contribute to safety on operations like this one.

it won't twist during the cut or break prematurely (Illus. 3-53).

Generally, tensioning is accomplished by a mechanism that provides for vertical movement of the upper wheel. The "correct" tension is easy to achieve because the machine will have a tension scale. The wheel is raised until the pointer on the scale indicates that the setting is correct for the blade being installed. Many experienced woodworkers establish tension by first supplying a maximum amount and then slowly relaxing it until they can flex the blade about 1/8 inch with light finger pressure. This is done at midpoint on the area of the blade above the table and with the blade guard raised to its highest position. At any rate, slight adjustments are easy to make if sawing operations indicate they are necessary.

The blade is correctly tracked when it stays

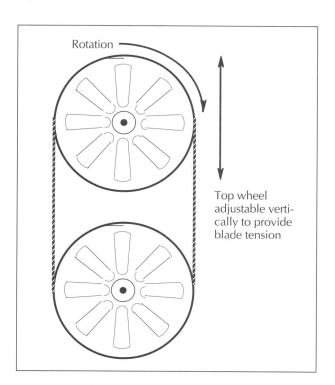

Illus. 3-52. Tracking, the first step, consists of centering the blade on the wheels.

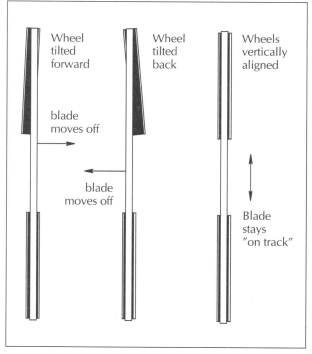

Illus. 3-53. The wheel is raised until the pointer on the scale indicates that the setting is correct.

close to the center of the wheel rims while it is running. Again, it's usually the upper wheel that supplies the control. Tilting it one way or the other will cause the blade to move to the front or back edge of the wheel. After the adjustment has been made, close the covers of the machine and turn it on for a few seconds. Make a visual check to see if the blade is tracking correctly.

Both tensioning and tracking must be done with the blade guides and the blade backup out of the way and with the blade guard at it highest point.

The next step is to adjust the table so the angle between its surface and the side of the blade will be 90 degrees (Illus. 3-54). The table will have an auto-stop that should be set at this point so the table can be returned to its horizontal position after any chore that involves tilting it.

Next, adjust the blade guides. A common system that serves as well as any other is to a use a strip of paper as a gauge to set the clearance between blade and guides (Illus. 3-55). This clearance prevails only when the blade is running free. The blade will rub against the guides when sawing, which is a good reason for replacing steel guides with "non-friction" or "cool blocks." Cool blocks are graphite-impregnated so they generate less friction and heat than metal guides. They supply the blade guidance that is necessary while reducing wear and tear on the blade.

The forward position of the guides is adjusted to suit the width of the blade; they must not contact the teeth. Set them so their front edges are on line with the gullets between the blade's teeth (Illus. 3-56).

The final step is to adjust the blade backup, the unit that prevents the blade from moving off the wheels during sawing chores. This is always a free-running bearing that is movable horizontally (Illus. 3-57). Set it to allow a slight clearance between it and the back edge of the blade when the blade is running free. Then it will work as it should, supporting the blade *only* when it is cutting.

Illus. 3-54. The band-saw table must be adjusted so the angle between it and the side of the saw blade is 90 degrees. Make this check after tracking and tensioning the blade.

Illus. 3-55. Clearance between the guides and the blade doesn't have to be more than the thickness of a piece of paper.

Illus. 3-56. The guides are set so the blade's teeth don't cut into them. Position them so their front edges are in line with the base of the blade's gullets.

Mental Mistakes

This section has nothing to do with alignment, but with a phase of band sawing that requires planning how a cut should be made. Sawing is generally straightforward, but you can easily box yourself in on some jobs and then have to saw your way out or do considerable backtracking to get back to where the cut was started. Usually, the problem occurs because we overlook how the arm of the machine can interfere with how the work can be moved (Illus. 3-58 and 3-59). This is a typical mental mistake that's easily avoided by some beforehand planning.

DRILL PRESS

To avoid drilling errors when using a drill press, it's essential that the angle between the surface of the table and the vertical centerline of the spindle be 90 degrees. You can check this angle

Illus. 3-57. The blade backup is a free-running bearing that is movable horizontally.

Illus. 3-58. This cut cannot be completed because the work is hitting the arm of the machine.

by locking a long piece of steel rod in the chuck and using a square to check the angle between it and the table. Another method is shown in Illus. 3-60. The rod, which can be retained as a per-

Illus. 3-59. If the cut in Illus. 3-58 had been mentally planned and started this way, it would have been completed without interference from the arm (in a single pass).

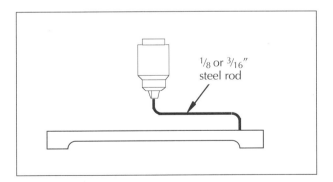

Illus. 3-60. Checking the alignment between the table and the spindle of a drill press. This test will also prove whether the table is flat. Turn the chuck by hand!

1/8 or 3/16″ steel rod

manent checking gauge, is rotated by turning the chuck by hand. It will reveal whether the alignment between spindle and table is correct, and if the table surface is as flat as it should be.

I've encountered some drill-press tables that needed attention. My remedy was to take down high spots with a belt sander, followed by an overall smoothing with a pad sander.

REMOUNTING THE WORK ON A LATHE CORRECTLY

It's often necessary to remove a spindle from between centers or the work from a faceplate so some off-lathe work can be done before final turning. To be certain of correct alignment when remounting the workpieces, I modified one of the blades on the spur center and drilled a small hole in the faceplate through which I could tap a nail (Illus. 3-61). Both techniques leave marks on the work that make it easy to remount them correctly.

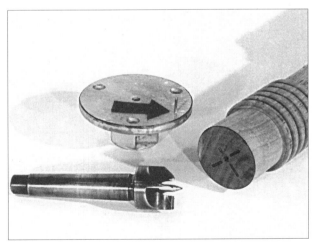

Illus. 3-61. A modified spur center and a nail that can be driven through a hole in the faceplate make marks in the work so it can be returned to its original position after it has been removed from the lathe for some other attention.

4

Miscellaneous Jigs and Woodworking Techniques

JIGS OVERVIEW

I've certainly made a lot of jigs over the years, but there isn't one that wasn't created to solve a problem, aid production, provide precision when many similar parts are needed, reduce shop expenses by eliminating the need to buy an "after market" accessory, provide additional safety, and, in general, reduce the possibility of human error. Practicality is essential, and shop testing must prove the jig's worth before I suggest it to others. There is the thought that jigs are only for amateurs, that advanced woodworkers have the expertise to function without mechanical aids. If so, there are many professionals who work in amateurish ways!

Jigs can be very simple, made to solve a current problem and then discarded. Other jigs must be more elaborate because they will be used for a particular, frequently performed operation, or they must be flexible enough for a variety of chores. Whatever the intended use of the acces-

sory, it must be made carefully. There is little point in producing one if it isn't accurate.

Jig-making often requires particular pieces of hardware that allow certain actions. Hold-downs that are part of some jigs have to be loosened and tightened, some components have to be moved and held in a new position, etc. Improvising with materials that are probably already in your shop is one way to operate (Illus. 4-1), but there are other options. Some manufacturers have become aware of the current interest in jig-making and are supplying units that are specially designed for such projects (Illus. 4-2).

DEALING WITH COMPOUND-ANGLE JOINTS

There is no sawing chore that can be more error-prone than making the joint cuts for projects such as shadow-box picture frames (frames whose components slant away from the wall), or taper-

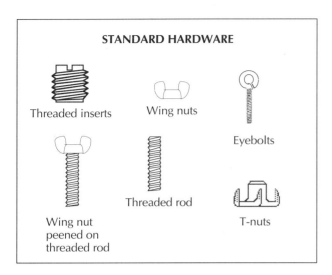

Illus. 4-1. Fasteners and other items required for jigs can be made by using standard pieces of hardware.

Illus. 4-2. Hardware designed specifically for jig-making is now available commercially. One source is home craftsman catalogues.

sided boxes, or the installation of crown or cove moldings. The warning about cutting accurately when sawing simple miters has already been issued. When making compound-angle joints, this warning is twice as important.

The conventional, and frustrating, cutting method on a table saw requires a miter-gauge setting *plus* a blade tilt. The two adjustments must mesh perfectly to result in the required slope angle to the sides and a 90-degree turn at the corners. Charts available in woodworking books and magazines indicate the settings for selected angles, but knowing the theoretically correct angles of the miter gauge and blade is only a start. You have to make test cuts to prove the settings are precise, but this can tempt you to depart from the shop and seek serenity somewhere else. Rarely is it possible to make the adjustments to machine-scale readings and produce an accurate joint. And making corrections is complicated by the fact that the two settings interact.

However, compound-angle joints can be made more easily and accurately by eliminating the critical factor of one machine calibration: the tilt of the saw blade. Let's consider this quick example: the blade is in normal crosscut position, and the miter gauge is set at 45 degrees. Place a workpiece so it slopes from the face of the miter gauge down to the table and make the cut. It's like sawing a simple miter, but since the work slopes, the cut is a compound angle. Of course, working this way freehand is chancy and should never be tried. That's why a jig like the one being used in Illus. 4-3 is needed: the work, braced against a stop, won't slip out from under your fingers.

Construction details for a jig that is improved over the one shown in Illus. 4-3 are shown in Illus. 4-4. The new design incorporates an adjustable stop that is secured with bolts, so the need for a tack-nailed strip of wood as a stop is eliminated. To make the jig, join its

Illus. 4-3. Sawing with the blade at 90 degrees but with the work sloped results in a compound-angle cut. The value of working this way is that it eliminates one critical machine setting.

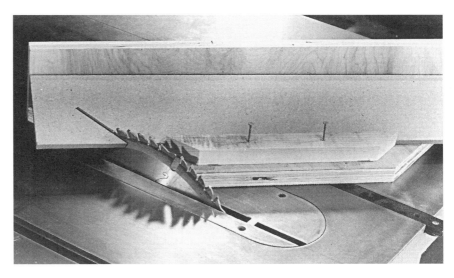

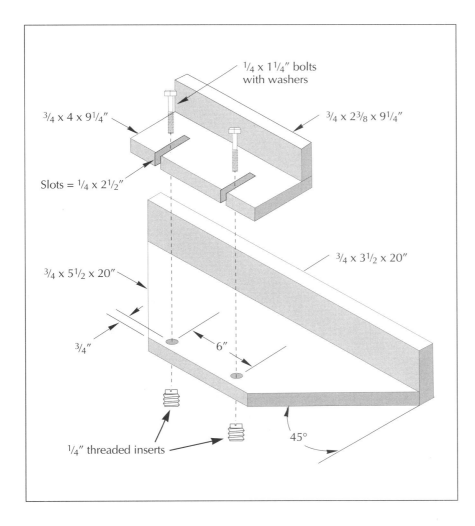

¹/₄ x 1¹/₄" bolts with washers

³/₄ x 4 x 9¹/₄"

³/₄ x 2³/₈ x 9¹/₄"

Slots = ¹/₄ x 2¹/₂"

³/₄ x 3¹/₂ x 20"

³/₄ x 5¹/₂ x 20"

³/₄"

6"

¹/₄" threaded inserts

45°

Illus. 4-4. A jig used for compound-angle cuts.

back and base. Then, after securing the assembly to the miter gauge, saw off the corners to a 45-degree angle (Illus. 4-5). A good way to form the slots in the base of the stop is to drill ¼-inch holes where the slots must end and then saw out the waste.

When using the jig, secure the workpieces at a slope angle by bracing them between the base of the jig and the stop, as illustrated in Illus. 4-6. The slope can be determined by using a bevel or a triangle template if one is suitable, but there is another option that may eliminate the need for a precise setting. Since the slope on many projects, as far as appearance is concerned, is not critical, it may be set at an angle that is visually pleasing. Anyone who judges, for example, a shadow-box picture frame on the basis of the slope angle is a pretty persnickety critic! Anyway, the point is, whether you approximate the slope angle by eye or measure it accurately, the joints will always fit.

Incidentally, there is no reason why the jig

Illus. 4-6. The work is braced between the jig's fence and the adjustable stop. The jig may be used on either side of the saw blade.

can't be used for simple miters. The work is just placed flat in the jig as shown in Illus. 4-7. Also, moldings used for inside or outside corners can be placed in the jig, as shown in Illus. 4-8. In these cases, the slope angle is determined by the material itself.

Illus. 4-9 shows how the jig, now mounted

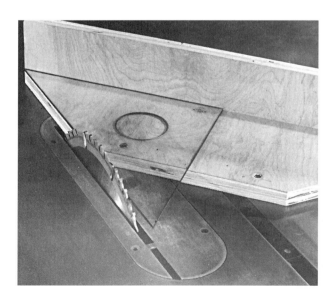

Illus. 4-5. Each end of the jig is sawed at 45 degrees.

Illus. 4-7. The jig is also usable for routine miter cuts.

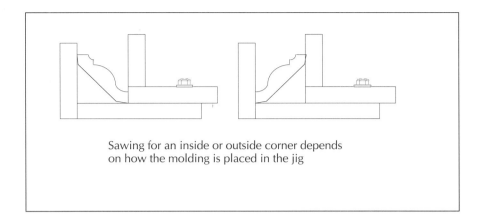

Sawing for an inside or outside corner depends on how the molding is placed in the jig

Illus. 4-8. How to place molding for inside or outside corners on the jig.

on a square platform, is used on a radial arm saw. Right-hand miters are cut with the jig on the left side of the blade. For left-hand miters, shift the jig to the right side of the blade and rotate it clockwise one quarter turn.

HOW TO CUT TENONS ACCURATELY

Since tenons are formed by making straight cuts, it's logical that the table saw is a prime candidate for the work. Tenons must be uniform

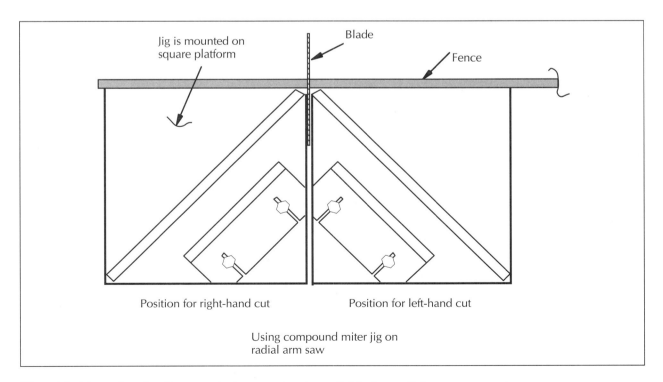

Jig is mounted on square platform

Blade

Fence

Position for right-hand cut

Position for left-hand cut

Using compound miter jig on radial arm saw

Illus. 4-9. Mounting the jig on a platform makes it available for radial-arm-saw work.

and have smooth cheeks and shoulders, so the first thing to consider is the best blade to use. A steel combination blade with set teeth *is not* a good choice. A hollow-ground blade will work okay, but some blades have a limited area of relief and can cause burn marks. The ideal choice is a quality, carbide-tipped combination planer blade (Illus. 4-10).

Most times, tenons are needed on the end of relatively narrow pieces, such as parts for frames, components like rails and stretchers, aprons, etc. Thus, making the cheek cuts without using a jig means hand-holding the work on its end as you move it past the blade. Since the work has little surface bearing down on the table, it's possible for it to tilt or wobble as it is moved. So, relying on hand guidance contributes nothing to accuracy or safety. Often the solution is to use a jig that positions and secures the work as the cut is made without help from you, other than moving the jig.

A tenoning jig is a fairly common workshop aid, but the ones most often used are designed to ride on the rip fence. I'm not going to criticize this idea (I've made them so myself), but there is a possible flaw because they must be free to slide on the fence. While the clearance between the jig and fence in such cases is minimal, there is still a chance the unit might wobble a bit and spoil the accuracy. Also, the design of the rip fence may not be compatible. A more advanced concept is an independent jig on a sliding platform that is guided by a bar in the table slot. Such a jig, as shown in Illus. 4-11, is more dependable. An optional feature is an improvised screw-feed that moves the sliding part of the jig to or fro for fine adjustments (Illus. 4-12).

Illus. 4-13 shows how the jig is put together. Begin the project by making the platform and the guide bar. The latter is sized to slide nicely in the table slot, but without permitting any lateral movement. Use glue and small flathead screws to attach the bar, but be sure the inside edge of the platform is about 2 inches away

Illus. 4-10. The ideal choice for cutting tenons is a quality, carbide-tipped combination planer blade.

Illus. 4-11. This tenoning jig has its own sliding table.

Illus. 4-12. The screw-feed on the jig is optional but recommended because it provides for fine adjustments that would otherwise have to be made manually.

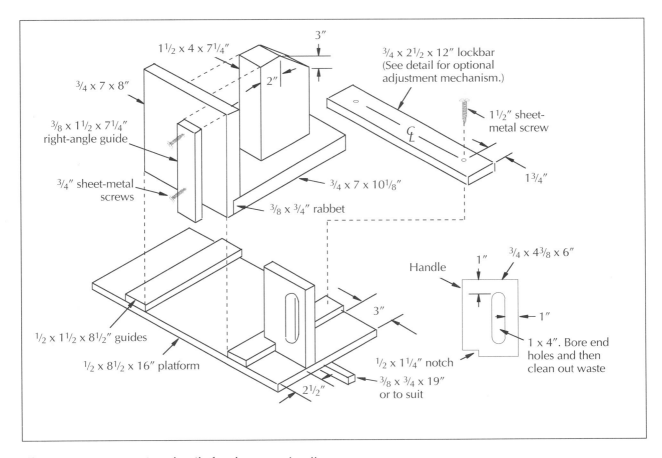

Illus. 4-13. Construction details for the tenoning jig.

from the saw blade and parallel to it.

Next, make the two guide bars for the platform and then attach the front one so it is 3 inches from the forward edge of the platform. The angle between the inside edge of the bar and the saw blade must be 90 degrees (Illus. 4-14). Do not attach the second guide bar until other parts of the jig have been made.

Next, make and join the base and the vertical face of the sliding unit. Be sure they form a perfect 90-degree corner. Before adding the brace that abuts the back of the unit's face, check Illus. 4-15, which shows how the screw-

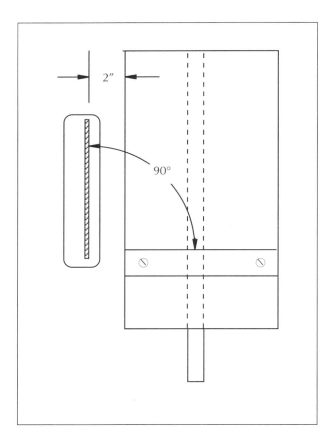

Illus. 4-14. After assembling the sliding platform, the first thing you should do is make sure the forward guide is 90 degrees to the saw blade.

feed is installed. As we said, it's an optional feature, but nice for making fine adjustments. If you opt for it, the brace must have the counter-bored hole before it is put in place.

All the parts of the screw-feed must be put together as a subassembly before the hardboard or aluminum plate is attached to the brace. The lock-nuts at the front end of the threaded rod are adjusted to allow the threaded rod to turn. The slight play that is needed there does not impair the accuracy of the jig.

Put the sliding assembly in place against the guide that's already on the platform so it can be used as a gauge to position the second guide. The assembly must move, of course, but it must be straight forward or back with no side play. It's okay if the fit is a little snug to being with; a little touch-up with sandpaper will make it right. Coating sliding parts with paste wax rubbed to a polish is a wise step.

For the jig to work accurately, two crucial alignment factors must be met. First, the angle between the face of the jig and the saw table must be 90 degrees (Illus. 4-16). Second, when installing the right-angle guide, be certain that the angle between its bearing edge and the table is also 90 degrees (Illus. 4-17).

Using The Jig

Forming cheek cuts for tenons is straightforward. Elevate the saw blade to suit the length of the tenon, and adjust the jig so the distance from its face to the *outside* surface of the blade will equal the width of cut that is required. For example, if the stock is 1 inch thick and the tenon must be $\frac{1}{2}$ inch thick, then the space between the jig and the outside of the blade must be $\frac{1}{4}$ inch. To make the cut, secure the workpiece in the jig and then move the jig past the saw blade. The second cut is made after reversing the position of the stock (Illus. 4-18).

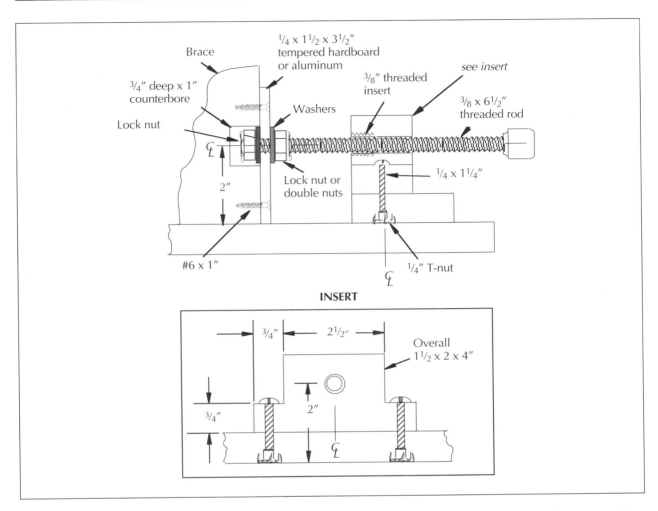

Illus. 4-15. Construction details for the screw-feed. It adds to construction time, but the results are worth it.

The shoulder cuts can be made either before or after the tenon's cheeks are formed. In either case, they are cut with the work flat on the table—like a crosscut, but with the blade having a particular projection (Illus. 4-19).

Here's a technique I often use when I have to produce many similar tenons: I mount *two* blades on the arbor so I can cut both cheeks in one pass (Illus. 4-20). The blades are separated with washers or something similar so the space between them equals the thickness of the tenon. A precaution: don't use this technique if you don't have enough thread on the saw's arbor for the locknut to seat securely.

You should also try to work with a special insert, one that leaves minimum clearance between and around the blades. Special inserts are made by using the regular insert as a template to mark a piece of hardwood or tempered hardboard. With the blade, or blades, lowered below the table, place the new insert and use the fence, or provide some other means to keep the new insert secure. Then, very slowly raise the blade so it cuts its own special slot.

Illus. 4-16. The angle between the bearing face of the jig and the table must be 90 degrees.

Illus. 4-18. The workpiece may be held by hand, but it's often better to secure it with a clamp.

Illus. 4-17. Install the right-angle guide so its bearing edge is 90 degrees to the table.

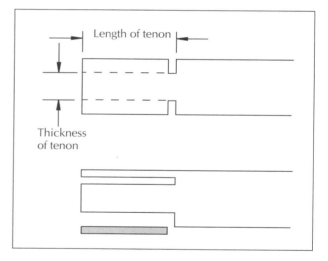

Illus. 4-19. Shoulder cuts can be made before or after you make the tenon's cheek cuts.

DRILLING SPACED HOLES ON A COMMON CENTERLINE

Drilling holes that must be on a common centerline is often accomplished by clamping a strip of wood to the drill-press table as a fence to position the work. This improvised fence takes some positioning and reclamping before its placement is correct, and it's a one-time approach that must be repeated for similar jobs. An improvement is a jig with a large table that provides ample work support, and a pivoting

Illus. 4-20. Twin blades make both cheek cuts in a single pass. Note the special shop-made insert that provides for minimum clearance around the blades.

Illus. 4-21. A drill-press jig. The pivoting fence can be adjusted for various stock thicknesses or widths.

fence that requires clamping at only one end. For on-line center drilling, I mark one hole location, bring the drill bit down to contact it, and then swing the fence to butt against the workpiece (Illus. 4-21).

The design of the jig is detailed in Illus. 4-22. The size of the U-shaped cutout at the back of the table and the base block is customized to suit the diameter of the drill-press column. Once this is done, the block is attached to the table with glue and flathead wood screws. The arrangement for securing the jig on the drill press is shown in Illus. 4-23. To avoid damage to the column when tightening the lock bolt, place a piece of hardboard between the end of the bolt and the column.

With the jig centered and secured, place a small drill bit in the machine's chuck and drill through the table and base block. This is done to establish the correct distance from the column to the centerline of the spindle. The hole is enlarged to about 2¾ inches for a reason we'll show later.

A valuable addition to the jig is a device that will automatically establish the correct distance between any number of holes (Illus. 4-24). The arm can be swung in any direction and moved forward or back. Thus, it can be adjusted to suit the edge distance of holes as well as the spacing, and it will function whether the stock is flat on the table or on edge.

When using the adjustable spacing guide, drill the first hole and then establish the position of the guide pin. Thereafter, inserting the pin in the last hole drilled will position the stock for the following hole. The guide is used for pilot holes that can be enlarged later if necessary. Illus. 4-25 shows how the spacing guide is made. A rod with a smaller diameter can be used as the guide pin if smaller pilot holes are preferable.

I said I would explain the reason for the large hole in the table. It makes the table usable for drum-sanding operations (Illus. 4-26). When curved edges are smoothed this way, you know they will be square to the surfaces of the workpiece.

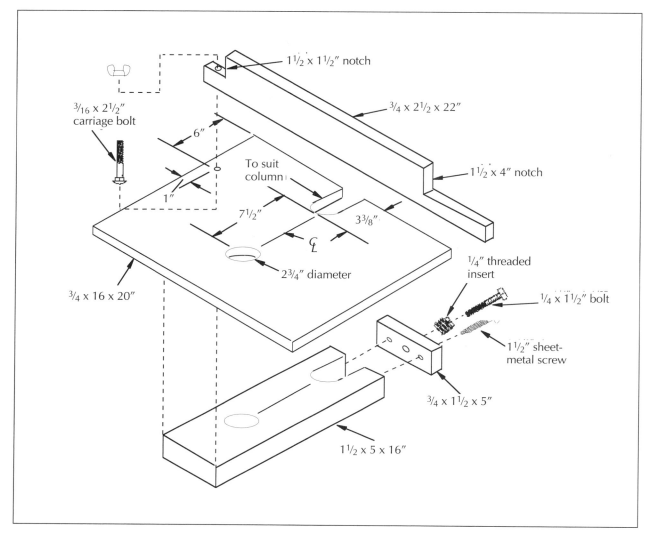

Illus. 4-22. Construction details for the drill-press jig.

ADDING FEATHERS TO MITER JOINTS

Feathers, which are triangular splines, reinforce cross-miter joints and, when they are made of a contrasting material, supply a decorative detail that adds to the appearance of the project. Cutting the grooves that are needed can be very difficult unless a device that will eliminate human error is provided. My aid is the miter-gauge V-block jig that is displayed in Illus. 4-27. As often happens, this accessory, which was made for a particular application, becomes usable for other functions. Having this jig led naturally into exploiting it for other cuts, some of which are displayed in Illus. 4-28.

The dimensions of the prototype, shown in Illus. 4-29, should be suitable for most miter gauges, but check them against your own equip-

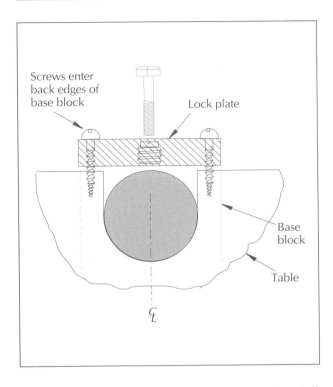

Illus. 4-23. How the jig is secured on the drill press. Use a slim piece of wood or hardboard between the tool's column and the lock bolt.

ment before doing any cutting. The crucial factor is the 90-degree angle between the front and back faces of the jig. There is no reason why the legs of the V can't be longer or wider.

Start construction by making the triangular block that is secured to the miter gauge. Check the 45-degree angle with a protractor to be sure it is correct, and then attach the component with screws driven through the holes in the miter-gauge head that are there for just such a purpose. Put the legs of the V support together with glue and nails or screws. Be sure not to use a fastener in the area where the saw kerf will be. Then, attach the V assembly to the triangular block with glue and several #10 x 1¾-inch flathead wood screws.

Using the Jig

Mating pieces that haven't been mitered yet are placed in the jig and held together by hand or with clamps as the jig is moved past the saw blade. Use a clamped stop block to gauge the edge distance of the kerf (Illus. 4-30). Make cuts

Illus. 4-24. The adjustable spacing guide in use. The pin, placed in the last drilled hole, positions the work for the next hole.

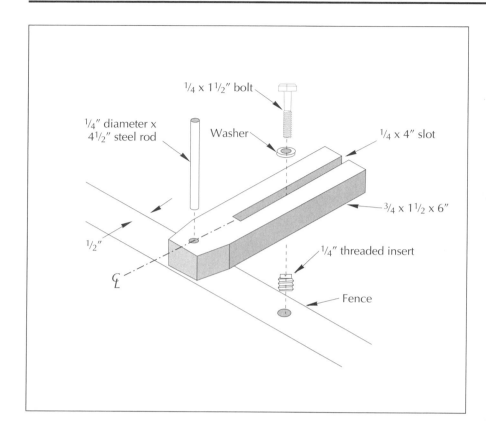

$\frac{1}{4}$ x $1\frac{1}{2}$" bolt

$\frac{1}{4}$" diameter x $4\frac{1}{2}$" steel rod

Washer

$\frac{1}{4}$ x 4" slot

$\frac{3}{4}$ x $1\frac{1}{2}$ x 6"

$\frac{1}{2}$"

$\frac{1}{4}$" threaded insert

Fence

Illus. 4-25. How the spacing guide is made. If you ever have to position it higher than the jig's fence, use a longer lock bolt and a spacer between the guide and fence top.

Illus. 4-26. The oversize hole in the jig's table provides for other uses like drum-sanding.

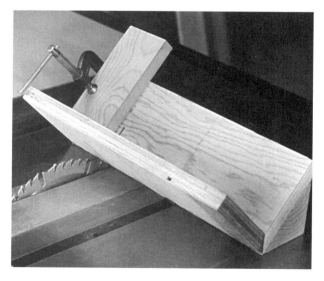

Illus. 4-27. This miter-gauge V-block was made for "feathering" miter joints, but it has other applications.

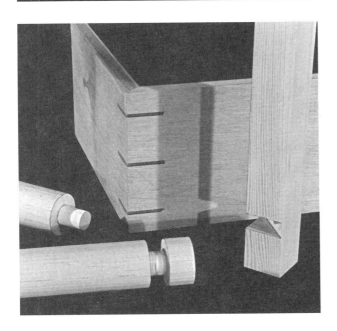

Illus. 4-28. Examples of work that can be accomplished with the miter-gauge V-block.

on all pieces before changing the position of the stop block for other cuts. Adjust the projection of the saw blade so it is only enough to cut partially through the miter joint. You can do the cutting with just a saw blade; most produce a $\frac{1}{8}$-inch-wide kerf, so standard material like plywood or hardboard can be utilized to produce the splines. If thicker splines will be better, the kerfing can be done by using a dadoing tool. The wider cut that will be formed in the jig will not interfere with the use of it with just a saw blade.

When ready, prepare the splines so they are a bit wider and longer than necessary so that after they are installed and the glue is dry, they can be trimmed and then sanded flush to adjacent surfaces (see Illus. 4-31 and 4-32).

Other work that can be done accurately with the V-block jig is shown in Illus. 4-33 and 4-34. Spline grooves for feathers that will reinforce

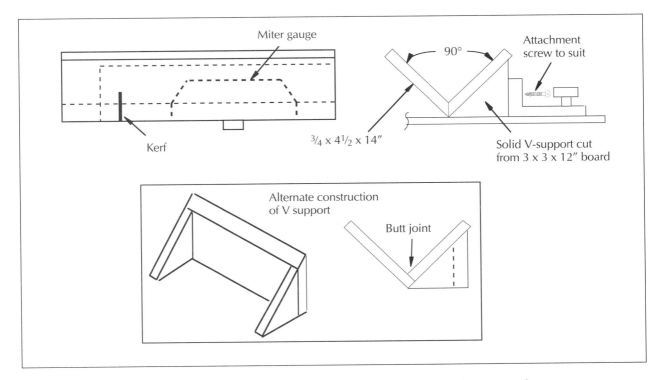

Illus. 4-29. Two ways to construct the V-block jig. The solid support allows less room for error.

Illus. 4-30. Cut the feather grooves by holding both parts of the joint in the jig. The stop block positions the work for edge distance.

Illus. 4-31. The feathers are made a bit wider and longer than necessary.

Illus. 4-32. The feathers are trimmed and sanded flush after the glue dries. Contrasting feathers add a decorative detail.

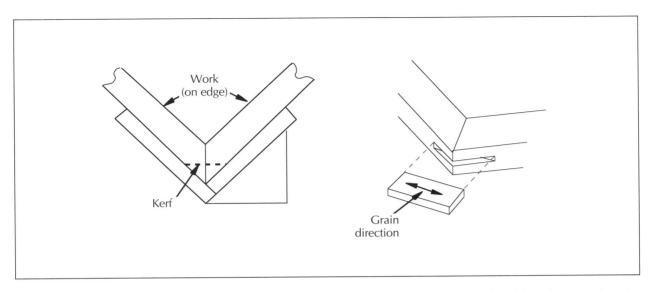

Illus. 4-33. Flat miter joints can also be grooved for feathers. It's just a matter of making the cut with the joint parts on edge.

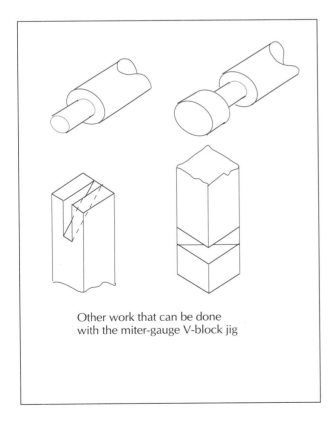

Other work that can be done
with the miter-gauge V-block jig

Illus. 4-34. More uses for the V-block jig.

flat miter joints are formed by holding the pieces on edge. To produce integral, round tenons, clamp a stop block to gauge the length of the tenon, and set the projection of the saw blade to suit the tenon's diameter. Shaping is done by rotating the cylinder as you make repeat, slightly overlapping passes.

Forming a dado across the corners of square stock or forming diagonal notches on the edge of boards (Illus. 4-35) are also accomplished by making repeat passes. Work of this nature can be expedited by using a dadoing tool instead of a saw blade.

STRETCHING YOUR TALENTS WITH DISC AND BELT SANDERS

If I were to rate the jigs in my shop, those that I use on belt and disc sanders would rank high. The jigs increase the tools' capabilities, make it easier to use them more accurately, ensure duplication when I need similar pieces, and they are useful for completing jobs like a miter cut to a line or just trimming one. That's a lot, but isn't that what jigs are for?

The pivot jig shown set up on a disc sander

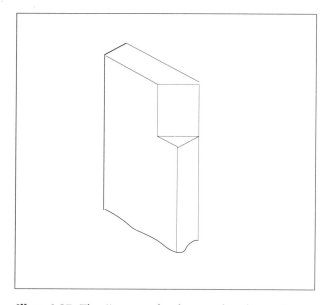

Illus. 4-35. The jig may also be used to form diagonal notches on the edges of boards.

in Illus. 4-36 offers a foolproof method of sanding circular components to exact size, and with the assurance that edges will be square to surfaces. You may have to alter the dimensions of the jig as shown in Illus. 4-37, but the construction will remain the same.

Cut the three pieces that comprise the body of the jig to overall size and then bevel the inside edges of the top parts to 45 degrees. Prepare the slide safely by cutting it from a piece of wide material. Attach the left, top piece to the base with glue and flathead wood screws; then use the slide to gauge the position of the second piece. Now that the three parts are assembled, you can cut the side tapers.

To add the guide bar, set it in the table's slot, place the jig on top of it, and then check two factors. First, allow a clearance of about $\frac{1}{8}$ inch between the forward edge of the jig and the disc. Second, be sure the angle between the dovetail slot in the jig and the disc is 90 degrees. Tack-nail the components together while they are in correct position and then

Illus. 4-36. The pivot jig for sanding circular edges set up on a disc sander.

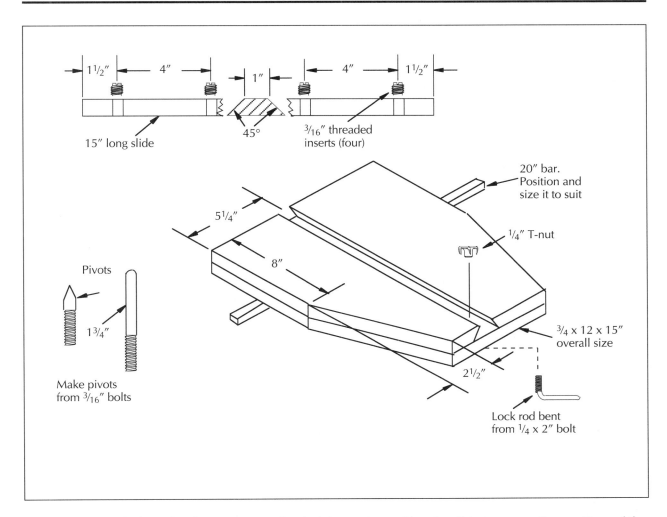

Illus. 4-37. The platform for the jig is comprised of three pieces. Use the slide to gauge the position of the top parts.

remove them from the tool so the bar can be permanently installed with glue and flathead screws driven through the bar.

Two pivot points are needed (Illus. 4-38). The longer one is used when the work can have a center hole. Work that does not need a center hole is just impaled on the point of the short pivot. Both pivots are made by chucking headless, $3/16$-inch bolts in the drill press and shaping their ends with a file.

Using the Jig

The jig is positioned so sanding will be done on the down-spinning side of the sanding disk. (The down side is that area of the disk that moves down toward the table.) Place the rough-cut work over the suitable pivot and then move it forward to contact the disk. Then, after securing the slide with the L-shaped lock rod, rotate the work to sand its edge (Illus. 4-39). When duplicates are needed, say, wheels for a cart, mark the position of the slide so it can be relocated accurately. When much sanding is needed, move the jig occasionally left or right to maximize use of the abrasive surface.

The jig is not limited to sanding circular work. For example, it can be used to round off the ends of narrow pieces or the corners of square stock (Illus. 4-40 and 4-41).

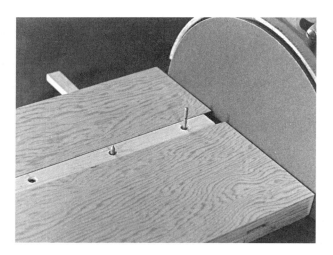

Illus. 4-38. The short, pointed pivot is used when the work does not have a center hole. The work is pressed down on the pivot.

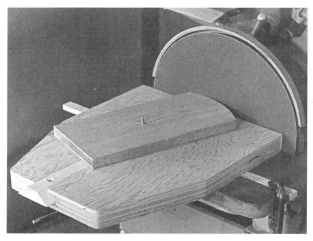

Illus. 4-40. Using the jig to round off the end of a board. Interesting variations are possible by mounting the work off-center.

Illus. 4-39. The work can be rotated in either direction. Sanding is done on the "down" side of the disk. Move the jig occasionally to avoid overuse of one area of the abrasive surface.

Illus. 4-41. Using the jig to round off the corners of a square workpiece.

SANDING MITERS

The mitering jig shown installed on a belt sander in Illus. 4-42 is a pretty simple affair, but that shouldn't cause you to be casual when making it. An accurate procedure is to make and assemble the platform and guide bar, being certain that the front edge of the platform is parallel to the platen of the tool and about ⅛ inch away from it. Make the left and right guides so their bearing edges will be exactly 45 degrees, and then install them on the platform (Illus. 4-43).

Workpieces can be sanded whether they must be placed flat on the platform or on edge (Illus. 4-44 and 4-45). Since there are both left- and right-hand guides, both ends of stock that can't be turned over (like molding) can be sanded.

A few words of advice concerning sanders. We forget that sanders should be used as *finishing* tools. Except in special cases where you might be working with very coarse-grit sandpa-

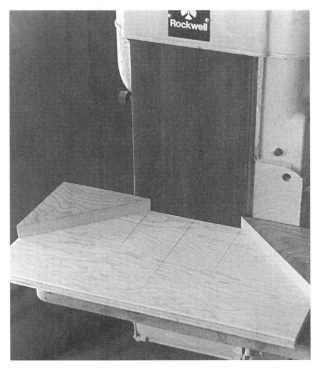

Illus. 4-42. The miter jig set up on a belt sander.

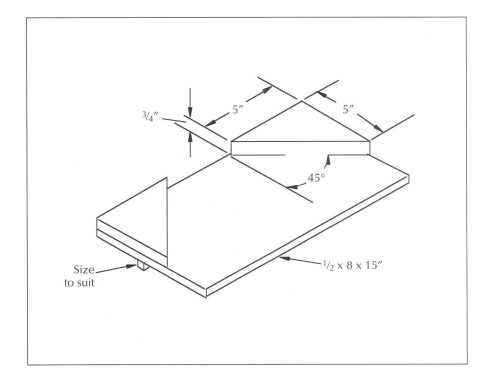

Illus. 4-43. The front edge of the miter-jig platform must be parallel to the machine's platen. Install the guides after that setting has been established.

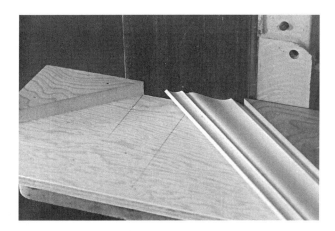

Illus. 4-44. Hold the work firmly against the jig and move it slowly to contact the abrasive surface. Light feed pressure gets the job done efficiently. Twin guides allow you to sand both ends of work that can't be flipped, like molding.

Illus. 4-45. Placing work on edge permits sanding of cross-miters.

per, they should not be used to *shape*. Always make saw cuts as close to layout lines as possible. Rely on sanding for the final touches. Forcing work against abrasive surfaces to speed up the job will only result in burn marks. Clean

belts and disks occasionally with one of those "rubber erasers" that are now available. (These are specially formulated erasers that, when held against a turning belt or disk, remove waste particles that would eventually clog the abrasive paper.) Lest we forget, abrasives are particles of cutting material. Allowing them to get clogged reduces the cutting action and causes glazing that isn't good for either the sandpaper or the work.

NOTCHED JIGS

What is a "notched jig?" Essentially, it's a combination gauge/guide that allows you to produce or make cuts in small parts accurately and safely. Often, they provide a solution for work that can't be handled by using just a rip fence or miter gauge.

If you take a piece of wood and cut a shape (notch) along one edge, you have a notched jig. The shape of the notch is the control for the part you want to keep, or for the waste piece that needs to be cut off from a project component. Major reasons for providing jigs of this type are: 1. a part is so small or so oddly shaped that it can't be held by hand safely, or it requires a lot of effort to be made accurately by conventional means; 2. the cut is such that normal use of the miter gauge and rip fence is negated; and 3. many small, identical parts are needed. Typical applications for notched jigs are suggested in Illus. 4-46–4-50.

One additional thought: Use this type of jig to form cheek cuts for tenons or for half-lap joints when a tenoning accessory is not available. This jig, which is just a ¾ - or 1½-inch-thick piece of stock, is dadoed so the work will fit snugly. The depth of the dado determines how thick the tenon will be, or in the case of a half-lap joint, how much material will be cut off. The jig, with the work in place, is used as shown in Illus. 4-51.

Illus. 4-46. A notched jig used for small wedges. Always use a jig that's wide enough for safe handling.

Illus. 4-48. Is there a better way to cut grooves in the end of round components than as shown here? Advance the jig only far enough to cut the groove.

Illus. 4-47. A quick, accurate way to produce short splines and similar parts. The width of the jig determines the length of the workpieces.

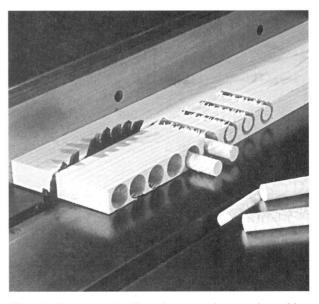

Illus. 4-49. Many similar plugs can be produced by first forming them with a plug cutter, and then sawing them off the stock.

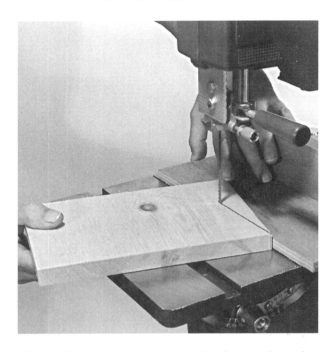

Illus. 4-50. Notched jigs can also be used on the band saw. The blade guard should not be so high as shown here. It's shown this high only for the sake of photo clarity.

Illus. 4-51. This unique notched jig is set up to make the cheek cuts for a tenon.

USING A PORTABLE ROUTER

The portable router is very popular these days, but it's a fact that to use it proficiently and to exploit its potential a jig must be used or the router guided in some way.

To start with, when the tool is equipped with a bit that has an integral or ball-bearing pilot, and is being used to shape an edge, it must be held truly horizontal through the length of the cut. It doesn't matter how much bearing surface for the router is provided by the work itself, there is always the chance that you will tilt the router. If the router is inadvertently tilted upward, away from the work's edge, the work will not be affected. But if it is tilted downward *into* the edge, the work will be gouged and will require repair. This blemish will be exaggerated if the bit's pilot doesn't bear sufficiently against the edge of the workpiece.

The way to avoid this type of error is so simple, it's foolish to ignore it. On straight cuts, place a strip of wood away from the work and parallel to it. Then the tool can span across the pieces so it can't tilt. On curved edges, uniform or otherwise, use the cutoff to provide "outboard" support (Illus. 4-52).

Woodworking jobs such as hollowing bowls or trays and forming recesses for large inlays require another type of error-prevention method. When the router can't span across the sides of the project, it must be equipped with a special, longer base (Illus. 4-53).

No-Mistake Centering Jigs

Forming mortises in the edge of furniture components and cutting centered, lengthwise dovetails or grooves are standard router applications. An edge guide, a commercial accessory that may be supplied with the tool or is available at extra cost, is often used to guide the tool paral-

Illus. 4-52. Always use a strip of wood as an outboard support when using a portable router to shape edges.

Illus. 4-53. The shop-made auxiliary base on this router ensures that the tool can't be accidentally tilted. This kind of extra attention eliminates mistakes while contributing to accuracy and, often, safety.

lel to the stock's edge. This calls for precise measuring and diligent control of the tool. The edge does not supply much support for the router so an accidental tilt one way or the other is a definite possibility. That's why centering jigs like the one at work in Illus. 4-54 are made. Their purpose is to hold the work securely, keep the bit centered in the edge throughout the cut, and to provide adequate support for the tool, thereby eliminating any mistakes waiting to happen.

The centering jig shown in Illus. 4-54 and 4-55 and detailed in Illus. 4-56 is based on the idea of using two parallel rules. The distance between its legs is constant and uniform; the router is centered as the jig is adjusted to suit the thickness of the stock. The end pieces are locked after the position of the jig has been established. The screws that hold the base are tightened enough for security, while still permitting the router to move.

The jig displayed in Illus. 4-56 provides similar accuracy and router support. An advantage is that the special base may remain on the router when the jig isn't needed for centering

Illus. 4-54. This jig for centering router cuts was modeled after the idea of using two parallel rules.

cuts. Illus. 4-58 shows how the jig mounts on the work. The scale, which must be carefully marked, allows settings for ¾-, 1½-, and 2-inch stock. Of course, in actual use, the work would be gripped in a vise. The parts that are required for the jig are shown in Illus. 4-59.

A vise clamp (Illus. 4-59) is an excellent companion for a centering jig. The length of the

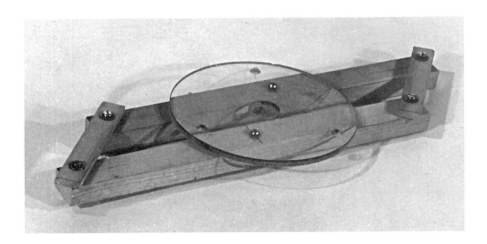

Illus. 4-55. The centering or parallel-rule jig has its own base plate, to which the router is secured.

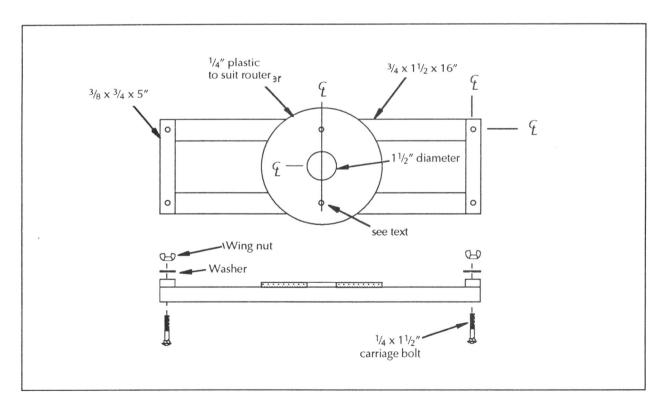

Illus. 4-56. How the parallel-rule jig is made. It can be used on workpieces of any length.

Illus. 4-57. This version of a centering jig uses heavy blocks to provide extra bearing surface against the sides of the work.

clamp's fences can be increased if you feel that the 24 inches called for in Illus. 4-60 might be limiting. Just be sure to use good, straight pieces of hardwood. The clamp may be gripped in a bench vise (Illus. 4-61) or it can be clamped to the edge of the workbench if the vise would interfere with positioning the workpiece. Actually, the clamp could be attached permanently to a bench so it would always be ready for use.

Illus. 4-62 and 4-63 show the setups being used to form an edge groove and a dovetail slot.

Accurate Spacing for Dadoes

Any dado cut with a router calls for moving the tool along a straightedge that is clamped or tack-nailed to the work. This is okay for a single cut, but if several, equally spaced ones are required, moving the straightedge for each cut is an error-prone procedure. To ensure accuracy, equip the router with a longer base to which is attached a guide strip whose thickness matches the width of the dado. The distance from the bit to the guide determines the spacing that is needed. Make the first cut with the guide strip riding the end of the workpiece, and the following ones with the strip placed in the last dado that was cut (Illus. 4-64). If the first dado requires a particular location, rout it by using a clamped T-square as a guide. The same system is practical for forming dadoes back-to-back. All you have to do is flip the stock.

Illus. 4-58. How the jig is used. The work, of course, must be secured in a bench vise. Be very accurate when making and placing the scale.

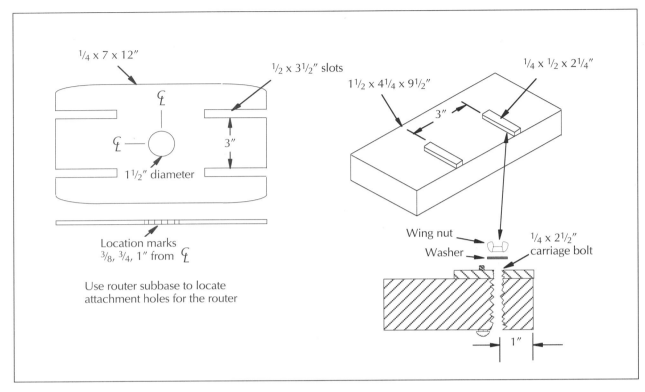

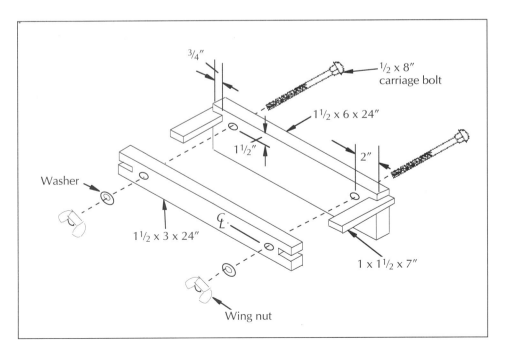

Illus. 4-59. Construction details for the centering jig. The guide blocks must have perfectly parallel, smooth sides.

Illus. 4-60. How to make a vise clamp for router work.

Illus. 4-61. The vise clamp and a centering jig make a fine combination. Strips of wood can be tack-nailed across the clamp to gauge the length of the mortise.

Illus. 4-62. Forming an edge groove. Deep cuts require repeat passes.

Illus. 4-63. Forming a dovetail slot. It's not possible to make repeat cuts for dovetails, so the pass must be made very slowly. When necessary, cut a straight groove first, and then switch to the dovetail bit.

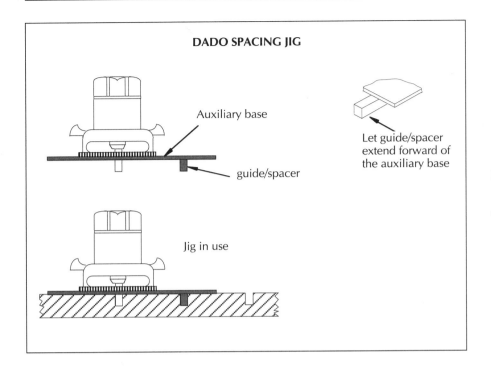

DADO SPACING JIG

Auxiliary base

guide/spacer

Let guide/spacer
extend forward of
the auxiliary base

Jig in use

Illus. 4-64. Using a special router base to gauge equally spaced dadoes.

Widening a Dado

When a dado or a groove is needed that is wider than the largest bit available, a common procedure is to reposition the straightedge after the first cut and then make a second pass. Again, this is okay for a single cut, but having to do it again and again for similar cuts increases the possibility of error. It's better to be able to make the second cut *without* moving the guide. A way to do this is to provide a special platform for the router. After the router's position on the new base has been established, the base is "reduced" on three sides when a portion of its edges is cut off (Illus. 4-65). After the first cut, with the base's full edge against the guide strip, the tool is rotated so a reduced edge bears against the guide. If you are, for example, working with a $\frac{1}{2}$-inch bit and need a $\frac{3}{4}$-inch dado, make the second pass with the edge of the base that was reduced $\frac{1}{4}$ inch against the guide strip.

Moving in Circles

Using a router to cut disks or to form circular grooves isn't a new procedure but, many times, accuracy and convenience are jeopardized by temporary improvisations. Often, a rod with a hole at one end for a nail-pivot is secured at the other end in one of the holes normally used for an edge guide, or a jig that is attached to the router's base is provided. The rod needs some maneuvering before the radius for the circle is established correctly; a jig that must be attached each time it's needed is a nuisance.

Illus. 4-66 contains construction details for an easy-to-use jig. To use it, all you have to do is place the router inside the jig's ring. The radius-adjustment holes should have a common centerline and be accurately spaced. Also, they should be drilled slightly undersize for the nail that will be used as a pivot. Illus. 4-65 calls for a $\frac{1}{2}$- or 1-inch spacing, but other holes can be added.

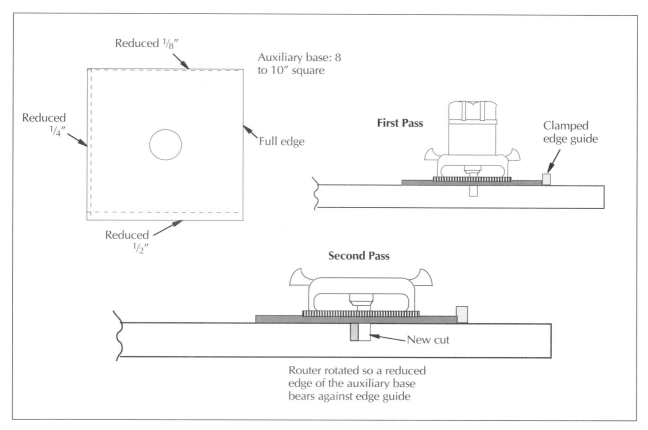

Reduced 1/8″

Reduced 1/4″

Auxiliary base: 8 to 10″ square

Full edge

Reduced 1/2″

First Pass

Clamped edge guide

Second Pass

New cut

Router rotated so a reduced edge of the auxiliary base bears against edge guide

Illus. 4-65. A base with reduced edges makes it easy to widen dado cuts without having to reposition the edge guide.

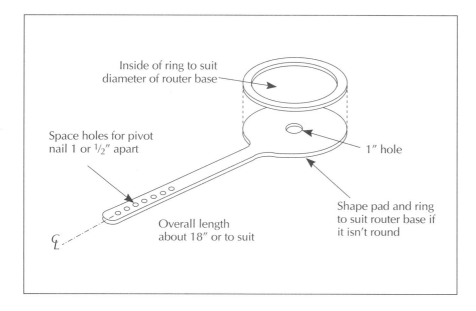

Inside of ring to suit diameter of router base

Space holes for pivot nail 1 or 1/2″ apart

1″ hole

Overall length about 18″ or to suit

Shape pad and ring to suit router base if it isn't round

Illus. 4-66. This pivot guide for circular cuts is more practical than one that requires that the router be attached to it. The router just slips inside the ring. The router end of the jig will have to be modified if your tool does not have a round base.

USING A SCROLL SAW

Bevel-Sawing with a Scroll Saw

I've been asked more than a few times why a bevel-sawed project failed. The answer usually is that the technique was not understood, or that there were operation errors. To begin with, bevel-sawing is a unique procedure that is used to produce bowl-type projects from a board whose thickness doesn't even come close to the project's depth. It is done to use wood economically, and to make maximum use of a small piece from an exotic or rare species that isn't usable for much else.

How does bevel-sawing work? This can be understood by studying Illus. 4-67. If you scroll-saw a disk from the center of a board with the machine's table in normal position, the disk will fall through the part it was cut from. However, if the table is tilted to a particular angle, the disk will fall through only partway, jamming into place. If you bevel-cut a series of concentric rings, they can be assembled to form the basis of the bowl shape (Illus. 4-68 and 4-69). The total depth of the project will depend on the thickness of the stock, the table tilt that is used, and the width of the kerf. Here's an example: If you bevel-cut six concentric rings from a ¾-inch-thick board that is 6 inches square, and each ring projects ½ inch, the project will end up 3¼ inches deep and its top diameter will be 6 inches. You can pretty much preview results by making a full-scale, cross-sectional drawing on paper.

The less table tilt you use, the greater the projection of each piece; the more pieces you cut, the greater the total projection. Be aware, though, that minimizing tilt can result in a difficult glue job when it's time to assemble the parts (Illus. 4-70). Also, with a very thin wall, it

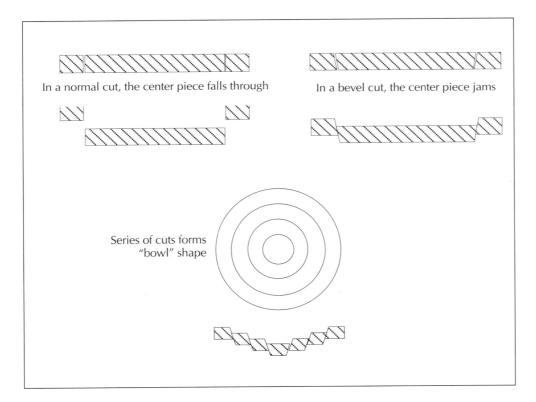

In a normal cut, the center piece falls through

In a bevel cut, the center piece jams

Series of cuts forms "bowl" shape

Illus. 4-67. The basis of scroll-saw bevel-sawing.

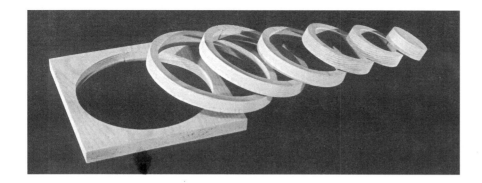

Illus. 4-68. The more rings that are cut, the deeper the project will be.

Illus. 4-69. Each ring will jam into its neighbor.

before being secured in the chucks (Illus. 4-72). On routine piercing work, the hole is drilled squarely through the stock, but when bevel-sawing, it must be drilled at an angle that is compatible with the tilt of the table. This is easy to do on a drill press because its table can be tilted. If you are using a portable drill, it's a good idea to make a gauge, which is just a small block of wood that is sanded at one or both ends to the angle required.

When doing the sawing, you must be sure to *always* keep the inside piece (the part that will project) on the same side of the blade.

may be difficult to avoid fractures when doing follow-up work like smoothing inside and outside surfaces, especially if the assembly will be used as a lathe turning (Illus. 4-71).

It can be difficult to anticipate the projections that will occur, so it's good practice to make a single experimental cut in a piece of scrap whose thickness matches that of the project material. In my own work, I have found that a table tilt of 2 to 5 degrees is acceptable on materials from $\frac{1}{4}$ to $\frac{3}{4}$ inch thick as long as the blade does not produce a heavy kerf. As a start, try a scroll-saw blade that has 15 teeth per inch (TPI) and is .020 inch thick and .110 inch wide.

Each of the rings to be cut will require an entry hole that the blade can pass through

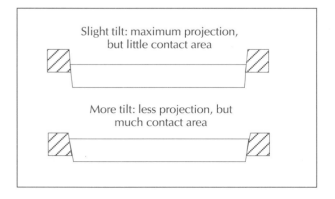

Illus. 4-70. The tilt of the scroll-saw table is important when you are cutting bevels. More tilt will lead to less ring projection and too much contact area, and less tilt leads to maximum ring projection but little contact area and a weak connection.

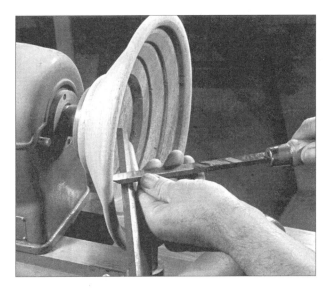

Illus. 4-71. Bevel-sawing is often used to produce a blank for lathe turning. That's one of the reasons why the contact area between rings is important.

Illus. 4-72. Blade entry holes must be drilled to match the tilt of the table. Saw carefully. Make sure the relationship between the work position and blade is constant throughout the cut. The blade entry holes make it easy to assemble the rings correctly.

Failing to do this will change the direction of the bevel, and the parts won't fit.

Bevel-sawing is not limited to bowl shapes. For example, it can be used to produce a raised lip for a round tray. Projects do not have to be circular. Why not an oval shape? Many hobbyists use bevel-sawing to produce hollow hulls for boat models. The latter application demands very close attention to the relationship between work and blade throughout the sawing task.

MISCELLANEOUS WOODWORKING TECHNIQUES

Cutting Angles on Panels

Angular cuts on large panels can be done by spanning the work across sawhorses and making the cut by guiding a saber saw or portable circular saw along a clamped straightedge. It's a common procedure, but the saws may not produce the smoothest of cuts, especially when the work is not supported adequately enough to prevent chatter. Also, when the cut is "in the field" (far from an edge), handling the tool for both accuracy and safety becomes awkward.

That's why cutting panel angles on a table saw is often recommended, but often with casual instructions. The gist of the operation is to tack-nail the panel at the angle needed to a board that will ride the rip fence so the cut can be made like any rip cut. To do the job accurately and safely, the guide board must be at least as long as the length of the cut, and the panel must be supported, as suggested in Illus. 4-73, so it can't tilt. It's also necessary to keep the panel on an even plane through the entire cut by using a stand, or calling for extra hands, to provide outboard support. If an assistant is used, be sure the person is briefed beforehand on what is going on and the kind of help required.

Good Riddance to Irregular Edges!

Providing a straight edge on a board or panel that, perhaps, is the cutoff from a saber-saw or band-saw operation is accomplished by using the same technique for making angular cuts on large panels. A change is to tack-nail the guide topside, so the work will be flat on the table throughout the cut (Illus. 4-74). Here, too, an anti-tilt strip of wood is in order, but this time, it is placed under the guide strip.

Another way to get such jobs done, and without fuss, is to clamp a long strip of wood to the rip fence. Sawing is done by keeping the high points of the irregular edge against the auxiliary fence (Illus. 4-74).

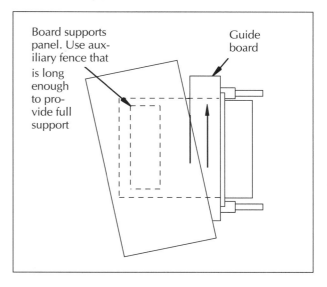

Illus. 4-73. Making an angular cut on a large panel. The support board will prevent the work from tilting during the cut.

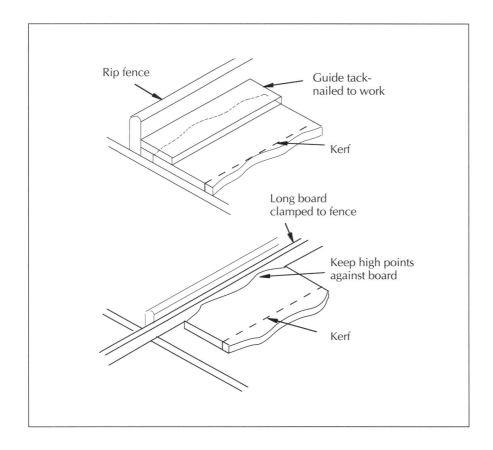

Illus. 4-74. Two ways that a board with irregular edges can be straightened.

Minimizing Rough Cuts

There are times with certain tools or when sawing particular materials, when taking an extra step eliminates, or at least greatly minimizes, the trimming of cut edges. When saber-sawing, no matter what blade is used, there is always a degree of feathering, and sometimes splintering, that we could do without. This is especially true when the job calls for a heavy blade that must have enough tooth set to cut freely. Help is on hand when you equip the tool with an auxiliary base that has a slot barely large enough for the blade to pass through (Illus. 4-75). This works because the new base bears down on the work immediately around the blade, thereby preventing surface fibers from being lifted by the blade action. A plus is the V-notch at the front that helps you follow the layout lines.

Eliminating the burring that happens when sawing sheet metal on a scroll saw is accomplished the same way. In this case, either add a special insert to the machine or clamp a piece of plywood to the table that has a tiny hole for the blade to pass through (Illus. 4-76). This technique also applies when cutting sheet metal on a band saw.

Some workers prefer the method that calls for sandwiching the metal between sheets of thin plywood. Either way, edges will be considerably smoother than they would be without the precautions.

Lengthening or Widening a Board

When you have a piece of material that's useful for a particular purpose, but isn't long enough or wide enough to suit, you might be able to salvage it by halving it diagonally and then putting the parts together as they are in Illus. 4-77. Obviously, lengthening reduces available width, and widening cuts down on length. The amount of sacrifice depends on how the pieces are rejoined. A small increase one way or the other is feasible, but it's not likely that an extensive correction will be practical.

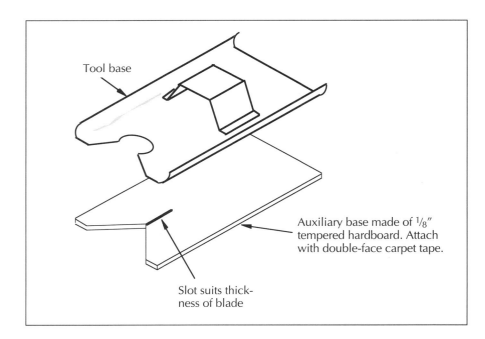

Tool base

Auxiliary base made of ⅛″ tempered hardboard. Attach with double-face carpet tape.

Slot suits thickness of blade

Illus. 4-75. A special base for a sabre saw provides for zero clearance around the saw blade. The result is greatly reduce feathering and splintering regardless of the blade that is used.

Illus. 4-76. A tiny hole, just enough to let the blade through, will eliminate jagged edges when you are sawing sheet metal on a scroll saw. The hole may be made through a special insert or, as shown here, through a clamped-on auxiliary table.

Lengthening a board by joining it to the end of a similar piece is another matter. This is where *scarf joints* come in. A common practice is to make the same slant-cut on the end of each piece and then to join them by gluing and clamping. To be sure of avoiding distortion around the area of the connection, use an assembly procedure like the one shown in Illus. 4-78.

A "Story Stick" for the Table Saw

Well, the miter-gauge extension shown in Illus. 4-79 doesn't look like a story stick pole, but it serves the same purpose: it establishes dimensions on a "gauge" (often just a strip of wood) so measuring when duplication is necessary needs to be done just once. In this case, I provided the extension when some projects required groups of similar parts, each group a different length. The dadoes in the extension are spaced to suit a specific length; the block of wood serves as a variable stop.

The tool provides convenience and ensures more accurate positioning than a plain extension with a clamped stop block that must be reset each time a new part is needed.

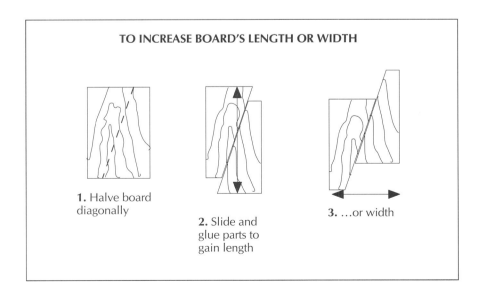

TO INCREASE BOARD'S LENGTH OR WIDTH

1. Halve board diagonally

2. Slide and glue parts to gain length

3. ...or width

Illus. 4-77. A board can be widened or lengthened by working this way. Widening the board decreases its length, and lengthening the board decreases its width. How severely the width and length decrease depends on how the separated parts are rejoined.

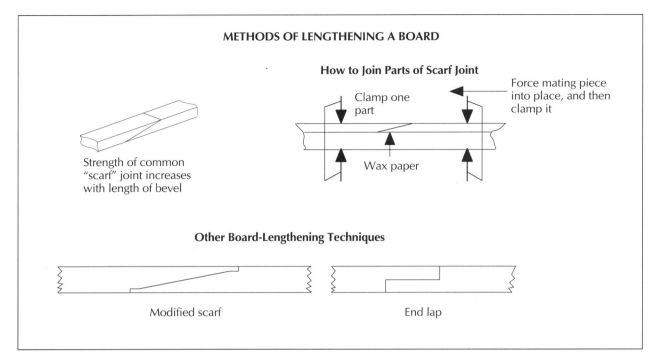

METHODS OF LENGTHENING A BOARD

How to Join Parts of Scarf Joint

Clamp one part

Force mating piece into place, and then clamp it

Wax paper

Strength of common "scarf" joint increases with length of bevel

Other Board-Lengthening Techniques

Modified scarf

End lap

Illus. 4-78. Scarf joints are used to assemble boards end to end. There are many joint variations, but those shown here are common.

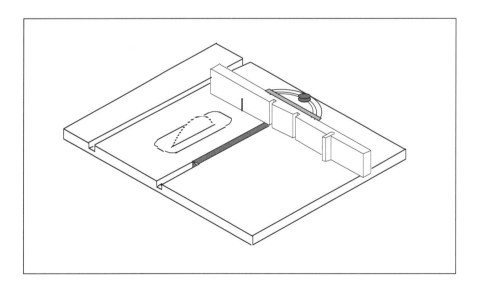

Illus. 4-79. This miter-gauge extension allows you to saw various pieces to a particular length. The stop block should fit snugly in the dadoes, so clamping won't be necessary.

5

Planning Projects

THE CONCEPT OF PROPORTION

Woodworkers have different tastes, tools, and skills. For example, if you were to ask a dozen woodworkers to design and construct a table, you would end up with a dozen tables of different sizes, styles, and shapes, despite the fact that a table is essentially a top supported by legs. There are many different table designs, including tables with round, square, oval, or free-form tops, with construction that might include stretchers or a drawer or a shelf, and there might even be one with a glass or marble top sitting on wrought-iron legs.

All these designs are acceptable, but only if the builder has, as a preliminary step, paid sufficient attention to the concepts of proportion. For any project to be successful, it's overall dimensions must be visually pleasing. The proportions of components like doors, drawers, legs, aprons, etc., must be compatible with the proportions of the project as a whole. A thick slab on skinny legs or a coffee table 17 inches high with rails that are 10 inches wide will disturb the eye. Would you feel that a paneled cabinet door with a top rail 2 inches wide and a bottom rail 8 inches wide is visually appealing?

DESIGN FACTORS AND INFORMATION

It's generally assumed that it was the Greeks, aware of a particular ratio in Egyptian architecture, who coined the phrase *golden section,* also known as *golden* rectangle and *golden moon.* What is the definition of a golden section? One dictionary definition is "a portion into which the ratio of the whole to the larger part is the same as the ratio of the larger part to the smaller" (Illus. 5-1). Actually, so we don't get too shook up, a smart furniture-designer friend of mine says that the numerical ratio is about 5 to 8. I can live with that.

Design elements, architectural and otherwise, that are based on the golden section are pleasing to most people. Developing the ratio for projects of different sizes isn't difficult if you use graphics and plan to scale. First, you can form a golden rectangle by starting with a square of any size and doing the geometrical construction shown in Illus. 5-2. Now, with a basic rectangle available, and knowing either the height or the length of the project, you can use the information in Illus. 5-3 to construct a suitable golden rectangle.

Now we're all set to plan the project, but are

135

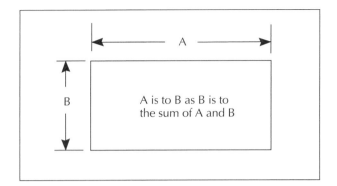

Illus. 5-1. The mathematical formula for the dimensions of a golden rectangle.

we? It isn't difficult to imagine situations where adherence to these procedures won't work. For example, the project may be a built-in whose dimensions are already established because it must fill an available space. Or you may be designing a dining table, in which the important factor is the number of people you want it to accommodate. And when building a chest, do we first dimension the drawers according to these procedures and then design the rest of the chest around them?

There are other facets of proportion that influence design. You might use the golden section for the overall structure, but ignore it for internal elements. You can design symmetrically around a centerline and achieve a most pleasing balance (Illus. 5-4). There are times when, out of necessity or as an option, making particular components of a structure asymmetric achieves a balance of the whole.

In the final analysis, a project is successful if it looks good and is functional. We can design by rote, but we have the freedom to be creative and express our individuality. The one thought we should bear in mind was stated many years ago by George Hepplewhite. He said that the purpose of furniture is "to unite elegance and utility, and blend the useful with the agreeable."

STYLE AND DESIGN

I make a distinction between *style* and *design*. Style is influenced by many things: personal tastes, the mode of the times, etc. Period pieces often bear the name of a monarch whose preferences made the style popular for that period. Style may relate to particular characteristics that identify the work of a designer or craftsman.

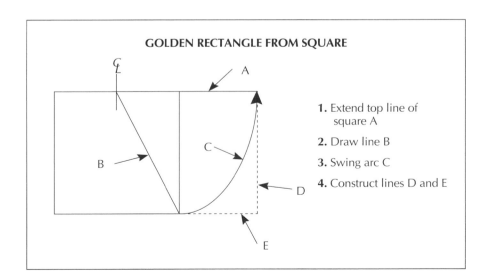

GOLDEN RECTANGLE FROM SQUARE

1. Extend top line of square A
2. Draw line B
3. Swing arc C
4. Construct lines D and E

Illus. 5-2. Start with a square and use this construction method to create an acceptable golden rectangle.

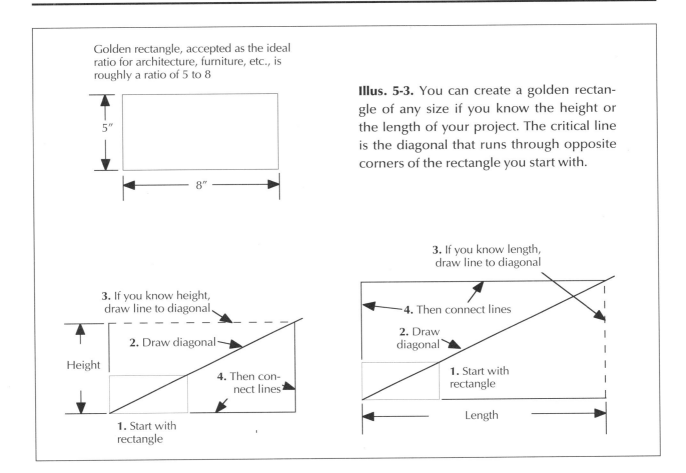

Golden rectangle, accepted as the ideal ratio for architecture, furniture, etc., is roughly a ratio of 5 to 8

5″

8″

Illus. 5-3. You can create a golden rectangle of any size if you know the height or the length of your project. The critical line is the diagonal that runs through opposite corners of the rectangle you start with.

3. If you know length, draw line to diagonal

3. If you know height, draw line to diagonal

4. Then connect lines

2. Draw diagonal

2. Draw diagonal

Height

1. Start with rectangle

4. Then connect lines

1. Start with rectangle

Length

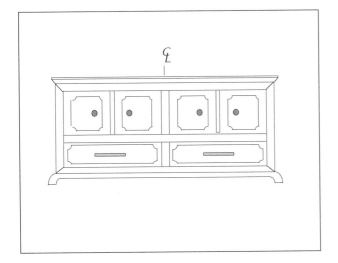

Illus. 5-4. Designing for symmetry around a centerline achieves a pleasant balance.

However, appearance alone will not make a project. Style, or how the piece looks, may be accepted or rejected by different people, but good *design*, which determines how a piece functions, should be a constant. You may not like the style of a piece, but if the piece is functional and comfortable, you will appreciate its design. Knowing the difference between style and design makes it easier to plan original projects or to adapt the ideas of existing pieces successfully.

One of the fundamental principles of good design is that the project be made to be used. A dining table may look great, but if it isn't close to the norm for height and doesn't allow room for individuals to eat, it won't be comfortable.

Adequate table spacing allows about 16

inches per place setting, with 8 inches in between each setting. A generous, rectangular table for six diners would therefore measure 36 x 84 inches, but being realistic, we can squeeze in another person or two when necessary (Illus. 5-5). There are options when the ideal size is too much for available space. A "small" table can be lengthened if it is designed with hinged ends or leaves that can be inserted between permanent components.

Why human anatomy should influence project specifications can be understood by using a desk as an example. When you lack a plan, you can quickly establish one for the main part—the top.

To do this, imagine sitting at a desk. Then reach forward and note the distance from your chest to your fingertips (Illus. 5-6). This dimension will establish a reasonable width for the project. Second, reach out to your left and right (Illus. 5-7). The total span of your arms suggests what the maximum length of the desk should be.

While using the desk, you should be able to reach anywhere on its surface. For a smaller unit where you might sit at one end, a practical length for the top can be determined by reaching to the left or right with one arm and then adding the width of your body.

Often, the dimensions you decide on are a compromise. In this case, consider the items you'll use on the desk. These may include books, a telephone, fax machine, or a computer. All these accessories have a specific dimension that you know beforehand and can allow for when you do the initial planning on paper.

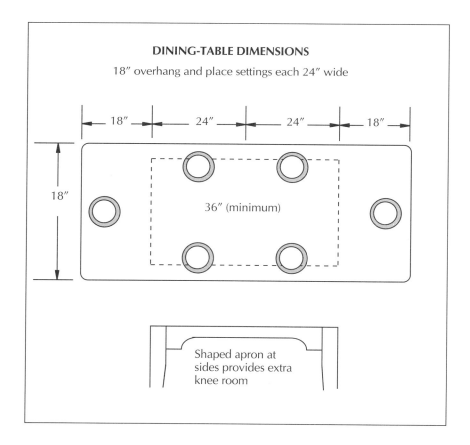

DINING-TABLE DIMENSIONS

18″ overhang and place settings each 24″ wide

18″   24″   24″   18″

18″

36″ (minimum)

Shaped apron at sides provides extra knee room

Illus. 5-5. Human proportions are factors to consider when establishing dimensions for a project. Shown here are the standards for pleasant dining. Point them out to some restaurants!

Illus. 5-6. You should be able to reach across a desk without straining. Its height and the space between pedestals must allow for comfortable sitting.

Illus. 5-7. Being able to reach either end of the desk easily adds to the practicality of the project. Other factors, which include the items you need on the desk, may prompt a deviation from the norm.

This kind of forethought also applies to components of the project. What will you store? A shallow drawer will accommodate a ream of writing paper, but file folders require more depth. Partitioning a shallow center drawer for pencils, paper clips, stamps, etc., adds to the utility of the project. There should be no guesswork here. Simply measure the items and design for them.

It's an error to arbitrarily decide the spacing of shelves in a storage cabinet. Good results depend on anticipating what you will store or, of course, installing adjustable shelves. But many times there is the opportunity to be a bit more creative.

BALANCING A PROJECT

Projects should be "balanced." By balanced I don't mean that the parts should be symmetrical, but that the unit as a whole should appear to have its weight equally distributed so there will be a visual impression of poise and stability.

A friend, a good craftsman, built a respectable chest of drawers, but there was something about the project that was disturbing. The drawers varied in depth and I felt the distraction occurred because the heavy drawers were at the top, causing the project to appear top heavy (Illus. 5-8). Is this nit picking? Maybe.

I asked the craftsman if he had overlooked this possible fault when he was planning the project. When he didn't answer, maybe puzzled by the question, I suggested that even from a practical point of view, if he had built the shallow drawer at the top to hold items like a wristwatch, wallet, coins, etc., it would have made storage and retrieval more convenient. However, we're still friends.

PROJECT MATERIALS

The materials used can make or break the project. Different materials may be combined, but you have to consider the overall visual impression. A high-gloss plastic laminate used for doors on a bookcase made of knotty pine that will be antiqued and distressed just isn't going to look right. Economy wood has its own suitable place when used as shelves in certain projects, as do the high-quality species such as walnut or Honduras mahogany.

Consider an area of emphasis, something that will attract the eye, such as the wood itself, a glorious finish, an intriguing detail like an eye-catching inlay or, when suitable, handcrafted hardware. It could be, and often is, a construction detail like classic joinery left exposed. It might be the visual impression of incorporating unfinished woodwork with a bold decorative element, such as a bookcase of unfinished boards with slim, steel bar stock for the uprights. How about a case painted pure white and with black, iron hardware?

Woodworking is a creative activity and the wood an art medium. As long as we do not go too far astray from some necessary standards, there is no reason why our creativity should be subdued. That's another mistake to avoid.

HOW TO PRODUCE A DESIGN

We start off with the intention of building a project that will fulfill certain needs. Then what? There are design options, but they must be preceded by an idea of what the project will look like. If you don't have an idea of what the project will look like, it's likely that errors will occur in design and construction. Sources of inspiration include illustrations in magazines, furniture stores, or furniture in a friend's house, commercial establishments, or even museums. And there is always the easy chair to sit in while your mind conjures up images.

I read a comment once that said woodworking can be enjoyable even without wood. I assume the author was alluding to planning stages, and that makes some sense. By working in your mind you can build a project as many times as you wish; you can even change the wood being used, substitute joints, or redo a finish, all without actually having to rectify errors. If you're enthused, it goes to bed with you, so tomorrow's chores and how they must be done

Illus. 5-8. Which of these similar designs do you find more acceptable? Does the small drawer at the bottom on the chest of drawers on the left seem crushed by the larger ones above it?

correctly are established tonight. However, I must inject a factor that is paramount over all others. It's when the lady of the house says, "I want a table *exactly* like that one!"

PROJECT DRAWINGS

Designing a project on paper can be simple or complicated and time-consuming. Which way to go depends on how much you feel you need to get from a drawing in order to work efficiently. Some woodworkers just start sawing. Forming a tenon without seeing the dimensions on paper is chancy, to put it mildly.

Types of Drawing

A "three-view" drawing is one that shows the project as if you were looking directly at its front and end, and down on its top. The drawing can show overall dimensions, and through the use of dotted lines, the relationships of components (Illus. 5-9). Details can also be dimensioned, but since such a drawing is usually done to scale, including the data can complicate the drawing. It's better to do a separate view, say, for the rail-to-leg connection, and to draw it full size. This depiction doesn't need more than a front and a top view for all dimensions to be shown.

The three-view drawing, with details added, provides enough information for you to work on the project in the shop, but if you wish to preview how the views, or "elevations," will appear in their actual relationships, you need to use an illustration.

A common follow-up is an *isometric* drawing, which is constructed by using three axes, one being vertical and the remaining two drawn to the left and the right, 30 degrees to the horizontal (Illus. 5-10). The true measurements (or scaled versions) of the height, width, and depth of the project are marked on the three axes. Each sur-

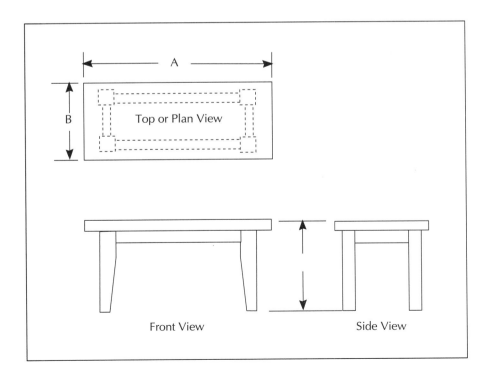

Illus. 5-9. A three-view drawing. You look directly at the front and side, and down on the top of the project.

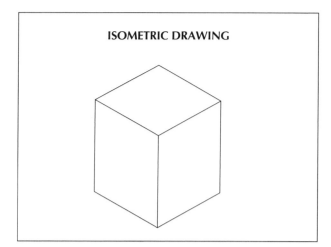

Illus. 5-10. An isometric drawing is based on three axes, a vertical one and two that are 30 degrees to the horizontal. This type of drawing is easy to make with a draftsman's 30- or 60-degree triangle template.

face, or view, is completed by drawing necessary lines parallel to those already established.

An advantage of the isometric drawing is that dimensions can be taken right from the drawing. However, it does not show the project as the eye would actually see it. A *perspective* drawing comes close to presenting an object as it appears to the eye, or as it would look, say, in a photograph. This style of drawing is based on the fact that all lines extending from an observer seem to converge at a distant point. Common examples of this phenomenon are railroad tracks that seem to come together, or a straight highway that gets narrower as it fades off into the horizon.

There are many ways to construct perspective drawings, but for our purposes, it's enough to draw a horizontal line that represents the eye level of the observer and to arbitrarily mark this line with left and right "vanishing" points. (Vanishing points are drawing representations of that spot on a horizon where two points meet.) After establishing a vertical line that represents a corner of the project, you will extend all other lines, except vertical ones, from it to one or the other vanishing point (Illus. 5-11). You can see that with the vertical line and the two base lines established, all other lines fall into perspective. The three beginning lines may have true dimensions, but other lines will not be accurate. The difference between an isometric drawing and a perspective one is that the latter shows the project as it will actually appear (Illus. 5-12).

Drawing to Scale

If you have a large enough drafting table or other smooth surface, you can draw projects full

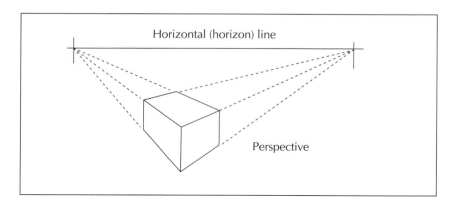

Illus. 5-11. One way to construct a perspective drawing is to draw a horizontal line and to mark it with left and right "vanishing" points. You can't take dimensions from this type of drawing as you can with an isometric drawing where lines are drawn actual size or to scale.

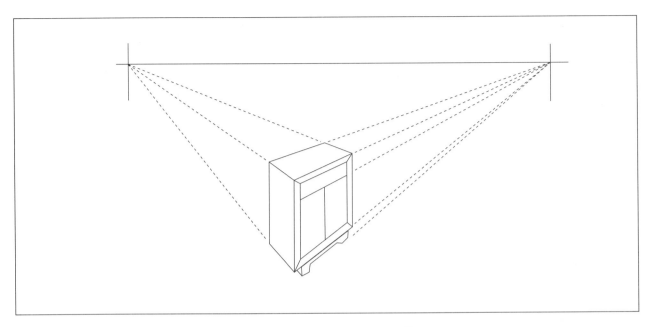

Illus. 5-12. A perspective drawing shows the project as it will actually appear.

size. That would offer advantages, but the more common practice is to work to scale. It's practical, and when the ruler and pencil are carefully used, it will offer accurate results. Drawing to scale simply means that, for example, ¼ inch on the drawing represents 1 inch, or 1 inch equals 3 inches, etc. The most convenient scale to use depends on the size of the paper you are drawing on. The drawing can be half-size, quarter-size, etc., but the larger you can make it the easier it will be to work.

My computer provides a great assist in this area because my drawing program allows me to automatically enlarge or reduce the size of a drawing, and I can set up the program's ruler to the scale I wish to use. It makes things easier, but it is not, of course, the only way to go.

An architect's scale, a common drafting implement, can easily be used even if you've had very little experience with it. The "stick," to use the vernacular, provides a wide range of scale reductions. The basic measuring faces, in addition to full size, are designated as 3, 1½, 1, ¾, ½, ⅜, ¼, 3/16, 3/32, and ⅛. Each scale represents the proportions to which a drawing can be reduced in relation to inches and feet. Thus, the measuring edge marked with a 3 indicates that 3 inches equals one foot, an edge labeled as 1½ inches means that 1½ inches equals one foot, etc. The sizes to which a drawing can be produced by using an architect's scale are shown in Illus. 5-13.

MODELS

Imagining the project and making drawings of it are good beginnings, but for a real preview of what the project will look like nothing beats taking the time to make a mock-up (Illus. 5-14 and 5-15). You don't have to complicate your life by treating them as museum-type miniatures or even by including intricate details, but they should, preferably, be made to scale, and include all important components.

CHART FOR SCALING DRAWINGS		
Size	*Scale*	*Equivalent*
Full	12″ = 1′	1″ = 1″
$^3/_4$	9″ = 1′	$^3/_4$″ = 1″
$^1/_2$	6″ = 1′	$^1/_2$″ = 1″
$^1/_4$	3″ = 1′	$^1/_4$″ = 1″
$^1/_8$	$1^1/_2$″ = 1′	$^1/_8$″ = 1″
$^1/_{12}$	1″ = 1′	1″ = 12″
$^1/_{16}$	$^3/_4$″ = 1′	
$^1/_{24}$	$^1/_2$″ = 1′	
$^1/_{48}$	$^1/_4$″ = 1′	

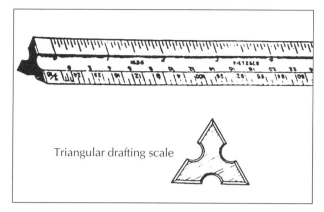

Triangular drafting scale

Illus. 5-13. The scale sizes that can be produced with an architect's scale, as shown on the right.

Illus. 5-14. It's easy to see how the project will finally look when you look at a miniature of it.

Many different types of materials can be used to make the models. These include $^1/_4$-inch plywood assembled with brads, foam core modeling board, blocks of scrap wood band- sawed to shape, and stiff cardboard held together with tape. If you use cardboard, avoid corrugated varieties unless you want to make a full-size mock-up. Small pieces are difficult to cut with a knife and will have shredded edges.

The advantage of models is that they can be viewed from any angle. And if you add a floor plan or the walls of a room scaled to match, they can even be viewed in the envi-

Illus. 5-15. Models don't have to be highly detailed, but they should be made to scale. They not only show the project, but how its different components relate to each other.

ronment they will be placed in.

When making a project from another person's plans, you are not obligated to clone the project, and you don't have to dismiss it if it isn't suitable as is (Illus. 5-16). Often, a few minor alterations can dramatically change the appearance of a project more to suit your preference or the decor of your home without altering its function.

AVOIDING THE MISTAKES OF OTHERS

If you like to scrutinize Readers' Letters columns in woodworking magazines, you'll know how frequently there appears a note from an unhappy woodworker who blindly obeyed the dimensions on a drawing or in a materials list and found that some of them were inaccurate.

Unfortunately, it isn't hard to come across such errors. The materials list for the outdoor bench in Illus. 5-17 listed the length of the backrest and the rail as 30 inches. Someone overlooked the fact that the parts are mortised into the back legs. In another example, the layout shown in Illus. 5-18 indicates how a number of project components could be produced from a single board. This technique is fine, but someone forgot that saw kerfs produce waste and that the real width of a 10-inch board is $9\frac{1}{4}$ inches.

Many culprits could be blamed if an inaccurate dimension is given in any magazine or book: the typesetter, the writer, or the artist who did the final drawings for the book. But let's face facts. The ultimate responsibility for avoiding dimension errors is the builder's. So what should a prospective project builder do? First, don't accept the dimensions on a drawing or in a cutting list as automatically accurate. *Never*

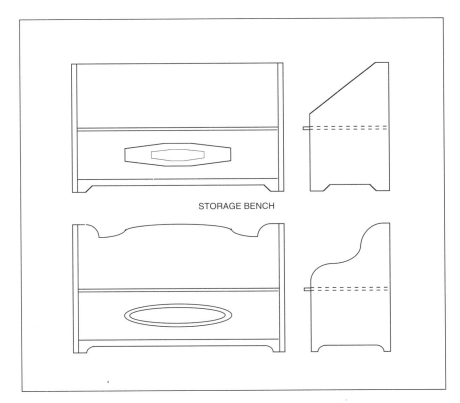

STORAGE BENCH

Illus. 5-16. You don't have to use the plans for someone else's project exactly as they are when building the project. Often, minor changes to the design that have to do with the project's appearance can transform the project into something that is more suitable for your environment.

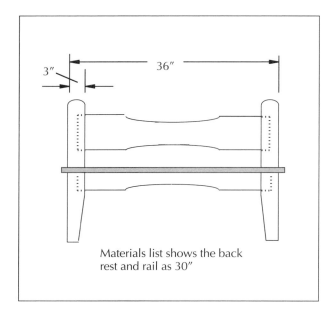

Materials list shows the back
rest and rail as 30″

Illus. 5-17. The materials list for this outdoor bench mistakenly lists the length of its back rest and the rail as 30 inches. Someone overlooked the fact that the back rest and the rail are mortised into the back legs. This type of error is not rare, which is why dimensions on a drawing or in a materials list should not be blindly accepted as accurate.

start a project by cutting to size all the parts in a cutting list or take such a list to a lumberyard that will cut material to size before checking the accuracy of the parts.

THE MAIN-PART SYSTEM

What is the best way to design a project? Well, I have my way, and it's as good as any and better than others. I give it the fancy name of The Main-Part System. Consider a desk. After making a sketch and maybe a model, I know the overall length, width, and height of the project. The main part of the desk is the top, and the length and width of the desk establish the dimensions for the top. With the top on hand, you have established the parameters of the substructure. On the underside of the top, mark them. Now, you have a frame within which all other elements must be contained.

You may have two main parts. On the desk example, they may be the top and the ends. Now, in addition to length and width, there is a limit on the desk's height. Once the additional parts are

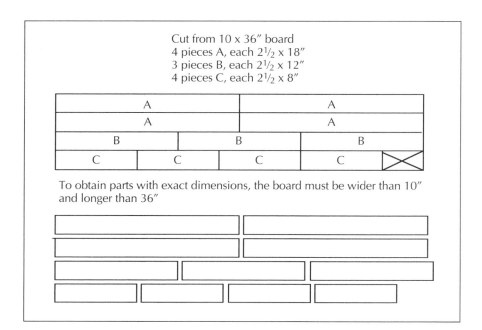

Cut from 10 x 36″ board
4 pieces A, each 2½ x 18″
3 pieces B, each 2½ x 12″
4 pieces C, each 2½ x 8″

To obtain parts with exact dimensions, the board must be wider than 10″ and longer than 36″

Illus. 5-18. Another goof that proves we must be somewhat skeptical about printed dimensions. Someone forgot that while the nominal width of a board is 10 inches, its real width is 9¼ inches and that a normal saw kerf is ⅛ inch wide.

made and positioned by the marked frame on the underside of the top, you work within the dimensions that are imposed. This is a check-as-you-go system that will work much more to your advantage than the complete fabrication of all parts before assembly that have dimensions based on those in a cutting list or on a drawing.

The system also allows for possible human error. If a plan calls for X number of inches between the side members of a desk's pedestal and you inadvertently cut them X minus ¼ inch, they would have to be discarded. But, when you check and build as you go, little discrepancies can be compensated for. In this case, bring the sides of the pedestal closer by ¼ inch.

This system can also be applied to making joints. If you need a number of mortise-and-tenon joints, it isn't wise to precut all the components feeling that you will be precise enough. It's better to form the tenons and then use one to establish the dimensions of the mortise. If you've made the tenons wider or thinner than they should be, it would be no problem to form the mortises to suit.

I don't wish to oversimplify the procedure for planning a project. There are times when it is good practice to make intermediate drawings to transfer dimensions of parts that follow those already on hand, such as establishing the length and width of shelves or web frames and their joint configurations after vertical members are on hand. This as-you-go drawing gives exact dimensions for cuts that are needed. This drawing can even include notes to remind you of critical factors (See Illus. 5-19 and 5-20).

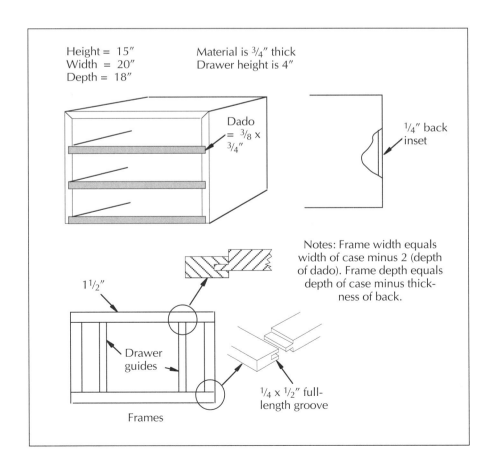

Height = 15″
Width = 20″
Depth = 18″

Material is ³⁄₄″ thick
Drawer height is 4″

Dado = ³⁄₈ x ³⁄₄″

¼″ back inset

Notes: Frame width equals width of case minus 2 (depth of dado). Frame depth equals depth of case minus thickness of back.

1½″

Drawer guides

Frames

¼ x ½″ full-length groove

Illus. 5-19. Intermediate drawings can be done during construction stages of a project. They may show an entire subassembly or just details.

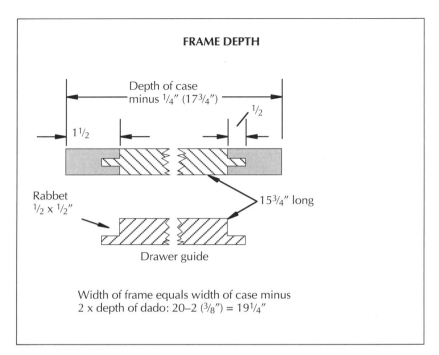

FRAME DEPTH

Depth of case
minus ¼″ (17¾″)

½

1½

Rabbet
½ x ½″

15¾″ long

Drawer guide

Width of frame equals width of case minus
2 x depth of dado: 20–2 (⅜″) = 19¼″

Illus. 5-20. This drawing, done after other components were on hand, establishes the dimensions of web frames. Measuring on assembly is a better way to ensure accuracy than precutting parts.

6

Dealing With Defects in Wood, and Other Woodworking Repairs

KNOTS

A knot is the place where the branch of a tree is attached to the main trunk (Illus. 6-1). Knots appear as either circles or spikes in sawn lumber, and are generally considered blemishes except when they contribute to the project's appearance, as in a project made of knotty pine.

The number and types of knots on lumber (plus other defects such as pitch pockets, checks, and shakes) are used to determine lumber grades. (A pitch pocket is an opening in wood that contains resin. Checks are separations of the wood fibers that can occur anywhere on a piece. Shake is a lengthwise separation of the wood.) Lumber in the Select-grade category is either clear and suitable for staining or natural finishes, or has minor defects that can be concealed with paint. There are various grades of Common-grade lumber that range

Illus. 6-1. Top: Knots detract from or add to a project's appearance, depending on what you plan to do with the wood. Bottom: The number, size, and type of knots (light, loose, decayed, etc.) that appear on boards are some of the elements that determine the grade of the wood.

from "sound with tight knots and limited blemishes," to lowest quality, which are boards that have value only as filler material.

Yet, even the less desirable grades will have areas of perfectly good material that might be suitable for the project on hand. When shopping for lumber, it's quite practical to take along the pattern of a project part to aid in selecting usable stock between defects. Studying a board with defects may reveal that it can be sawed so that the defects are discarded and narrow, better-quality boards are produced (Illus. 6-2), or that using one end as waste provides a good, although shorter board. Tight knots do not diminish the strength of the board, and we can opt to eliminate those we don't want. A loose knot or even a knot hole shouldn't prevent us from using the board if the board as a whole looks good. With lumber prices as they are, shrewd shopping is essential. Price-wise, there is a substantial difference between "select" and

"common" grades of lumber. And, by making maximum use of every stick of wood, we help to preserve a diminishing resource.

Knots in the Field

I generally use Forstner bits in a drill press to eliminate knots in the field (Illus. 6-3). They can't be beat for producing clean, flat-bottom holes, and their center point is so shallow they can even be used on thin material without the center point breaking through.

After cutting the knot out, the next step is to make a plug for the hole. It would be nice if we could use a hole saw to make the plug, but such tools are equipped with a pilot drill and the plug would have a hole through it, which defeats the purpose. I have used hole saws without the pilot, but only under the following strict conditions: 1. the hole saw must be clean and sharp; 2. use the hole saw only in a drill press and at

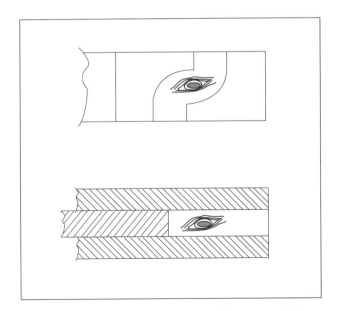

Illus. 6-2. It's often possible to eliminate defects in boards by working around them or by judicious sawing.

Illus. 6-3. Forstner bits produce clean, flat-bottomed holes. They are available in sizes from ¼ inch up to as much as 3 inches.

the machine's slowest speed; 3. feed pressure must be very light; and 4. the work must be securely clamped.

If you follow these rules but still get chatter or a rough cut, or if you feel uncomfortable working so, don't do it. Instead, cut a disk with a coping saw or on a scroll saw and then smooth the edges. It's a good idea to sand the edges to a slight bevel, so it will be easier to force the plug into place (Illus. 6-4). Make the repair piece from wood that matches the work-piece, and plan for grain patterns to be compatible. After the glue is dry and the repair area is sanded smooth, it will be difficult to discern that the job was done (Illus. 6-5).

If you are thinking of cutting disks from round shapes, remember they will show end grain. The woodworker friend I keep mentioning, faced with a number of knots to hide, turned a cylinder of suitable diameter on the lathe and then sliced off disks like so much sala-mi. Exposed end grain may or may not be important, depending on how the project will be finished. It won't be visible at all if the intention is to seal and paint it.

A similar technique is used when the knot

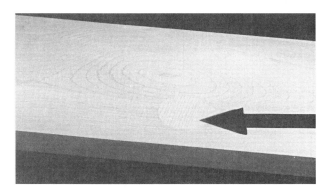

Illus. 6-5. If you sand the repair area after the glue on it has dried, the plug will be barely noticeable. Matching the grain of the plug with that of the board isn't especially critical if the project will be painted.

or other blemish can't be covered with a single hole. Use a Forstner bit to bore a series of over-lapping holes and then clean away the remaining waste with a chisel. Cut the patch to a size and shape that fits the hole (Illus. 6-6).

Knots on Edge

It's not rare to find a knot on the edge of a board that's graded to fall in the "select" or even "common" category (Illus. 6-7). Getting rid of this flaw is another job for a Forstner bit (Illus. 6-8). One of the values of this type of boring tool is that it can be used efficiently on edges, and even when the center point is not contacting the wood. Form full-circle patches for this type of recess. Saw off and sand the section that must be compatible with the edge of the stock after the glue dries.

Another way to treat this problem, one that eliminates the chore of having to produce a round patch, is to cut out a notch that's deep and long enough to remove the knot, and then to cut a rectangular patch to fit the hole (Illus. 6-9). The thickness of the patch is not critical because you

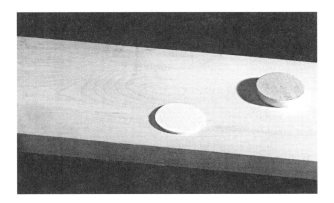

Illus. 6-4. Bevel the edge of the plug so it can be forced tightly into the hole. Prepare the plug so it is thicker than necessary.

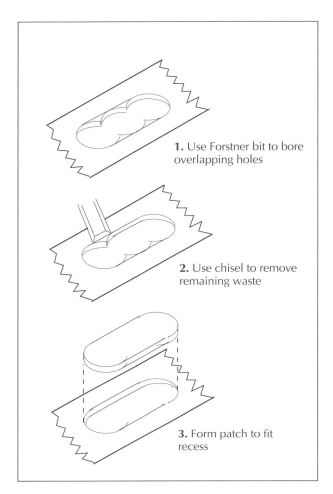

1. Use Forstner bit to bore overlapping holes

2. Use chisel to remove remaining waste

3. Form patch to fit recess

Illus. 6-6. Forming overlapping holes with a Forstner bit takes care of long knots.

Illus. 6-7. Knots on the edge of a board. These types of knots can be trimmed off, or they can be replaced without sacrificing any of the board's width.

Illus. 6-8. Forstner bits are practical tools for cutting partial holes on edges. Make a full-circle plug for this type of repair. Trim off the excess plug after the glue dries.

will be sawing off and sanding the excess, but it should only be a fraction of an inch longer, so gentle taps with a mallet will seat it securely.

Another idea, one that works nicely on plywood, starts with the setup shown in Illus. 6-10. It involves using a table saw. Lower the saw blade under the table and then set the rip fence so the distance from its surface to the *outside* face of the blade equals the thickness of the stock. Clamp the work to the rip fence and slowly raise the blade until the arc it forms is deep enough and wide enough to cover the defect. If one cut doesn't do the job, repeat the process after bringing the rip fence a bit closer to the blade. Then, cut a patch to fit (Illus. 6-11).

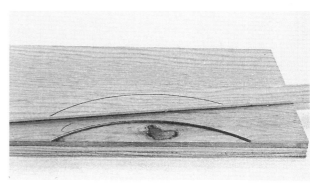

Illus. 6-11. Surface veneer can be sliced from a similar piece of plywood and then shaped to fit the arch.

Illus. 6-9. Another way to eliminate an edge knot. Don't make the patch too long. A snug fit is good, but having to force the patch into place will create unwanted stresses.

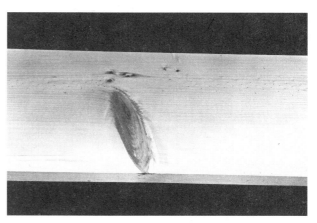

Illus. 6-12. Groups of knots, like this array, require special treatment, and you must be sure the patched area is sound.

Illus. 6-10. This method of eliminating edge knots, done on a table saw, works fine and is particularly good for plywood. The setup can be organized so just the surface veneer is removed.

How about a long knot that just happens to fall at midpoint in a board that otherwise would fit nicely into your plans (Illus. 6-12)? Use a dadoing tool to form a recess that's just deep enough and wide enough to clear away the unwanted material. Make the patch thicker than you need so it can be sanded flush, but don't make it so wide it must be forced into place. The patch should fit snugly, but without creat-

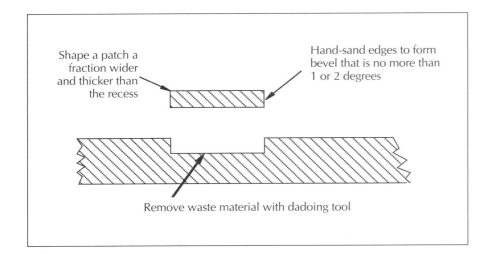

Shape a patch a fraction wider and thicker than the recess

Hand-sand edges to form bevel that is no more than 1 or 2 degrees

Remove waste material with dadoing tool

Illus. 6-13. Use a dadoing tool to remove the flawed area and then cut a patch to suit. Keep the depth of the cut to a minimum.

ing stresses that might cause trouble later on (Illus. 6-13).

One time, when I needed an assortment of candlesticks, I thought it would be nice to have a tool that would form tapered holes for the candles. The answer was in the form of a spade bit that I modified as shown in Illus. 6-14. What does this have to do with knots? Well, as often happens, a tool made for one purpose serves another. In this case, I used the new modified spade bit to cut out a knot that passed through a board, and then shaped a plug to fit the hole. The plug fit tightly, and after it was sanded, I had a neat appearance on both surfaces of the board.

RIGHTING A WRONG IN VENEER

Blistering, a kind of half bubble that appears in veneer without invitation, is usually caused by insufficient glue in spots under the surface veneer or maybe a bad patch in the core panel. One repair method is to first drill a small hole through the blister and then get some glue into the cavity using a glue syringe or maybe just a toothpick (Illus. 6-15). Use just enough glue to get under the blister. If you flood the cavity with glue, the pressure required to flatten the

blister may spread excess glue to surrounding areas and cause further damage. Next, cover the blister with wax paper and keep weights in place overnight. The last step is to fill the hole with a wax stick of suitable color. Special sticks of carnauba wax mixed with resins and coloring pigments are available, but often, a

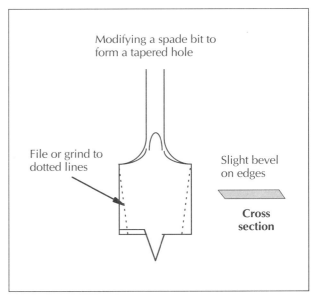

Modifying a spade bit to form a tapered hole

File or grind to dotted lines

Slight bevel on edges

Cross section

Illus. 6-14. How to modify a spade bit so it will form tapered holes.

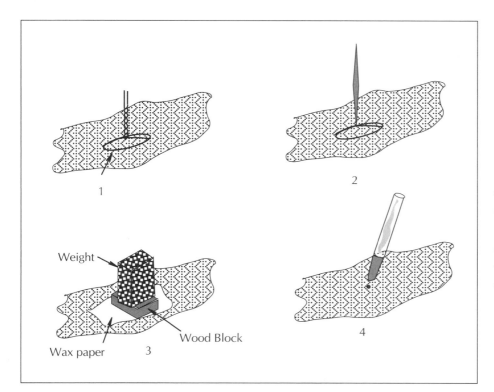

Illus. 6-15. The four steps involved in repairing a blister. First, drill a small hole through the blister. Second, using a toothpick put some glue into the cavity. Third, cover the blister with wax paper and leave weights on it overnight. Last, fill the hole with a wax stick of suitable color.

crayon can do the job satisfactorily.

Another way to repair a blister, especially on straight-grain veneer, is to slit the bubble lengthwise with a single-edge razor blade. Then, very carefully lift each half of the culprit just enough to get some glue inside the cavity. When the work is done this way, it is rarely necessary to do anything else to the surface. The razor slit won't be visible after the blister is weighted down to where it should be.

Tenting is another veneer flaw. It's like a half-bubble that appears at the edge of a panel, often along the line where two pieces of veneer are matched. This type of problem is often caused by moisture, either from the environment or a spill. If this is so, just gluing and clamping won't work because the "tent" may fracture or fold back on itself. Therefore, a good job depends on first drying out the area. This can be accomplished with a hair dryer or heating pad, or by placing a wad of newspaper over the flaw and heating it with an iron. The heat must be minimal. Too much can soften surrounding areas.

After the flawed area is dry, use glue after scraping away the old application and then, over wax paper, use weights to flatten the tent.

Repairing a Damaged Veneer Area

A damaged area or maybe a spot that's been sanded through requires special attention, namely, removing the flawed section and replacing it with a patch that will match the parent stock. There are several ways to go.

A common method is to start by placing a sheet of tracing paper over the damaged area and taping it in place, but leaving one or two edges open (Illus. 6-16). Use a pencil to trace the outline of the damage. If the damage has irregular edges it will be difficult to cut a patch

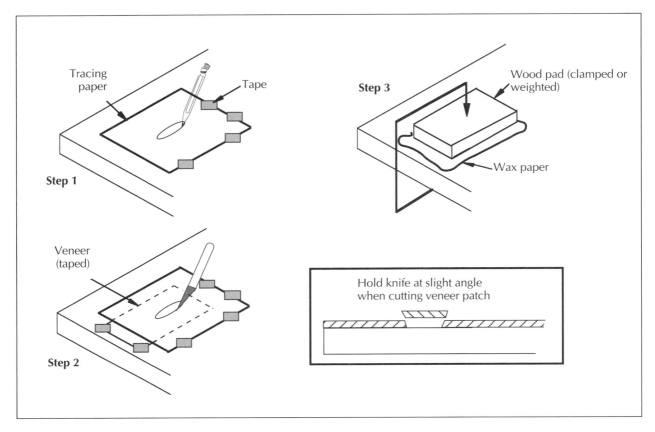

Illus. 6-16. The step-by-step methods for producing a veneer patch. This technique allows you to cut through the patch and the flawed veneer at the same time.

that will match. Therefore, it's a good idea to draw a circle, rectangle, or oval that's just large enough to cover the flaw. Next, slip the veneer patch under the tracing paper, aligning it as closely as possible with the grain pattern of the original veneer, and tape it firmly in place. Then, using a utility knife with a new blade, cut through both the patch and the old veneer, but staying a smidgen outside the line. Hold the knife at a slight angle as you cut.

After removing the tracing paper and the patch, use a chisel to clean out the damaged veneer and to scrape away the old glue. Test-fit the patch and, if necessary, use fine sandpaper to make the patch conform. Wipe a thin layer of glue on the wood base and the underside of the patch and press it carefully into place. Finally, place wax paper and a wood block over the patch and use a clamp or weights to keep it in place overnight.

Repairing Veneer with an Inlay Kit

This procedure is similar to the hand method that was just described, but with mechanical assistance supplied by a portable router that makes it easier to achieve accurate results. The kit, normally used for inlay work, consists of a template guide for the router, a bushing that fits over the sleeve of the guide, and a special bit whose diameter equals the wall thickness of the bushing (Illus. 6-17). The kit can be used to outline the damaged area *and*, without fuss, to form the matching patch. There is one restriction: you can't turn a sharp corner because of the diameter of the bushing. Any turn must be an arc whose radius is one half the bushing's diameter. But this is a minor factor, and it's not likely that you would want to design a patch with sharp corners, anyway.

Here are the steps for repairing veneer using an inlay kit (Illus. 6-18):

1. Make a hardboard template with a central cutout that is the shape of the patch you wish to make. Make the template large enough so there will be ample support for the router.

2. Use clamps, if feasible, or double-faced tape to attach the template to the work so the cutout is situated over the damage. Adjust the projection of the bit to match the thickness of the template plus the depth of the recess. Then, with the template guide and the bushing in place, run the router around the edges of the cutout. This establishes a groove that is the exact shape of the pattern.

3. Use the router or work manually to clean out the waste. It's possible that you may be able to lift out the waste with a chisel. Softening the adhesive with a little heat will help.

4. Use double-faced tape or some other means to attach the same template to the patch material and a backup. The only change you have to make is to remove the bushing from the template guide. Then run the router around the edges of the cutout. The result will be a patch (inlay) that will precisely fit the recess formed in Steps 2 and 3 in Illus. 6-18.

A Storehouse of Patches

I (and I'm sure others) make it a practice when veneering my own panels of saving trimmings and leftovers from the veneers I use and storing them for possible future repair chores. This eliminates problems should it ever be necessary to have a piece with a grain, figure, and color that is compatible with the project's. The alternative is to visit a lumberyard or craft store that stocks veneers and attempt to locate a helpful piece. Success is not likely, so save all scrap for such times when they will be ideal for making a project right again.

CRUSHED CORNERS

Some projects may have crushed corners. This may occur because the boards used were

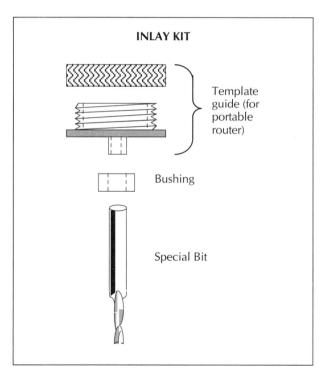

Illus. 6-17. An inlay kit consists of a template guide for a portable router, a bushing that fits the sleeves of the guide, and a special bit. As the name says, it's made for inlaying, but isn't installing a patch an inlaying technique?

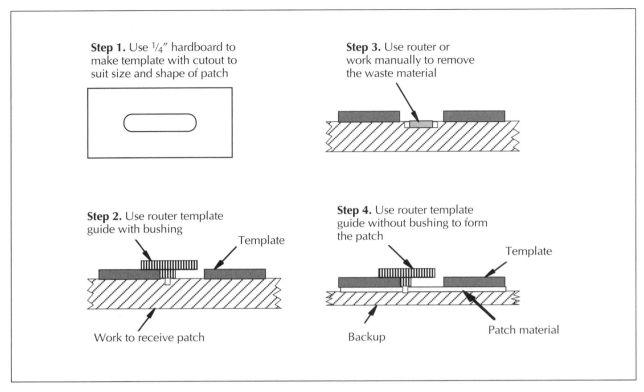

Step 1. Use ¼" hardboard to make template with cutout to suit size and shape of patch

Step 2. Use router template guide with bushing
Template
Work to receive patch

Step 3. Use router or work manually to remove the waste material

Step 4. Use router template guide without bushing to form the patch
Template
Backup
Patch material

Illus. 6-18. How the inlay kit is used. One template is used for both the recess that removes the flaw and the patch that will fill it.

dropped or fell off a shelf or because we didn't check closely enough when we bought the boards. The simple solution is to saw off the end of the board, but that may make it short for its intended purpose. The way to repair crushed corners is to pare off the corner and replace it with new wood (Illus. 6-19). Don't be skimpy when adding the patch. It's better to have a substantial surface for glue, and making a "large" patch piece is easier than shaping a tiny one. In any event, make the replacement larger than actually needed. Use fine sandpaper wrapped around a wood block to smooth the contact areas, and then glue the parts together, using tape as a clamp. For an "instant" bond, use cyanoacrylate glue. The parts will bond if held together for several seconds, thus eliminating

the need for any kind of clamping. Finishing is just a matter of sanding to bring the patch flush with adjacent areas.

We can, of course, damage edges or create dents in the field. In such cases, the ideas suggested for eliminating knots and replacing veneer can also be utilized to rectify these woodworking goofs. A tried-and-true method for raising a small dent in wood is to steam it. Place a small wad of dampened cloth over the dent and then heat it with an iron. It's likely that the heat will "coax" the bent fibers in the dent to return to their original positions. The moisture may also raise some "nap" (slight surface fibers) on the wood, so a little sanding will be in order after the rescued area has dried.

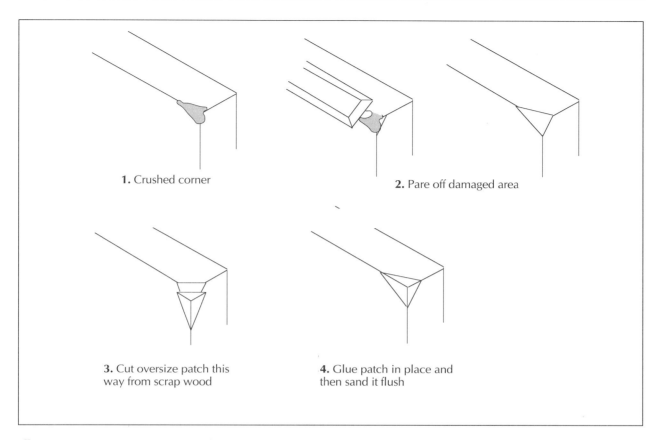

1. Crushed corner

2. Pare off damaged area

3. Cut oversize patch this way from scrap wood

4. Glue patch in place and then sand it flush

Illus. 6-19. How to repair a crushed corner. When the patch is made this way, its grain direction will be compatible with that of the board.

DEALING WITH CUP, CROOK, BOW, AND TWIST

It would seem that nature resents having its trees cut up, since boards, even after kiln- or air-drying, will often take one of the forms shown in Illus. 6-20. In all cases, the board has to be treated before it can be considered usable, but the work can't be done casually, and there is always a price to pay. For example, a cupped board (warped across its width) can be straightened, but with a sacrifice in thickness.

The machines you have, and their capacity, have a bearing on *what* can be done and *how* it should be done. It's easy to suggest, for exam-ple, that you joint the concave side of a cupped board and then resaw the opposite surface. But what if the board is 8 inches wide and you have a 4-inch jointer? You might make a pass to reduce one high point and then turn the stock end-for-end and make a second pass. It will help, but success isn't guaranteed, and one pass will be against the grain, which isn't the best way to do jointer work.

Resawing on a table saw is limited to a bit less than twice the maximum projection of the blade. Here, too, making a second pass after turning the board end-for-end will help. If the board is too wide for a double pass to do the job completely, there will be a raised band down the

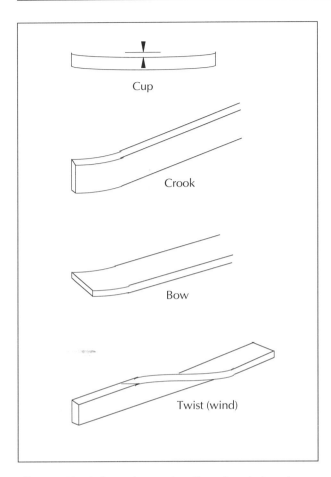

Cup

Crook

Bow

Twist (wind)

Illus. 6-20. A board may be flat after it has been kiln- or air-dried at the mill, but then it is subjected to uncontrolled atmospheric conditions. So, we're often confronted with distortions of this type.

center of the board, but that can be removed with a hand plane or maybe a belt sander.

Resawing on a band saw is limited by the tool's depth of cut. There is no double pass solution here. But the band saw is the tool to use to straighten a dished board, one where the warp is lengthwise.

A board in *wind* (that is a board that has a twist running down its length) is too troublesome to bother with. The best bet is to just cut out usable sections. Take similar action with boards

that have a crook or a bow at one end; sacrifice the part with the problem area by sawing it off.

In all cases, it's wise to study the wood before taking any action. It's very possible that the bulk of the work can be done efficiently and safely with a hand plane or belt sander. We can become so reliant on power tools that we overlook some of the advantages of working with hand tools.

DECIDING WHICH SIDE OF THE WORK TO PLACE UP

Are you careful about what side of the wood you place "up" when doing sawing operations? Paying attention to the good side of the work and how it relates to the cutting action of a saw blade can noticeably improve cutting quality, especially when you are sawing plywood.

A cut is smoothest where a blade enters the work. Feathering is more apparent at the bottom of the kerf. A table-saw blade, viewed from the side, rotates counterclockwise, and one on a radial arm saw rotates clockwise, but they both cut with a "downward" action. Therefore, on both tools, work should be placed with its good side up. The blade of a portable circular saw rotates counterclockwise, but because of the way the tool is used, the blade enters the work from beneath, so the good side should be down.

It isn't difficult to decide how to place material. Just check the direction in which the teeth of a blade point and how they move when sawing (Illus. 6-21).

RESIZING HOLES TO THEIR CORRECT SIZE

To resize holes that were drilled too large or too small, it's necessary to find the center of the hole before we can redrill it accurately. Guessing where the center is won't work, and

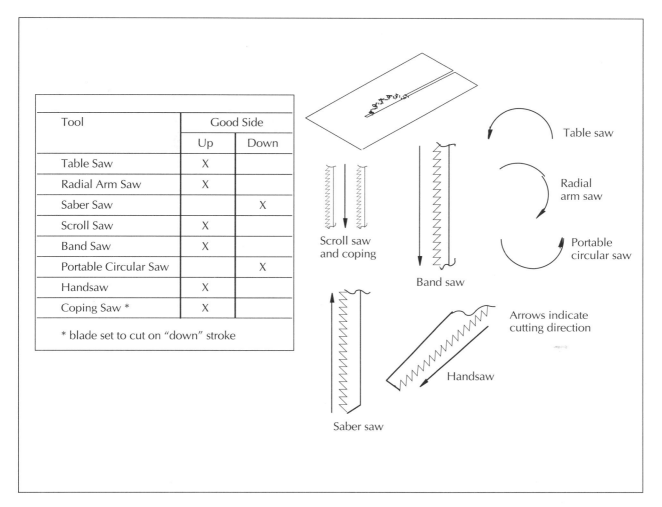

Tool	Good Side	
	Up	Down
Table Saw	X	
Radial Arm Saw	X	
Saber Saw		X
Scroll Saw	X	
Band Saw	X	
Portable Circular Saw		X
Handsaw	X	
Coping Saw *	X	
* blade set to cut on "down" stroke		

Illus. 6-21. Cutting quality improves when you place work so the saw blade cuts "down" into the good face of material. This is especially important when sawing plywood. The chart on the left indicates whether you should cut the material with its good side up or down when using a specific tool.

redrilling without the bit's point having something to contact isn't good practice. In either case, the existing hole should be plugged so its center can be determined and so the bit will enter solid stock.

If the hole is too small, any piece of dowel will serve as a plug. If it's too large, then a special plug, cut from material that matches the work, should be provided (Illus. 6-22).

CONCEALING FASTENERS

One of the jobs that always bothers me is concealing nail holes. Whether I use a commercial filler or make my own from sawdust, I'm never satisfied with results—unless the project will be painted. When I want a perfect result, I use the classic method shown in Illus. 6-23. You have to be careful when lifting the sliver. It must be flexi-

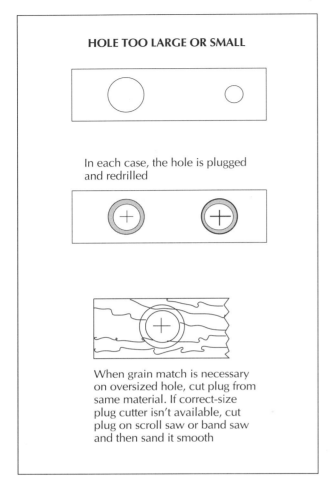

HOLE TOO LARGE OR SMALL

In each case, the hole is plugged and redrilled

When grain match is necessary on oversized hole, cut plug from same material. If correct-size plug cutter isn't available, cut plug on scroll saw or band saw and then sand it smooth

Illus. 6-22. How to resize a hole. For accurate results, the hole must first be plugged—no matter whether the hole must be reduced or enlarged.

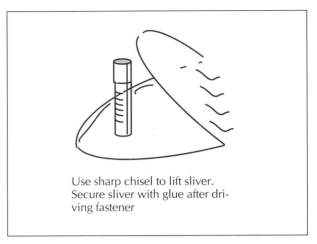

Use sharp chisel to lift sliver. Secure sliver with glue after driving fastener

Illus. 6-23. How to use the wood itself to conceal a nail.

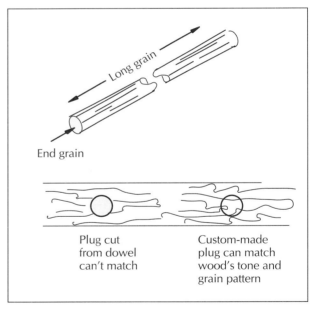

Long grain

End grain

Plug cut from dowel can't match

Custom-made plug can match wood's tone and grain pattern

Illus. 6-24. Plugs cut from commercial dowels are okay to use on end grain, but not on surface or edge grain—not if grain compatibility is important.

ble enough to allow driving the nail, but not to the point where it will break when it's bent.

There is no problem concealing screws by using plugs, but if appearance matters, most commercial dowels are not practical (Illus. 6-24). The way to ensure good-quality plugs is to use special cutters to custom-make them from matching material (Illus. 6-25). This way, in addition to choice of material, you can choose to cut into the surface or an edge of the stock, an option that lets you decide the grain pattern of the plug.

There are some commercial plugs that might

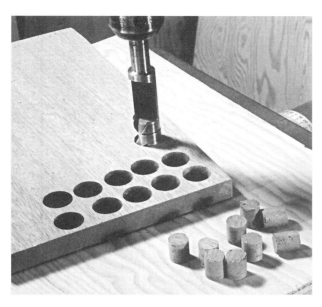

Illus. 6-25. Special cutters can produce plugs from any material, and *you* can decide the grain direction of the plug.

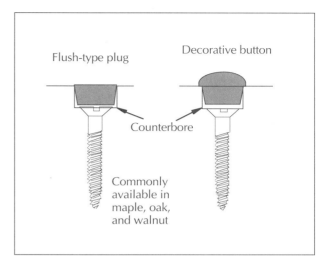

Illus. 6-26. Examples of ready-made plugs. Flush types are produced so their exposed ends will show surface grain.

be applicable if you wish to avoid making them. Flush commercial plugs are made so they have surface grain, which makes them compatible with the grain direction of the project material, if not the grain pattern (Illus. 6-26).

COUNTERSINKING SHEET METAL

If you have ever been involved with a project that required countersinking sheet metal, you know that ordinary methods won't do; a conventional countersink will enlarge the hole to the point where the head of the screw won't have anything to bear against.

The better way to go—actually, the only way—is to *dimple* the metal as demonstrated in Illus. 6-27. The backup under the metal is countersunk to suit the screw, so forcing down a rod whose end is shaped to suit will make the metal conform to the model countersink. The drill press is not turned on; it just serves as a press.

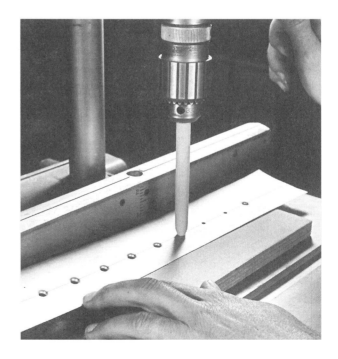

Illus. 6-27. "Dimpling" is the answer when you must countersink sheet metal. The rod attached to the drill press presses the metal so it will conform to a model countersink in the backup block.

FIXING A SPLIT

Splits can appear in a board even after a project has been in use for a while. Take, for example, a cutting board that merited saving shown in Illus. 6-28. It would have been a mistake to break the board apart and then to reshape the edges. That would have resulted in splinters and pulled-apart fibers. It's better to

Illus. 6-28. Unfortunately, a split can occur at any time. It might be in the field or on a joint line.

try to cut along the split with a saw; this hopefully will result in edges that do not require further attention. In this case, it worked (Illus. 6-29). We're not always so lucky, but the idea is always viable. If the split is not so straightforward, the piece can be cut apart, for example, by making a cut through the split with a band saw. The sawed edges can then be sanded to make them suitable for rejoining. What we should avoid is making cuts that remove more than the split itself. This will remove more wood than necessary and interfere with "reestablishing" the grain pattern. A kerf-size line minimizes that kind of problem.

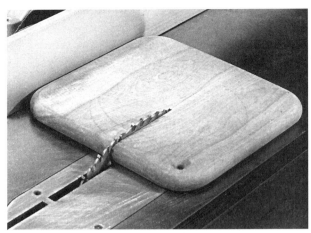

Illus. 6-29. Sometimes making a simple, straight saw cut along a split will result in edges that are straight and splinter-free. When this won't work, the piece can be sawed apart on a band saw.

DISTRESSING

Have you ever designed a new project with the intention of making it look used or like the product of a woodworking environment that wasn't preoccupied with fancy joinery—like the little table displayed in Illus. 6-30 and detailed in Illus. 6-31? It's not unusual to see projects of this nature in decorator or specialty shops with prices that would shock you. The wood is sound, but it has flaws. The project's construction is very basic. I can make tables like that in no time and retire early!

Making a new project look old or used is called "distressing." Distressing can take many forms, one of them the result of beating boards with a chain or some implement like a ball-peen hammer. When you think about it, it's unlikely that an old piece of furniture will have overall, uniform dents unless they were caused by deliberate abuse. It's more likely that wear and tear will be revealed by such things as a crushed corner, a split, a ding or

Illus. 6-30. This small table was intentionally designed to look used.

two long edges, a cavity that reveals a splinter was removed from the bottom end of a chair leg, etc. The dents and gouges that may occur over a long period of time will not be identical. Another point to consider is that normal wear places will appear on the edges of tables and components like the rungs and arms of chairs.

The trick to making the project look worn or aged is to make it look natural or to design it so it is an absolute departure from the sleek, highly polished furniture in stores. It's okay, for example, to utilize a board with a split end or to imitate a split (Illus. 6-32 and 6-33).

If you wish to stain a project, remember that dirt accumulates as a project ages, so you don't want the coating to be uniform. Apply the stain generously, but then wipe it, removing most of it from surfaces but allowing it to remain in

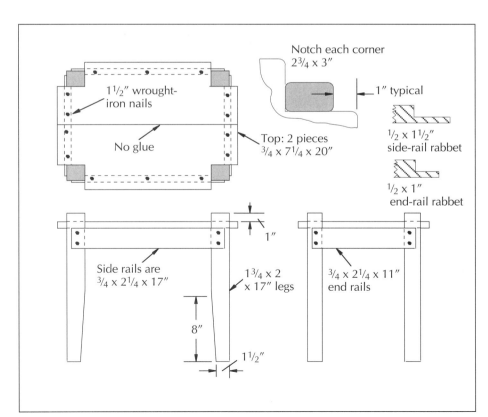

Illus. 6-31. Construction details for the small table shown in Illus. 6-30.

grooves, corners, and crevices (Illus. 6-34).

Really, there are no firm rules for distressing. Much depends on the effect you wish to achieve. Try your thoughts on a piece of scrap wood. Use items like rasps, wire brushes, sandpaper, a utility knife to create the flaws that can happen over time. It's nice to be successful from the very beginning.

Illus. 6-32. You can create a split by making a long, narrow V-cut with a saber saw or on a band saw.

Illus. 6-33. You can smooth the edges caused by a split by using a strip of sandpaper as you would a shoe-polishing cloth. The idea is to simulate the results of age and use—but not of abuse.

Illus. 6-34. Apply stains so crevices and corners will appear darker than surfaces.

7

Avoiding Assembly Errors

You are looking at a project with misaligned parts and thinking: Darn! My math was correct. I rechecked measurements. My cuts were clean and accurate. Then what happened? The parts do not fit together properly.

One of my recent projects was a storage unit I needed for my supply of disk caddies—not fancy, just straightforward and practical. The caddies were to slide in grooves cut into opposite sides of a small case. Everything proceeded satisfactorily as I sized the material and cut dadoes in it. I did the assembly and set the project aside to allow the glue to set. I even got to doing final sanding. Then I became aware of the goof shown in Illus. 7-1. I had accidentally inverted one side.

I recall similar glitches: installing one of the

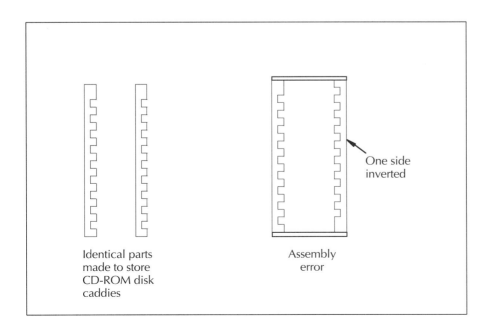

Identical parts made to store CD-ROM disk caddies

Assembly error

One side inverted

Illus. 7-1. To avoid assembly errors like this one, you must anticipate that they can happen and concentrate on avoiding them during all stages of construction.

plywood shelves in a bookcase with the good surface of the material facing down instead of up; and placing a cabinet door upside-down, advancing to a point in an assembly and then becoming aware that I have neglected to install a component that now could not be fitted. "Once burned, twice shy" may apply to lovers, but it doesn't seem to affect woodworkers.

Mistakes like the few I've mentioned are the hardest to forgive, and the easiest to avoid. The answer, as I've said before, is the proper mental concentration. Below I discuss ways to ensure that your project will be assembled accurately.

CLAMPS

Clamps act just like extra hands in the workshop. They hold parts together until glue sets, keep assemblies in order while you install fasteners, and act as a vise to keep parts secure as you work on them. You can get by with a single combination saw blade, one hand plane, and one hammer, but working with one, two, or even three clamps is very restrictive, especially when you consider the many types of clamps and their particular applications.

Gluing and clamping—the last stages of a project—should be approached calmly and with the confidence that you know exactly what must occur, and what *might* occur. Therefore, it's good practice to do a dry run, that is, to assemble the components without glue, so you can be sure they will be put together accurately, and in order. Putting parts together as subassemblies makes clamping procedures easier and will help ensure accuracy. For example, don't put together the substructure for a table in one operation. Instead, assemble the legs and end rails as separate units and, when they are ready, unite them with the side rails. Put together the shelves and sides of a bookcase first, and then add the back, top, and bottom. There's another

reason for doing this. Let's say we goofed a bit on the length of the shelves. With the shelves and sides together, we can check other components on assembly and compensate for the error.

Apply glue thinly and evenly on all mating surfaces. Too much glue is wasteful and may cause joints to stay open or slip, or even create stresses due to hydraulic pressure. A bead of glue is not recommended. You may apply it that way to begin with, but then spread it evenly with a brush. Also, use the brush to remove excess glue, wiping it on a cloth as you proceed.

Whenever possible, do final assembly at the end of the workday so the glued assembly can remain undisturbed overnight. But don't rush it. If you are anxious to get to dinner, put off the assembly for another day.

Proper Cleaning Procedures

Sometimes we use too many clamps on an assembly, or do not apply them properly. Clamps are for bringing surfaces together firmly, and not more. Excess pressure can cause distortion of individual pieces and force joints out of alignment. Move from clamp to clamp as you tighten them, so pressure will be spread evenly. Pay attention to the following clamping guidelines:

1. Slab assemblies must be flat. Be aware that the tail stop and the sliding head of bar or pipe clamps must have some clearance in order to move, so it's possible for them to exert uneven pressure (Illus. 7-2). One way to counteract this tendency is to use a cylinder or a piece of half-round molding between the work and the jaws of the clamp (Illus. 7-3).
2. When pieces of wood are placed between the work and clamp jaws to protect edges, they must be placed in line with the direction of pressure. A block that is situated too low or too high can "misdirect" pressure.

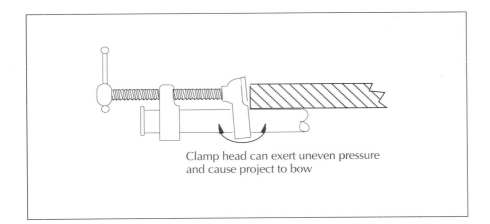

Illus. 7-2. The sliding head on a bar or pipe clamp needs clearance in order to move. Thus, it can tilt enough so pressure isn't directly forward.

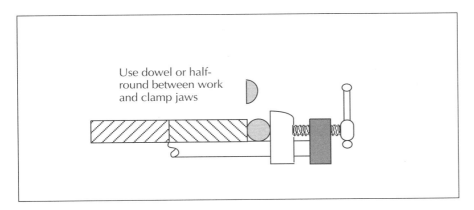

Illus. 7-3. Using a cylinder or a piece of half-round molding between the clamp and the work will direct pressure forward even if the sliding head should tilt a bit.

3. Clamp pressure can cause parts to bow, especially on wide slabs. A common and practical solution is shown in Illus. 7-4. Strips of wood, held with clamps, will keep the work flat until the glue sets. Synchronize placing the boards with applying the clamp pressure. There's not much point in placing the boards *after* the bow has appeared.

    My shop has a little collection of shop-made *glue bars* that I use when doing slab assemblies (Illus. 7-5). They're always ready, and I can place them on the slab wherever they do the most good. Another thought, and it's a good one, is to do the project in partial slabs. For example, if you must glue together six boards, do them three at a time.

4. Special faces for pipe or bar clamps, like those mounted on a pipe clamp in Illus. 7-6, actually do triple duty. The holes through them are sized to fit snugly on the pipe so as to counteract clamp-jaw movement; they serve as pads to protect the work so you don't have to add pieces of wood that are sometimes difficult to keep in position when applying pressure; and they serve as stands for the clamps so they will stay put as you place workpieces. Ideas for making the pad/stands for pipe or bar clamps are offered in Illus. 7-7 and 7-8.

5. The method shown in Illus. 7-9 is one I use when I want to be certain that a trim strip on lumber or a plywood slab will be perfectly positioned. It's not standard procedure because some jobs don't require this type of

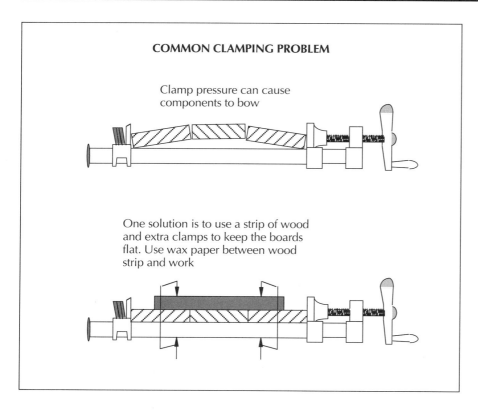

COMMON CLAMPING PROBLEM

Clamp pressure can cause
components to bow

One solution is to use a strip of wood
and extra clamps to keep the boards
flat. Use wax paper between wood
strip and work

Illus. 7-4. Clamp pressure
can cause parts to bow.
Clamped blocks are good
preventive measures, but
they should be placed as
clamp pressure is applied.

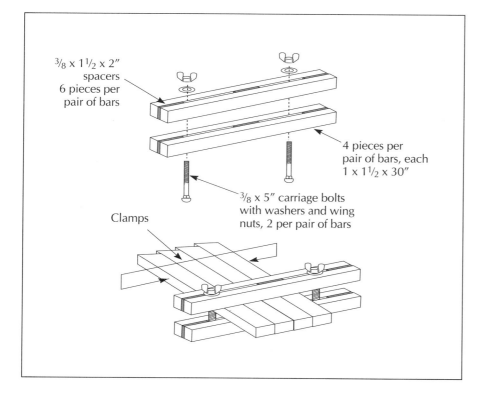

$^3/_8$ x 1$^1/_2$ x 2"
spacers
6 pieces per
pair of bars

4 pieces per
pair of bars, each
1 x 1$^1/_2$ x 30"

$^3/_8$ x 5" carriage bolts
with washers and wing
nuts, 2 per pair of bars

Clamps

Illus. 7-5. Glue bars are better than having to resort to
clamped strips of wood.
They are always on hand
and can be placed any-
where on the assembly.

Illus. 7-6. Special faces that fit snugly on pipe or bar clamps are a big help. In addition to minimizing head tilt, they protect the work and allow the clamps to sit firmly so the parts to be bonded will be easy to place.

attention. I use it when the trim is configured (like molding), so the clamp can't grip without harming the work. The shape for the clamp block can be cut on a band saw or scroll saw.

Keeping Things Square

Unfortunately, it isn't difficult to throw frames and case goods out of alignment when applying clamp pressure. Two things can happen: the project might twist, or corners will not be square. To prevent twist from occurring be sure you have a large enough, flat, level surface on which to support the project while you are assembling it. If the project doesn't have support at all points, it will "warp." You may discover this belatedly when you place the project on a level surface and find that it rocks.

You can examine a frame or case for squareness by using a square to check each corner. However, it's better to check the assembly as a whole by using the "diagonals" method. This system is based on the fact that if the diagonals (lines from opposite corners of a square or rectangle) are equal, the form will have square corners.

You can check the assembly for squareness by measuring the diagonals with a tape, but you will be more certain if you use a special gauge. The gauge can be two slim pieces of wood, pointed at one end, that you hold and spread between two opposite corners. Then, while

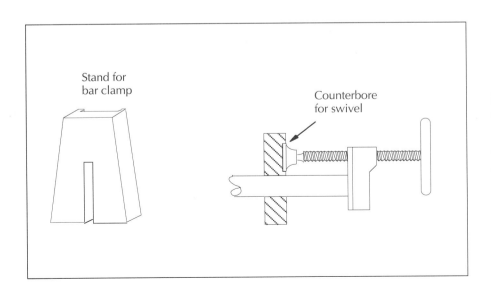

Stand for
bar clamp

Counterbore
for swivel

Illus. 7-7. Auxiliary faces for bar clamps need a slot instead of a hole. A counterbored hole is needed for clamps that have a swivel-type head.

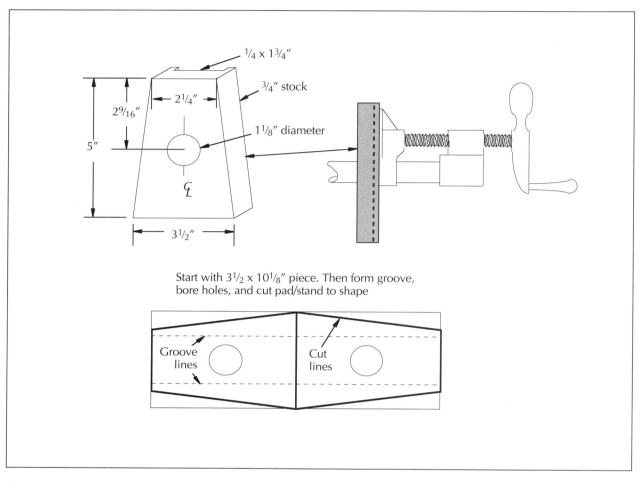

Start with 3¹⁄₂ x 10¹⁄₈″ piece. Then form groove, bore holes, and cut pad/stand to shape

Illus. 7-8. How to make auxiliary faces for pipe clamps. Both the groove for the head and the hole for the pipe should provide for a snug fit.

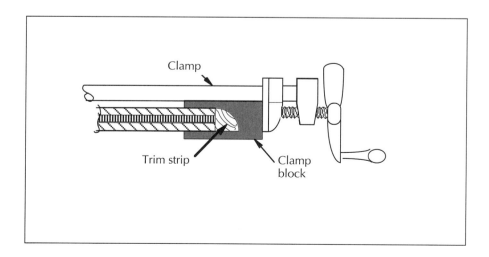

Illus. 7-9. Configured trim strips, like molding, can be attached easily and accurately if you supply special clamp blocks.

retaining your grip, lift these wood pieces out and fit them into the other diagonal. Holding these pieces in your hands can be chancy, especially if you have to repeat the process several times. It's much better to make a special gauge that can be locked to secure a dimension, as shown in Illus. 7-10 and 7-11. The gauge will always be ready and can be useful in other ways, like checking inside, horizontal distances between side members of a project.

The length of a diagonal can also be determined mathematically. Two adjacent sides of a square or rectangle plus the diagonal form a right triangle; the diagonal is the hypotenuse. The length of the hypotenuse (the diagonal) is the square root of the base (squared) plus the altitude (squared). Calculations can be done full-size or to scale (Illus. 7-12).

OTHER HELPFUL ALIGNMENT PROCEDURES

Squaring Jig

A squaring jig will ensure accuracy whether you are assembling picture frames or web frames for a case. The idea is simple: secure two straight pieces of wood to the end and edge of an arbitrar-

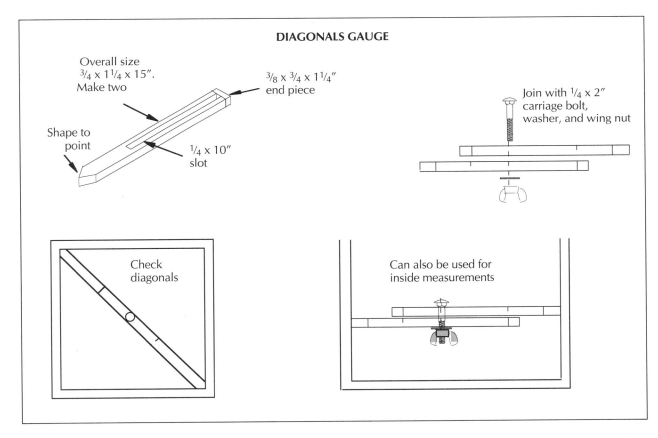

Illus. 7-10. A diagonals gauge can be used for checking square or rectangular assemblies and for other tasks like taking inside measurements.

Illus. 7-11. Other designs for diagonal gauges.

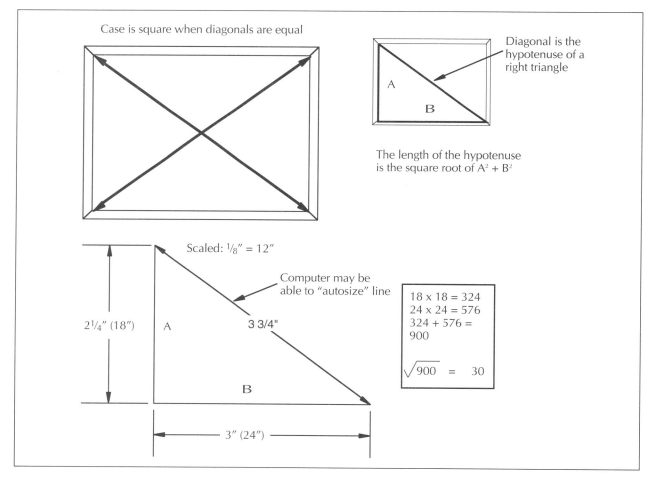

Case is square when diagonals are equal

Diagonal is the hypotenuse of a right triangle

A

B

The length of the hypotenuse is the square root of $A^2 + B^2$

Scaled: $\frac{1}{8}'' = 12''$

Computer may be able to "autosize" line

$2\frac{1}{4}''$ (18")

A

3 3/4"

B

3" (24")

18 x 18 = 324
24 x 24 = 576
324 + 576 = 900

$\sqrt{900}$ = 30

Illus. 7-12. The diagonal of a square or rectangular case is the hypotenuse of a right triangle. Thus, the formula that is shown here can be used to determine its length.

ily sized plywood panel so they form a 90-degree corner. When two adjacent sides of the frame are placed in the jig, the remaining parts will fall into place (Illus. 7-13). An advantage for the jig is that you'll know immediately if the parts do not have square ends or if you have goofed when cutting parts to length.

The jig can be used whether the project has butt joints, is mitered, or has corners with some other connection like an open mortise.

Squaring Gauges and Corner Blocks

Band clamps (also called web clamps) are fine for pulling together large structures, especially "odd" assemblies like chair substructures, where bar clamps won't do. However, on square or rectangular frames and cases, you want to be sure that components are in correct alignment before applying pressure. As usual,

the critical factor is that each corner must make a 90-degree turn.

One system I use to ensure that components are in correct alignment calls for making "squaring gauges" like those in Illus. 7-14. If you adjust the components to the gauges and exert pressure with the band clamp at the same time, the job will be done correctly.

Another idea, especially useful when assembling frames, is to make a set of corner blocks (Illus. 7-15). These would be difficult to place on case goods, but they pose no problem with frames since they sit flat on the assembly platform.

Let the Back Square the Case

The back of a case, carefully cut to exact size, can be the gauge for squaring the case itself (Illus. 7-16). Align the case with the bot-

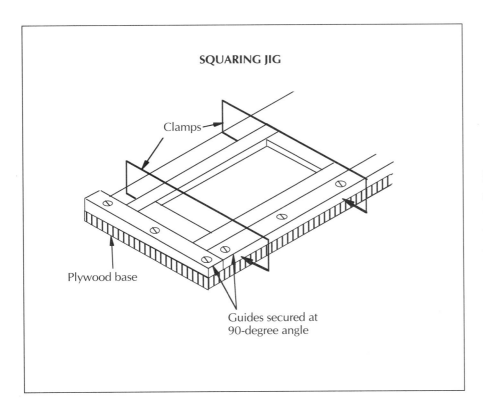

SQUARING JIG

Clamps

Plywood base

Guides secured at 90-degree angle

Illus. 7-13. Example of a squaring jig. The accuracy provided by fixtures like this justifies the time need-ed to make them.

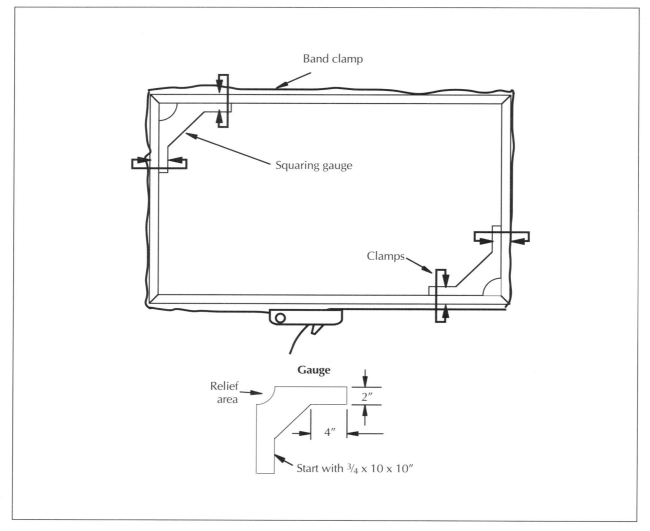

Illus. 7-14. Squaring gauges, used in opposite corners, will ensure that the project as a whole will be square.

tom end of its back, and secure the back with whatever fasteners you are using. Nudge the case one way or the other until one side is even with the vertical edge of the back. Then add a fastener at that top corner. The case will now be square, so you can continue adding fasteners. It goes without saying that this system will be successful *only* if the back has square corners.

Fixing Corners

A less-than-perfect miter joint can often be adjusted without drastically altering the dimensions of an assembly by clamping the parts together at a 90-degree angle and then using a fine-tooth saw to cut directly on the joint line (Illus. 7-17).

The same technique will work when a

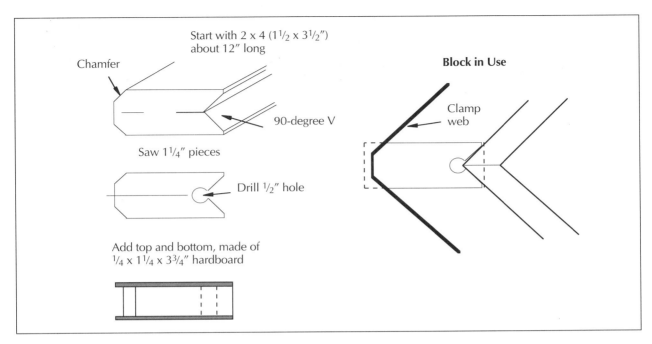

Start with 2 x 4 (1½ x 3½″) about 12″ long

Chamfer

90-degree V

Saw 1¼″ pieces

Drill ½″ hole

Add top and bottom, made of ¼ x 1¼ x 3¾″ hardboard

Block in Use

Clamp web

Illus. 7-15. Corner blocks are good accessories for band clamps, but they are more convenient for flat frames rather than case goods.

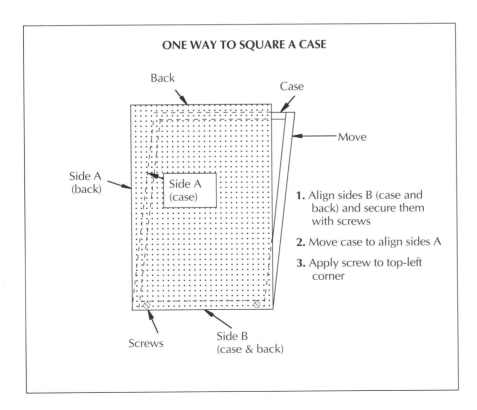

ONE WAY TO SQUARE A CASE

Back

Case

Move

Side A (back)

Side A (case)

1. Align sides B (case and back) and secure them with screws

2. Move case to align sides A

3. Apply screw to top-left corner

Screws

Side B (case & back)

Illus. 7-16. If the back of a case is made with square corners and used this way, it will ensure that the case as a whole will be square.

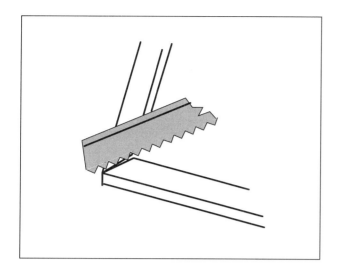

Illus. 7-17. Miscut miter joints can often be saved without drastically reducing dimensions by holding parts so they form a 90-degree corner and then using a fine saw to cut directly across the joint line.

frame will have butt joints and the end of one component isn't exactly square. However, the same cut will have to be made at the opposite corner in order for the entire frame to be square.

Miscut components on a butt-jointed frame will require other attention (Illus. 7-18). If the frame size is not important (which isn't likely), you can realign the parts properly by recutting those that were miscut. Otherwise, to save material, you can salvage the part or parts by using a wedge to supply a new end for the wood.

Spacing Partitions

You can establish equal spacing for partitions more accurately with simple mathematics than by making trial-and-error markings on the work. To arrive at the total spacing, subtract the thickness of the sides plus the total thickness of

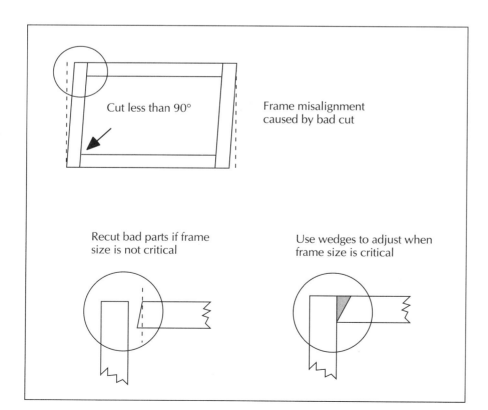

Cut less than 90°

Frame misalignment caused by bad cut

Recut bad parts if frame size is not critical

Use wedges to adjust when frame size is critical

Illus. 7-18. Misalignment of butt-jointed frames can be caused by flawed cuts on one or more pieces. How to save the project depends on whether the overall size of the project is important.

the partitions from the overall width of the project. Divide that figure by one more than the number of partitions to get the individual spacing (Illus. 7-19).

Too often, the answer includes a fraction that makes the layout more difficult than it should be. One solution is to equalize the two outside spaces and let the center one fall where it may, as shown in Illus. 7-19. If the center space is off $\frac{1}{32}$ inch or so, it will not be visually distracting.

Story Pole

A story pole is simply a strip of wood that is marked to indicate specific dimensions that have to be applied in different locations. In a sense, it's a way of measuring once so you don't have to do it twice, or more. For an example of how one is used, let's apply it to the partition spacing we just discussed.

Use a strip of wood that has some rigidity—something that is $\frac{3}{4}$ inch square or $\frac{3}{4}$ inch x 1 inch. Cut the strip to overall length and then carefully mark it for the spaces required. Use it at the bottom of the case and again at the top (Illus. 7-20). Without the stick, spaces would have to be measured individually, and you can see how that might lead to errors.

The story pole can have many purposes.

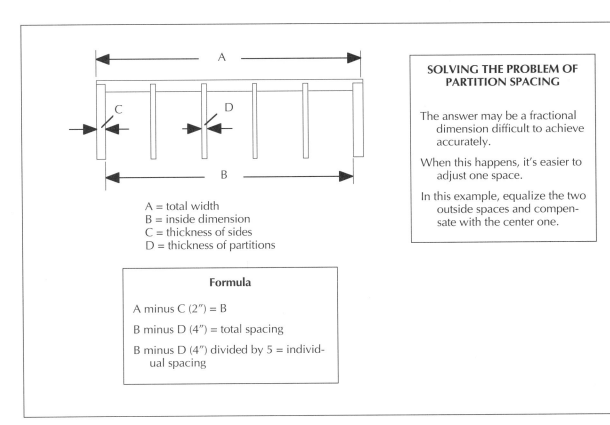

A = total width
B = inside dimension
C = thickness of sides
D = thickness of partitions

SOLVING THE PROBLEM OF PARTITION SPACING

The answer may be a fractional dimension difficult to achieve accurately.

When this happens, it's easier to adjust one space.

In this example, equalize the two outside spaces and compensate with the center one.

Formula

A minus C (2″) = B

B minus D (4″) = total spacing

B minus D (4″) divided by 5 = individual spacing

Illus. 7-19. Using simple math to determine the spacing between partitions.

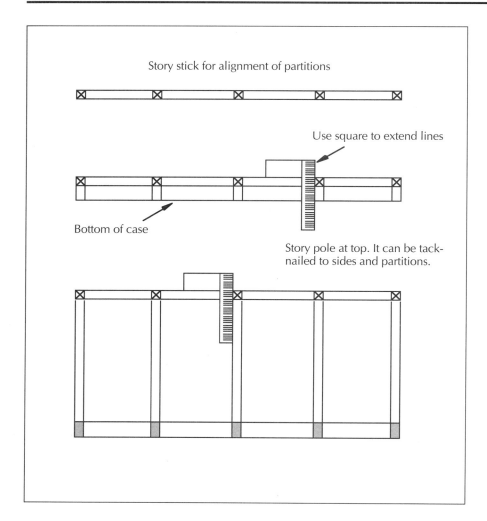

Story stick for alignment of partitions

Use square to extend lines

Bottom of case

Story pole at top. It can be tack-nailed to sides and partitions.

Illus. 7-20. An application for a story pole.

For a complex project, it can be marked on two or more sides to show positions of components in various areas. *Don't* mark one edge of the stick to show different sets of dimensions. I bear witness to the fact that such use can be pretty confusing!

8

Surface Preparation

What a disappointment! You were happy with the quality of the project that emerged from the stack of wood you started with, and then you applied the stain. A few minutes later you wiped off the excess stain, and now your enthusiasm has turned to despair. There are blotches, unsightly steaks running across the grain, and corners where the stain didn't take at all. The finish isn't at all uniform. What happened? You can bet that it's not how you applied the stain, but the attention, or lack of it, that you paid to *sanding*.

Sanding is done to prepare surfaces for the application of stain, paint, or for a natural finish. It's the final phase of fabrication, and any negligence in this area can negate all the time and effort that went into construction. The purpose of using abrasives is to eliminate any marks left by tools, and to make all surfaces *equally* smooth so the beauty of the wood and its grain will be enhanced by the finishing coats. Remember, it's not very professional to rely on thick coats of paint to hide imperfections—and paint does not conceal all mistakes totally.

SANDPAPER: A CUTTING TOOL

Sandpaper is paper or cloth that has sharp particles of a natural or man-made substance bonded to one surface. Not too long ago, flint was widely used, but it's been superseded by the introduction of harder, more durable materials like garnet and aluminum oxide. Sandpaper removes wood by various degrees depending on its coarseness and the number of the cutting particles on the paper (Illus. 8-1 and 8-2).

The terms "open coat" and "close coat" indicate how much of the surface of the backing material is covered with the abrasive. Close-coat products have overall coverage and produce the smoothest surfaces. Open-coat products have 50–70 percent coverage, which leaves ample space between particles so the paper doesn't clog so easily. That's why open-coat sandpaper is a logical choice for working on old, rough, or resinous wood, and for refinishing jobs.

Abrasive particles do cut (or shave, if you

181

ABRASIVE GRITS

Grade	Grit	Number
very	400	10/0
fine	360	
	320	9/0
	280	8/0
	240	7/0
	220	6/0
fine	180	5/0
	150	4/0
	120	3/0
medium	100	2/0
	80	1/0
	60	$1/2$
coarse	50	1
	40	$1 1/2$
	36	2
very	30	$2 1/2$
coarse	24	3
	20	$3 1/2$
	16	4

Illus. 8-1. Common abrasive grits. Most sandpaper sheets are identified by the grit number printed on their back.

want to look at it that way), so the finer the abrasive, the less obvious will be the ridge or groove that is left by each piece of grit. The general rule is to work through progressively finer grits until the wood is satiny smooth, but automatically choosing a coarse grit to begin with is not always the ideal way to operate. The condition of the wood should dictate what to begin with. It would be overkill, and probably would do more harm than good, to obey this general rule if the wood is smooth enough so just working with a fine-grit paper will get the job done. So much of the wood and wood prod-

ucts that we use today are offered in pretty respectable shape. Good practice calls for examining the wood before and after fabrication and judging how to get the work done with the least amount of sanding. The idea is to work efficiently, not harder.

GENERAL SANDING GUIDELINES

A finish will emphasize the color and grain of the wood, but it will also accentuate any glue spots, tool marks, or dents. Fortunately, all these flaws can be eliminated if you pay careful attention to the surface of the material when sanding it. I find that I produce as flaw-free a surface as possible when I get as many pieces as possible ready for finishing *before* assembling them. Take the substructure of a table, for example. It's so much easier to sand legs and rails individually than after they are joined. I can keep the pieces flat on a bench, even hold them in a vise, if I'm using something like a powered pad sander. Also, checking components individually makes it easier to spot imperfections, such as saw marks, ridges left by a planing operation, or a goof that occurred when an edge was routed.

Sandpaper is disposable. The abrasive particles get dull like any cutting tool, so you don't want to get to burnishing with a dull sheet instead of sanding. Sanding makes dust that can fool you into thinking that things are smoother than they are when you check with your fingers. The best way to remove dust is with a vacuum cleaner, which will also remove any particles that have loosened from the paper and that can cause their own scratches when you change to another piece of sandpaper. How the surface looks is the ultimate test. One way to determine how it looks is to shine a light across the surface of the work.

Always sand *with* the grain. It's sometimes suggested that sanding diagonally or across the

TYPES OF ABRASIVE AND SUGGESTED USES

Abrasive	Available Grits	Available in	Used for		Applications
			Wood	Metal	
Flint	Very fine to very coarse	Various sizes of sheets	X		Used for rough wood and refinishing. It lacks toughness and durability.
Garnet	30–220		X		Used for general woodworking applications
Aluminum oxide	30–220		X	X	Good for hardwoods and usable on non-wood materials. It is long-lasting.
Aluminum oxide, cloth-backed	30–120	sheets, belts, disks	X	X	Cloth-backed belts are strong and recommended for power sanding.
Silicon carbide (waterproof)	220–400	sheets	X	X	Used for sanding between finish coats, and often used with water & other lubricant

Note: Many abrasives are available in sizes that are just right for power tools like pad sanders. Some have self-adhesive backing for pad sanders

Illus. 8-2. Types of abrasive and suggested uses for each. Garnet and aluminum oxide are those most commonly available.

grain is permissible when you wish to remove a lot of material quickly. Cross-grain sanding may be quicker, but the scratches produced absorb more stain and will always appear darker than adjacent areas. If you ever decide to break the with-the-grain rule, be prepared to use a lot of time and sandpaper to get rid of cross-grain scratches.

Glue spots are the result of glue squeeze-out when parts are under clamp pressure. They can't be hidden because they act as a sealer that stain can't penetrate. Other than being careful about not being overgenerous when applying glue, what can you do? I find that I'm not always successful when removing excess glue by using the "classic" moistened-cloth method.

I often spread more of the glue than I remove. Instead, I allow the glue to set awhile, at least to the point where it develops a skin. Then I remove it by using a sharp chisel, bevel-side up.

A professional finisher made this suggestion: Add a tiny amount of food coloring to the glue so dried spots will be visible enough to guide you when sanding. Choose a color that closely matches the wood stain that you plan to use. Then, any errant spots that you overlook during sanding will blend in.

End grain, being more absorbent than edge or surface grain, requires some extra effort which consists of finishing it with a finer-grit paper than you use elsewhere. The end grain will then get less dark than it would otherwise.

This technique will also work on raised panels. Sand the top and bottom ends (which will be end grain) with much finer abrasives than you use on other edges and surfaces.

Except for end grain, it's important that the final sanding over the entire project be done with the same grit of sandpaper. If you fail to do this, coarser surfaces will appear duller under a clear finish, and they will appear darker when pigmented stains are used. I'm not so picayune about this when using dye stains because they do not affect the surface as drastically as the pigmented varieties.

HAND SANDING

While the bulk of smoothing operations can be done with power tools, the last "fine tuning" is best done by hand, but using your fingers to back up the sandpaper is not the way to go. Each finger will apply its own area of pressure and the result will be troughs instead of overall smoothness. Uniform finishes on surfaces and edges are easiest to obtain when the abrasive paper is mounted on a block of wood that you can grip comfortably. A rigid backing provides a leveling action for broad surfaces and cuts down ridges and irregularities. The backup block also provides greater abrasive-to-work contact than fingers can supply, so you reduce working time while doing a better job.

The key to producing a uniformly flat surface by hand is to use a sanding stroke of uniform length and with equalized pressure. It's not a good idea to stroke as far as you can reach in opposite directions over a large area because your pressure will decrease at the end of individual strokes, so you get an uneven surface. Short, straight, overlapping strokes as you move to-and-fro along the length of the work are best.

Since final sanding can make or break a project, it's often a good idea to make a special

abrasive applicator that is exactly right for the job on hand (Illus. 8-3). The simple block can be fitted with a felt pad, indoor/outdoor carpeting, or even thick foam rubber, so it will conform more readily to cylinders and contoured surfaces. A strip of thick, flexible material will back up sandpaper so it can be used like a shoeshine rag, making it good for rounding off edges, for example.

A way to sand molding is suggested in Illus. 8-4. Here a piece of the molding itself, with its edges trimmed to suit, becomes the applicator for the bulk of the material's contours.

Commercial products that I keep on hand for tasks like the one being done in Illus. 8-5 are abrasive cords and tapes. They're fine for getting into crevices that are difficult to smooth by other means, but they must be used carefully. A light touch is in order. If you apply too much pressure or work too long on one area, you may be forming grooves instead of doing sanding.

SANDING EDGES

When sanding a surface, whether it's wide or narrow, be especially careful as you approach the edges of the component. It's easy to mistakenly round off edges that should be square. Don't allow the sanding block to extend more than about one quarter its width beyond the edge. The idea is to make it easy to keep the sanding device on a horizontal plane. The least amount of tilt will cause a slope or a rounded edge.

If you want to guarantee square edges, think about making a device like the one shown in Illus. 8-6. Let your fingers keep the sandpaper taut as you use the tool. Attach the two parts with screws to allow for sandpaper changes.

There are times, especially when sanding small components, when it's better to apply the work to the sandpaper. This can be accomplished by supplying a "stationary" sanding

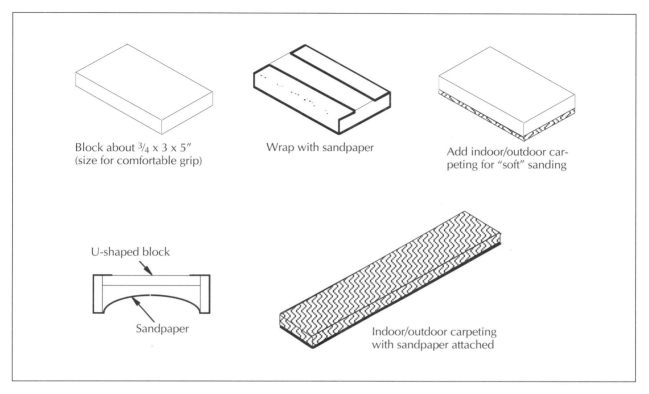

Illus. 8-3. Examples of shop-made sanding devices.

Illus. 8-4. A piece of the original stock, with its edges trimmed, makes an ideal sander for molding.

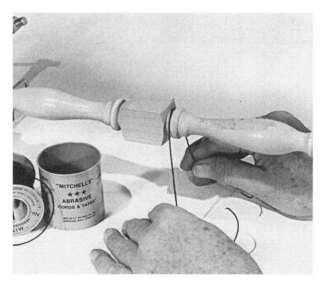

Illus. 8-5. Abrasive cords and tapes let you get into tight places, but they must be used carefully to avoid creating grooves.

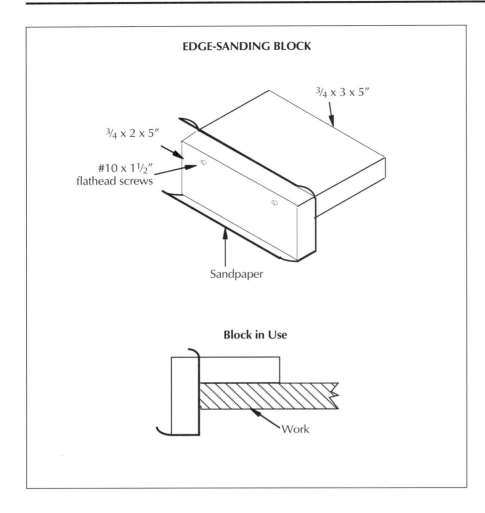

EDGE-SANDING BLOCK

$3/4 \times 3 \times 5''$

$3/4 \times 2 \times 5''$

#10 $\times$ 1$\frac{1}{2}''$
flathead screws

Sandpaper

Block in Use

Work

Illus. 8-6. An L-shaped sanding block will guarantee square edges.

block (Illus. 8-7). The block can be held steady by tack-nailing it to a firm surface or, if its size permits, by gripping it in a vise. A better idea is to use a block that is large enough to take a full sheet of sandpaper while leaving edges that can be clamped. That setup will also make it easy to replace worn paper or to change to another grit.

SANDING WITH STEEL WOOL

It won't replace sandpaper, but it's a worthwhile tool for woodworking and related shop tasks like removing pitch and gum from saw blades. Like sandpaper, steel wool is available in vari-

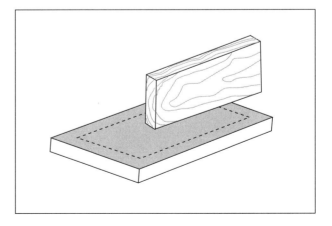

Illus. 8-7. A "stationary" sanding block is a good way to work when sanding small components.

ous numbers of grades; the larger the number, the coarser the grade (Illus. 8-8).

Steel wool is actually composed of strands that are shaved from special steel wire and then formed in bulk shapes or as pads or rolls. We know about the pads that are impregnated with a cleansing agent for cleaning pots and pans. Those that can be used for woodworking are similar, but sans soap.

The coarser grades of steel wool are usable

GRADES OF STEEL WOOL

Grade (#)	Texture	Comments	
		Used dry	Used wet
3	Very coarse	Used for preliminary smoothing of very rough surfaces, and to remove dry paint from glass and rust from metals	Used with lubricating oil to remove rust from garden tools and similar items
2	Coarse	Used to clean glass and brick, and on ceramic tile to remove paint, wax, and excess grout, and to eliminate scratches on copper	Used to remove rust from cast iron with turpentine as a lubricant, and can be used with stove polish on cast-iron stoves
1	Medium	Used to prepare copper or galvanized materials for soldering, and to clean soldering irons, and to create satin finishes on metals like copper and brass	Used with water to clean vinyl floors, with paint thinner (or paint remover) to remove old paint, and with scouring powder and water to clean whitewall tires
0	Fine	Used for preliminary smoothing of hardwoods, and between-coats sanding of polyurethane for finishes	Used with mineral spirits to remove pitch and gum from saw blades, and with soap to polish aluminum
00	Very fine	Used to polish copper pipe before soldering, to clean copper and brass, to polish wood floors, and for "secondary" sanding on wood	Used to remove burns from leather with soap and water, and with oil to buff surfaces
000	Extra fine	Used for intermediate wood smoothing and to remove paint spots from furniture	Used with soap and water to clean and polish stainless steel
0000	Super fine	Used for final wood smoothing, and for dulling gloss on finished surfaces	Used to rub in penetrating wood finishes, with oil and rubbing compound for satin finishes, and to rub laquer finishes satin-smooth

Illus. 8-8. The grades of steel wool and their suggested applications.

for many cleaning tasks, but it's the finer grades that are most eligible for woodworking. Often, they can be used to produce a mirror-like finish on wood that is difficult to achieve even with the finest of sandpapers.

One of steel wool's major advantages is its extreme flexibility. The fact that you can "mold" it to conform to odd shapes makes it particularly suitable for smoothing curves and angles and the arcs and curves on pieces like molding (Illus. 8-9). When working with steel wool in bulk form, you can make whatever size ball or shape that seems appropriate for the job. It can even be twisted rope-like and used like a shoe rag to refinish or to smooth spindles with fancy shapes. I find that it's a fine polisher and finisher for lathe work, especially hardwood turnings, on which it will leave a high-gloss surface that is difficult to obtain by other means.

In addition to finishing the wood, steel wool can be used on lathe work to polish finish coats. The finer grades, used with a delicate touch, do a fine job of smoothing lacquers or varnishes, even shellac or enamel.

Illus. 8-9. Steel wool easily conforms to compound arcs and curves, so it is especially suitable for smoothing moldings.

The general rule is to apply the material with minimum pressure and, like sandpaper, to stroke with the grain of the wood. Strike a new pad a few times over the edge of the workbench to free any broken strands. Do this a few times as you work, to clean out dust and waste for more effective cutting action.

POWER SANDING

Of all the woodworking chores we become involved with, the one most of us want to get through as quickly and efficiently as possible is sanding—no matter whether we're on a new project or refinishing an old one. Thus, we're happy to relegate the chore, or most of it, to power equipment. However, no one tool is acceptable for all phases of sanding, and each tool has characteristics that must be considered in relation to the *type* of sanding they are best suited for.

A logical sequence when completely power-sanding would be to start with a *belt sander,* shift to a *pad sander,* and then go on to a *random-orbit* machine and a *detail sander*. Not all the tools would be required for every project. You might get by with just a belt sander for an outdoor project, but it's not likely that the tool could be used to finish a fine furniture project. Knowing the tool and how it is used leads to efficiency with minimum fuss, and errorless results. Below I discuss the different types of sanders and how they are best used. Before proceeding, however, please note that the Appendix on pages 197–213 contains troubleshooting charts for using disk, belt, and drum sanders.

Belt Sanders

Just looking at a typical belt sander (Illus. 8-10) is revealing to a woodworker. It looks rugged and *is* rugged. No other portable tool

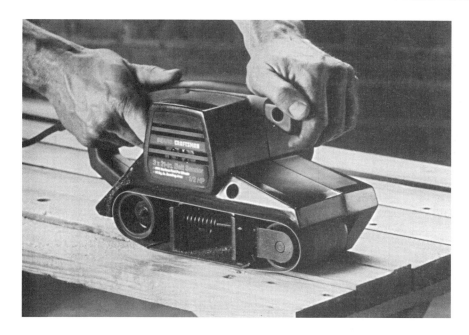

Illus. 8-10. A portable belt sander is fine for removing a lot of material quickly and for doing preliminary work to even surfaces. It is not a finishing sander, and it should not be used on thin-veneered plywood.

can compete when it comes to removing a lot of material quickly. Let's assume you have completed the task of gluing up boards for a benchtop or tabletop. The clamps are off and the glue is dry, so it's time to inspect the joints and check the slab for flatness. It doesn't matter whether you have done such work before or if it's a first effort, there will be glue to remove and possibly high points due to mis-alignment and ridges along joint lines. Even the best effort will require some surfacing before the component is ready for *final* sanding and finishing.

You can get the job done with a hand plane and muscle, but a belt sander will get the work done more quickly, and with little effort will produce a uniform surface even though there might be changes in grain direction. As with all sanders, controlling the degree of smoothness is just a matter of changing to another abrasive grit. I like the belt sander for such work because I can control the amount of material to remove more easily than I can with a plane, and remov-

ing hard glue with a plane doesn't do the tool's blade much good.

But there are a few precautions you must take when using a belt sander. A belt sander's non-stop action, its weight, and the fact that it can travel quickly combine to make it one of the more difficult sanding tools to control. If you place the tool on a surface and then turn it on, it will travel on its own and pull you along with it, but it won't do any sanding. So an important rule is to grip the tool securely and start it before contacting the work. Initial contact must be with the platen flat on the work. Only part of the belt will work if the tool is tilted in any direction, and the gouges that will happen will be difficult to remove. Allow the tool to keep moving; hold it in one spot and you'll have a rectangular dent the size of the platen.

A major feature of a belt sander is its straight-line cutting action, which makes it easy to sand parallel with the wood grain. Use strokes only as long as you can comfortably control, and overlap them a bit as you move to and fro. Don't bear down on the tool; its weight alone will supply sufficient feed pressure. Forcing won't accomplish much and can interfere with belt tracking. Keep the sander on the same plane as you come off the work. Allowing it to tilt will form a gouge or will round off edges. Another error to avoid is lifting the tool before the stroke is complete.

Just as the belt sander can cut too much wood unless it is held firmly, it can grip wood and throw it back at the operator. Unless the workpiece or project is heavy enough to stay put on its own, attach it to a bench or across sawhorses with clamps or weights. Secure small parts by bracing them against a backup strip that is clamped or tack-nailed to the bench.

The belt sander is not a very forgiving tool, so if you are just getting acquainted it's wise to clamp a board in the bench vise and do some practicing. You can even see what will happen when you move the tool diagonally or across the grain.

Pad Sanders

Pad sanders, which are either palm-size sanders that work with a quarter sheet of sandpaper or larger units that take a third or even a half sheet of abrasive, are often called finishing sanders (Illus. 8-11 and 8-12). Pad sanders are designed to move the pad to which sandpaper is attached in one or two ways—to and fro in straight-line strokes, or orbitally so the abrasive grits move in very tiny circles. There are also dual-action models that offer a choice of both motions—a switch or lever lets you choose whether the sanding will be done in a straight line or orbitally. Why choose? Orbital sanding,

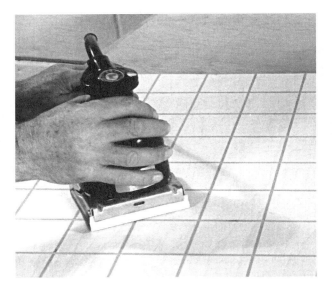

Illus. 8-11. A palm-size pad sander fitted with very fine sandpaper comes close to producing a "final"-sanded surface. Units like this usually work with ¼ sheets of abrasive. Always be certain the paper is taut over the pad.

Illus. 8-12. Larger-size pad sanders have a rectangular pad. Some are designed so you can switch from a to-and-fro sanding action to an orbital sanding action and vice versa.

depending on the size, weight and power of the tool, will remove material faster than straight-line sanding, but since orbital sanders are literally sanding in circles, they will leave swirl marks since part of the orbit is cross-grain. The marks are not easy to see on the raw wood, but they can become obvious after oil or stain is applied. If you have used an orbital sander with, say, 100-grit paper, a good follow-up would be to do a little hand sanding with the same grit paper. The straight-line sander does not leave swirl marks, but it sands slowly and on soft wood tends to sand out soft layers deeper than harder areas.

Pad sanders are equipped with a soft pad of felt or rubber or some similar material that provides about the right flexibility for average work. On some materials with a pronounced alternating hard- and soft-grain structure, such as fir, a soft pad can create depressions between hard-grain areas. In such cases, a hard pad will provide a more efficient backing for the sandpaper since it spans across greater areas.

You can provide a hard "shoe" by placing a piece of thin hardboard between the original pad and the paper. Slim brads of suitable length will hold the new pad in place or, if the design of the tool allows it, you can mount the new pad in place of the standard one (Illus. 8-13). If you use brads, be sure they are set flush or slightly below the surface of the auxiliary pad.

On the other hand, a pad that is thicker (softer) than the original one can be an advantage. It can be used, for example, to sand curves or cylinders, some moldings, or to smooth a finish with a very fine abrasive. The special pad might be available as an accessory, but you can easily improvise with pieces cut from an old rug, sponge, or foam rubber. There are many options. How soft a pad to use will depend on what needs sanding. Be sure the new pad is exactly the size of the original one.

Illus. 8-13. A thin piece of hardboard can provide a hard sanding surface. Whether it can be "nailed" to the original pad or used as a replacement depends on the design of the tool.

Using Pad Sanders Before you begin sanding, and when replacing worn sheets, make sure that the abrasive paper is drawn taut over the pad and held securely by whatever means is provided. If it is slack, even just a bit, it won't move with the pad as it should and sanding efficiency will be greatly reduced.

Accept that the weight of the tool is enough to make the abrasive work. Excessive pressure taxes the tool and you, and can result in exaggerated swirl marks, especially when you are using coarser grits of paper.

Be careful when sanding edges, especially when the tool has a soft pad. The pad will "bend" over corners and the edge will be convex instead of square. When it's imperative for an edge to be square, clamp strips of wood to each side of it so the sander will have a broader plane to rest on. Also, be careful when "leaving" a panel. You can rotate the tool as you leave the edge of a panel if you want a rounded corner, but if you don't, keep the sander on the same horizontal plane that served on surfaces (Illus. 8-14).

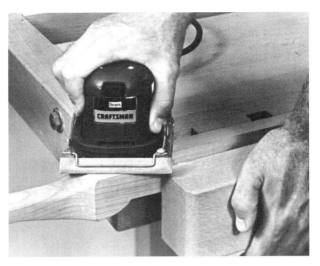

Illus. 8-14. How you handle the sander along edges will determine whether the edge will be square or rounded over.

Illus. 8-15. Sanding results are always better when the work is gripped so it can't move.

Keep workpieces firm. If you are working on small parts and they are not secured in some way, they can move along with the action of the tool and little sanding will be accomplished. Unless the workpiece or project is substantial enough to stay put on its own, secure it to something solid with clamps or grip it in a vise (Illus. 8-15). You should set up for sanding so you can concentrate on controlling the sander, not the work.

Random-Orbit Sanders

Random-orbit sanders are relatively new sanding machines that rate high marks in wood finishing. As far as woodworkers are concerned, they are a giant step toward errorless finishing (Illus. 8-16).

Essentially, random-orbit sanders combine the actions of two sanders—a disk sander and an orbital sander. As a disk sander, its pad

Illus. 8-16. Random-orbit sanders combine a circular action with an orbital one. They come closer to producing swirl-free finishes than any other sanding tool.

rotates as much as 12,000 rpm. As an orbital sander, its off-center bearing causes the pad to also move in tiny circles. The size of the circles (or orbits) can vary from $5/32$ to $3/8$ inch depending on the model. The important point is that as you guide the tool along a surface, the two actions overlap in a nonrepeating pattern that virtually eliminates the kind of swirls you normally get from an orbital machine.

It's characteristic of how random-orbit sanders operate that the rpm of the pad decreases along with increased feed pressure. Thus, they perform most aggressively when you use them with a somewhat gentle touch. My own experience has been that random-orbit sanders are harder to control at high speeds. Therefore, variable-speed models are the best choice in the long run even though they cost more.

Detail Sanders

Detail sanders are also newcomers to wood finishing. The value of a detail sander is the way it can efficiently work close to obstacles and in tight corners. These are the areas that show up as "errors" under finishes because they are difficult to get to with other sanding tools or even by hand (Illus. 8-17). All detail sanders have roughly triangular pads that operate as high as 20,000 rpm (depending on the model) and have an oscillating pattern that is less than $\frac{1}{16}$ inch.

What I like about the tool, in addition to the sanding help it provides, are the practical accessories that are available—items like thick or thin, and hard or soft pads, buffing pads, pad extenders, and even a steel scraper blade, an item I am particularly grateful for at times when I must remove some obnoxious hard glue that's hiding in a corner.

SCRAPERS

Scrapers are not the most popular woodworking tools, probably because we rely so heavily on powered sanders and hand planes. Yet, there are many situations where a well-tuned scraper is a

Illus. 8-17. Detail sanders work with triangular pads that can get into tight corners. Like other sanding tools, they should be kept moving.

better alternative. A scraper does a better job of smoothing irregular or interlocking grain than even the sharpest plane. Properly used, this humble tool severs wood fibers cleanly, leaving a smooth, even surface behind (Illus. 8-18).

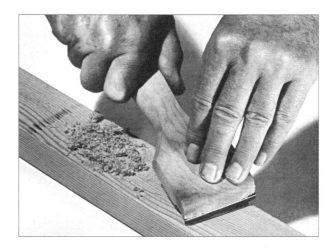

Illus. 8-18. One of the assets of scrapers is that they can quickly remove mill marks or smooth out rough grain.

Illus. 8-19. Refinishers will do well to have scrapers on hand. Many shapes are available, so you can work on contours and get into tight corners without too much fuss.

Scrapers can quickly take down high spots and can efficiently remove flaws, say in the mid-areas of slabs where you wish to isolate repair work. If you used one just to remove dried glue, it would be worthwhile. And if you are into refinishing, it would be unwise not to have scrapers on hand. They can quickly get down to bare wood, often without the nuisance of solvents and paint strippers (Illus. 8-19).

The most-common types of scrapers are either a rectangular piece of specially tempered steel or the so-called "cabinet scraper" (sometimes called a "scraper plane") that looks some-

Illus. 8-20. A "cabinet scraper" looks like a spokeshave. The operator determines how much of the scraper's edge will be exposed.

thing like a spokeshave (Illus. 8-20). But there is a wider variety available today, many of which require less expertise for efficient use than the plain steel blade (Illus. 8-21 and 8-22).

Unlike other tools like chisels and plane blades, a scraper has a burr or "hook" along each side of its working edge, so it can be pulled or pushed, and can get into tight areas and corners you couldn't possible reach with a plane (Illus. 8-23).

As the name tells us, scrapers *scrape*, but, at the same time, they should remove small shavings, not sawdust. The best way to use a scraper is to pull it *with* the grain of the wood whenever possible. Use strokes only as long as you can comfortably reach, and bear down only enough to keep the blade cutting. If you have never used one, take the time to practice on a piece of scrap wood.

Sharpening Scrapers

The edge of the scraper must be maintained in a certain way if it is to work correctly. With a plain blade scraper, secure it between blocks in a vise and then use a mill bastard file to square

Illus. 8-21. A few of the many scraper designs that are available today.

Illus. 8-22. Double-blade scrapers that are installed in handles are available in various widths. This one practically spans the width of a small project.

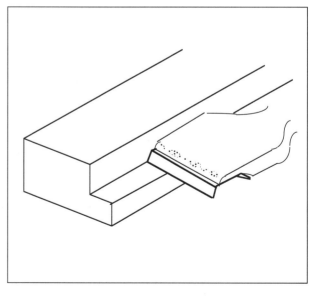

Illus. 8-23. Using a scraper to clean out the corner of a rabbet cut.

Illus. 8-24. The first step when renewing the edge of a plane-blade scraper is to file it square. This first step also removes dull burrs.

the edge (Illus. 8-24). Use light pressure and move the file uniformly along the scraper's edge. Place a few drops of oil on a sharpening stone and, with the scraper flat, remove any roughness that was produced by the filing.

The final step is to form the burr, which is done with a burnisher, a tool that is not much more than a length of highly polished, hardened steel with a round or oval cross-section. Place the scraper so its edge projects a bit over the edge of the workbench, and stroke the edge firmly several times with the burnisher. Repeat this step after inverting the scraper. The last step is to create the burr. Secure the scraper as you did when filing it and make several passes in one direction with the burnisher held level. Finally, repeat the process, but this time with the burnisher held about 10 degrees above horizontal. This will cause the edge to "swell," thereby providing the necessary hook. The stronger you use the burnisher, the bigger the hook.

Renewing the edge on double-edge scrapers, those that are secured in handles, is simpler. Grip the scraper component is a vise and then, with the file angled to match the bevel on the scraper, stroke several times along its edge (Illus. 8-25). Take light strokes in only one direction. Do not remove the slight burr that remains after the filing step.

Illus. 8-25. The edges on double-blade scrapers are easy to renew. Just let the original beveled edge guide the position of the file. Stroke *away* from the body of the scraper.

TROUBLESHOOTING CHARTS FOR POWER TOOLS

I. Table Saw
Ripping

Problem	Possible Cause	Solution
Work too narrow	Measuring from wrong side of blade	Always measure from side of blade facing fence
Edge isn't square to surface	Blade-to-table angle incorrect Distorted stock	Check alignment and reset "0" stop Surface material before ripping
Bevel cuts not accurate	Poor alignment or careless settings	Make settings carefully, make test cuts, and check auto-stops
Edges gouged or excessive tooth marks	Blade chatter	Don't feed blade too fast, and make sure it is sharp
	Careless handling of work	Keep work firmly against fence and use splitter
	Bad blade	Recondition or replace blade
Blade stalls or burn marks on sides of cut	Blade fault	Blade may need sharpening or replacement
	Forcing the cut	Allow blade to cut at its own pace
	Dense wood	Feed wood slowly and make repeat passes for deep cuts
	Poor maintenance	Clean blade frequently to remove residue
	Blade projection (on hollow-ground blade)	Requires more projection than conventional blade
Kerf closes and binds blade	Moisture content in wood	Keep splitter in place—use wedge in kerf if necessary
Work moves away from fence and blade	Alignment	Check for parallelism between blade and fence
	Poor work handling	Keep work against fence throughout pass
	Stock distortion	Edge that rides fence must be true
Work won't pass splitter	Misalignment	Be sure splitter lines up with saw blade
Kickback	Misalignment	Check fence position, and adjust anti-kickback fingers
	Pass not completed	Always move work completely past the blade
	Work handling	Use pusher when sawing narrow stock
		Keep work firm and moving directly forward

TABLE SAW CONTINUED

Crosscutting

Problem	Possible Cause	Solution
Cuts aren't square	Misalignment	Check miter gauge 90-degree setting
	Work handling	Keep work firmly against head of miter gauge
Work jams or is hard to feed	Misalignment	Be sure table slots and saw blade are parallel
Cuts not accurate	Misalignment	Check miter gauge auto-stop
	Work handling	Keep work firm throughout pass and use miter gauge hold-down if available
		Use care when lining up cutting line on work with blade
Cut has slight bevel	Misalignment	Be sure angle between side of blade and table is 90 degrees and check blade-tilt auto-stop
Miter gauge binds or the work is hard to move	Poor tool maintenance	Keep table, slots, and miter-gauge bar clean by applying paste wax occasionally and rubbing to polish
Blade binds	Blade fault	Sharpen or replace
	Work overhang	Supply adequate outboard support to keep work level
	Work handling	Keep work firmly against miter gauge throughout pass

Dadoing/Molding

Problem	Possible Cause	Solution
Bottom of dado or groove not flat	Tool fault	Have blades and chippers jointed and sharpened or invest in better tool
	Placement of blades and chippers	Mark blades and chippers so they can be lined up consistently when mounted on arbor
Widths not accurate	Tool adjustment	Make test cuts whether using a dado assembly or adjustable dado
There is chatter or a tool stalls	Cutting too fast or too deep	Use slower feed or use repeat passes for deep cuts whether dadoing or molding

Problem	Possible Cause	Solution
There is chatter or a tool stalls	Tool fault	Be sure dado tool and molding knives are sharp
Burns on cutters or wood	Feeding too fast or cutting too deep	Don't force work or make repeat passes for deep cuts
	Tool maintenance	Maintain tools in pristine condition
Excessive splintering or feathering at end of cut	Breaking out of cut too fast	Slow up at end of cut, especially when cutting across the grain
Molded edges not uniform	Work handling	Keep work firmly down on table or against fence throughout the pass

II. JOINTER

Jointing or Surfacing

Problem	Possible Cause	Solution
Jointed edge has slight bevel	Misalignment	Angle between fence and table must be 90 degrees
	Work handling	Keep work firmly on table and against fence throughout pass
Work hits edge of out-feed table	Knives too low	Reset for alignment with out-feed table
Work gouged at end of cut	Knives too high	Reset for alignment with out-feed table
Inaccurate depth-of-cut	Misalignment	Check depth-of-cut scale and its indicator
Raised line on planed edge or surface	Nick in knives	Regrind and sharpen
Rough or chipped cuts	Cutting against the grain	Make passes so knives cut with the grain
Rippled cuts	Feeding too fast	Slow feed produces smoothest cuts
	Work handling	Keep work firmly on table throughout the pass
	Misalignment	Just one knife cutting?
Cutter stalls	Cutting too deep	Take light cuts; make repeat passes when necessary

JOINTER CONTINUED

Beveling

Problem	Possible Cause	Solution
Inaccurate results	Misalignment	Recheck fence setting and check auto-stops
	Work handling	Hold work firmly against fence throughout the pass and use clamped blocks to keep work in position
Cut is tapered	Work handling	Keep downward pressure on work uniform while feeding

Rabbeting

Problem	Possible Cause	Solution
Work hits out-feed table	Misalignment	Adjust lateral position of knives
Cut wider at one end	Work handling	Do not force work against fence or use fence only as guide
Uneven cutting depth	Work handling	Keep uniform pressure on work throughout pass and use clamped hold-down block
Wrong cutting width	Inaccurate setting	Be sure to measure from fence to end of knives

III. RADIAL ARM SAW

Crosscutting

Problem	Possible Cause	Solution
Not 90 degrees to work edge	Misalignment	Blade travel must be 90 degrees to fence— check auto-stop
	Work handling	Keep work firmly against fence
Edge has slight bevel	Misalignment	Angle between side of blade and table must be 90 degrees; check blade-tilt auto-stop
Bevels or miters not accurate	Misalignment	Recheck settings before cutting, make test cuts, and reset auto-stops

Problem	Possible Cause	Solution
Blade drags, kerf is too wide, or there are rough cuts or excessive feathering	"Heeling"	"Back" teeth of blade not following line of "front" teeth, so saw needs yoke adjustment. Follow instructions in owner's manual
Blade "climbs"	Work handling	Don't rush cut; let blade saw at its own pace
	Blade fault	Sharpen or replace blade
Blade binds	Blade fault	Sharpen or replace blade
	Work overhang	Provide out-feed support to keep work level
	Work handling	Keep work firmly in place through pass

Ripping

Problem	Possible Cause	Solution
Blade drags, kerfs are too wide, or there are rough cuts		*See* "Heeling" in Crosscutting
Work moves away from fence		See "Heeling" in Crosscutting
	Work handling	Keep work firmly against fence throughout pass
Work binds or is hard to feed	Misalignment	Arm must be 90 degrees to fence, and blade and fence must be parallel
	Work practice	Work edge against fence must be true
	Tool fault	Sharpen or replace blade
Kickback	Misalignment	Check all alignment factors
	Work practice	Adjust anti-kickback fingers, use the splitter, always move work completely past blade
	Blade fault	Sharpen or replace blade
Rip cuts too narrow	Work practice	Measure from side of blade facing fence
Sawdust thrown at operator	Work practice	Tilt guard correctly (check owner's manual)

Dadoing or Molding

Problem	Possible Cause	Solution
Dado depth not uniform	Misalignment	Table and arm must be parallel
Bottom of dado or groove is rough, not flat	Tool fault	Have dado assembly jointed and sharpened. (It might be characteristic of adjustable dado.)

RADIAL ARM SAW CONTINUED

Dadoing or Molding (continued)

Problem	Possible Cause	Solution
Bottom of dado or groove is rough, not flat (continued)	Work habit	Mark components of dado assembly, and line up marks each time parts are mounted on arbor
Dado width is inaccurate		See "Heeling" under Crosscutting
	Work habit	Set adjustable dadoes carefully (assemblies often require shims for exact width setting), and make test cuts
Dado "climbs"	Work habit	Don't force cuts; make repeat passes for very deep cuts
Chatter or stalling	Tool fault	Molding knives and dadoing tools must be sharp and kept in pristine condition
Burn marks on cutting tools or wood	Work practice	Don't force cuts; make repeat passes when necessary
	Tool maintenance	Keep all cutting tools clean
	Tool fault	Sharpen cutting tools and keep them sharp
Molded edges not uniform	Work handling	Keep work firm; use clamps if necessary
Rough molding cuts	Cross-grain passes	Move cutter very slowly. If molding adjacent edges, make cross-grain cuts first.
	Cutting against the grain	Cut with the grain whenever possible

IV. BAND SAW

General Cutting Problems

Problem	Possible Cause	Solution
Blade veers from cutting line	"Lead"	Replace or recondition blade and hone "lead" side
	Misalignment (blade guides)	Reset guides to accommodate the blade
	Work handling	Use one hand to guide, the other to move the work, and feed the work slowly
	Wood knotty or with uneven grain structure	Use a heavy blade, and feed the work slowly and carefully
	Bad blade	Recondition or replace blade

Problem	Possible Cause	Solution
Edges have slight bevel	Misalignment	Angle between side of blade and table must be 90 degrees; check table auto-stop
Blade binds	Turns are too tight	Don't try to saw curves that are too tight for the blade in use
Blade breakage	Forcing the cut	Make easy cuts; allow blade to cut at its own pace
	Tight turns	Don't saw radii too small for the blade in use
	Blade is dull, worn, or damaged	Recondition or replace blade
	Misalignment	Recheck positions of blade guides and backup
Difficult to backtrack	Clogged kerf	Cut slowly, especially with fine blades. If necessary, stop the machine and clear the kerf
	Work handling	Backtrack carefully to keep blade in the kerf
Rough cut	May be characteristic of blade	Blades with heavy set leave rough edges
Blade scrapes when running free	Misalignment	Check for clearance between blade and guides; also check backup
Blade makes knocking noise	Blade is kinked, or bent	Remove blade from machine and straighten it, if possible, or discard it
	Lumpy weld	File weld so back of blade is straight
	Limited width-of-cut	No solution on some jobs
Arm interferes with cut	Poor work planning	Visualize cut before starting. If possible, plan cutting procedure to avoid arm
Bevel cuts not accurate	Misalignment	Check bevel scale and reset auto-stops
	Work practice	Check first cut and adjust table tilt if necessary

Resawing

Problem	Possible Cause	Solution
Side of cut is bowed	Blade is too narrow	Generally, use widest blade possible; narrow blades will work okay if stock is not too thick
	Wrong tension	Adjust tension to suit the blade being used
Blade moves off line when fence is used	Blade has "lead"	Recondition or hone "lead" side
	Work practice	Use shop-made resaw guide
	Blade fault	Sharpen or replace blade

BAND SAW CONTINUED

Dadoing or Molding (continued)

Problem	Possible Cause	Solution
Blade moves off line when fence is used	Wood fault	Better to resaw tough, grainy wood by guiding it freehand
Rough cut	Characteristic of wide blades with heavy set	No solution, but try narrower blade

V. SCROLL SAW

General Cutting Techniques

Problem	Possible Cause	Solution
Blade breakage	Blade selection	Use the correct blade for the operation, material, and material's thickness
	Speed selection	Use ideal speed or stay as close to it as possible
	Blade tension	Adjust to correct tension for the blade and operation
	Forcing the cut	Allow the blade to saw only as fast as it can
	Work handling	Don't try to make turns that are too tight for the blade's width
Bowed edge on work	Blade tension	Increase blade tension
	Blade selection	Don't use very fine blades to saw thick stock
Difficult to keep blade on line	Misalignment	Recheck positions of blade guide and backup
	Blade guide flawed	Replace blade guide
	Poor cutting practice	Feed work slowly; accuracy is more important than speed
	Blade tension	Adjust tension to suit the blade and operation
Slow cutting action	Blade is too fine	Change blade to suit the material and material's thickness
	Worn blade	Discard blade
	Hold-down too tight	Adjust hold-down so stock isn't forced down on table
	Wrong speed	Increase speed until cutting action is right

SCROLL SAW CONTINUED

General Cutting Techniques (continued)

Problem	Possible Cause	Solution
Work edge not square	Misalignment	Angle between side of blade and table must be 90 degrees
Work lifts from table	Hold-down not set correctly	Adjust hold-down for light pressure down on work
Vibration or chatter	Excessive speed	Reduce speed until cutting action is smooth
	Hold-down	Adjust hold-down for light down-pressure on work
Sawdust obscures cutting line	Air tube clogged or kinked	Remove and clean air tube; replace it if damaged
	Faulty blower mechanism	Consult owner's manual for repair or replacement

Sawing Metal

Problem	Possible Cause	Solution
Edges of sheet metal bend or there is excessive burring	No support at cutting area	Make special insert, or tape work to a backup block
Blade breakage or there is fast dulling	Wrong blade or speed	Use blades designed for metal work; adjust speed for smoothest cut
Very rough edges	Blade too coarse	Change to finer, more suitable blade

Sawing Plastics

Problem	Possible Cause	Solution
Kerf closes and binds blade	Heat causes plastic to fuse	Use plastic cutting blade or change to blade with coarser teeth
Plastic marred	Bad cutting practice	Keep protective paper on plastic while sawing

Bevel Sawing (Special Technique)

Problem	Possible Cause	Solution
Parts don't jam together	Wrong table tilt	Best table tilt is about 4–5 degrees
Parts don't mesh	Bad sawing procedure	Maintain same relationship between blade and work throughout sawing procedure

SCROLL SAW CONTINUED

Saber Sawing (If Applicable)

Problem	Possible Cause	Solution
Hard to keep blade on line	Wrong blade	Use special saber-saw blade or heaviest scroll-saw blade
	Forcing cut	Feed slowly and guide work very carefully
	Blade support	Use lower blade backup for support and use special backup if supplied

Filing/Sanding (If Applicable)

Problem	Possible Cause	Solution
File or sandpaper clogs too quickly	Speed (usually too fast)	Slow down to more suitable RPM
	Forcing file or sandpaper	Don't rush or force work against file or sandpaper

VI. DRILL PRESS

General Cutting Problems

Problem	Possible Cause	Solution
Cutting tool overheats or work shows burn marks	Excessive RPM	Use correct speed for the job or stay as close as possible
	Accumulation of waste chips	Retract cutting tool frequently to remove waste chips
	Dull cutting tool	Sharpen or replace cutting tool
	Feed pressure	Apply only enough pressure to keep tool cutting
Bit moves off center	Work habit	Use punch to mark location of hole
	Bit drifts	Supply pilot holes, and then enlarge them
Splinters where drill breaks through	Work habit	Use scrap wood under work as backup
Bit grabs when breaking through	Work habit	Slow up at end of cut, especially when drilling metal
Work twists or is torn from hands	Work habit	Safety calls for clamping work to the table, or fence if one is used
Bit dulls quickly	Feeding too slow	Apply pressure so bit is continuously cutting
Cutting tool slips	Poor practice	Always use chuck key; do not rely on hand-tightening chuck

Problem	Possible Cause	Solution
Incorrect hole depth	Depth stop has wrong setting	Check and reset depth stop
	Not allowing for point on bit	Allow for end of twist drills, point on spade bits, etc., when setting depth stop
Bit binds	Work pinches bit	Support work directly under or as close to drilling area as possible
	Feed pressure	Don't force bit to cut faster than it can
Angular holes are off center	Edge of bit contacts work off center	Work with a leveling block whenever necessary

Mortising

Problem	Possible Cause	Solution
Mortise has serrated edges	Misalignment	Angle between side of chisel and fence must be 90 degrees
Work, bit, and chisel overheat	Misalignment	Check clearance between end of bit and corners of chisel
	Waste chip buildup	Retract cutters frequently. Position chisel so escape slot is not against side of mortise
	Wrong speed	Check manual and change speed to correct RPM
	Cutting tool fault	Sharpen or replace cutting tool
	Feed pressure	Allow chisel and bit to cut; don't force them
Walls of mortise are tapered	Chisel moves during cut	Make overlapping cuts about $3/4$ of the chisel's width
	Work moves	Clamp work securely; use hold-in if available
	Lack of support when forming side mortise	Always use a backup
Excessive feed pressure required	Cutting tool fault	Sharpen or replace cutting tool
	Dense wood	Some wood species require extra feed pressure
Work pulls up when chisel is retracted	Work habit	Always use mortising hold-down and add clamps if necessary
Mortise lengths not equal	Work habit	Use stop block on fence as gauge to control length of mortises
Splintering on breakthrough	Work habit	Use backup under the work

VII. SHAPER

General Cutting Techniques

Problem	Possible Cause	Solution
Work or cutters burn	Heavy cuts	Light cuts, especially on hardwoods, are best; make repeat passes when necessary
	Forcing work	Use slow, steady work feed; quality is more important than speed
	Cutter fault	Sharpen or replace cutter
Work lacks support after passing cutter	Misalignment	Adjust out-feed fence to compensate when entire edge of stock is removed
Work hits out-feed fence	Misalignment	Fences must be on same plane when only part of the work edge is removed
Work gouged at end of cut	Misalignment	Check fence alignment whether removing part or entire edge of stock
End splinters on cross-grain cuts	Characteristic of cut	End such cuts very slowly. Make cross-grain cuts first when shaping adjacent edges. With-the-grain cuts will remove imperfection. Shape oversize piece and then remove flaw by sawing or sanding. Using a backup block will minimize if not eliminate flaw.
Irregular cutting depth	Misalignment	Check and adjust fences
	Work habits	Maintain uniform pressure against fences (or collars) and use hold-downs when ever possible
Kickback	Feed direction	Always feed work *against* the cutter's direction of rotation
Cut quality (smoothness)	Cutter speed	Use high speed if machine has variable or a set of speeds
	Cutting against the grain	Cut with the grain whenever possible
	Cutter fault	Sharpen or replace cutter
	Heavy cuts	Make repeat passes to achieve full depth of cut
	Rushing cuts	Slow down feeds. Slow feeds produce smoothest cuts
	Feed pressure	Hold work firmly and apply uniform pressure against fences (or collars) throughout pass

Problem	Possible Cause	Solution
Edge irregularity	Lifting work during pass	Keep work flat on table, especially when cutter is over the work. Use hold-downs whenever possible
Cutting inaccuracies	Work habit	Check profile of cutter against work edge. Cutter adjustments are made with the motor off!

Freehand Shaping

Problem	Possible Cause	Solution
Marred work edge	Tool maintenance	Clean collars frequently, keep them smooth, and store them carefully
Problem holding work	Bearing surface on collars	Work must have sufficient bearing surface against collars; this is also a very important safety factor!
Kickback	Work practice	Move work very slowly into cutter until there is firm contact against collars
	Fulcrum pins	Brace against in-feed pin at start of cut and against out-feed pin toward end of cut
Shaped-edge irregularities	Work handling	Keep work down on table throughout pass; use hold-downs
Shaped-edge gouges	Cutter setup	Work with cutter *under* the work whenever possible so inadvertently lifting work during pass won't cause gouging
Cut quality (smoothness)	Work habit	Feed work so cutting is done with the grain whenever possible

VIII. LATHE

General Shaping

Problem	Possible Cause	Solution
Work burns at cup center	Friction	Ease pressure between centers
		Clean cup center and apply some paste wax

LATHE CONTINUED

General Shaping Problems (continued)

Problem	Possible Cause	Solution
Excessive vibration	Wrong speed	Use lower speeds on large work
	Work not on true centers	Relocate centers if necessary. Slight vibration is not critical, and will be cured as work becomes true round
Chatter	Wrong speed	Use lower speed, especially when starting work
Chisels hard to control	Shaping tool fault	Sharpen and hone shaping tool
	Cutting too deep	Good shop practice calls for slow feed and moderate "bite"
	Poor support for chisel	Adjust tool rest position whenever necessary
Work slips	Loose between centers	Make necessary adjustment
	Spur center abrades wood	Reseat spur center; renew damaged end of work if necessary
Scored lines left by sanding	Wrong abrasive grit	Work through progressively finer grits
	Over-sanding in one area	Keep sandpaper moving
Hard to achieve super finish	Stubborn "nap" on wood	Reverse work between centers; wipe it with slightly dampened cloth before final sanding
Spindle turning whips	Lack of support	Use a steady rest
Excessive vibration or chatter on faceplate work	Speed fault	Reduce RPM, especially when starting job
	Work practice	Shape piece to round, or remove corners
	Faceplate not centered	Remount faceplate; slight vibration not critical
	Mounting problem	Tighten mounting screws or replace them with heavier ones if necessary
Excessive splintering when rough-turning square to round	Work habit	Work from centers toward ends of spindle
		Saw off corners of work before mounting
	Cutting too deep	Don't rush; quality is better than speed
Lathe labors when switched on	Forced grip on spindle turning	Ease off pressure between centers
Sanding burns work	Excessive pressure	Sanding builds up heat, especially on dense wood. Apply paper lightly and keep it moving
	Lathe-speed fault	Reduce RPM
Work on screw center loosens	Can be due to soft wood	Use heavier screw if necessary. Check screw center frequently, and do not use chisels aggressively

Problem	Possible Cause	Solution
Work on screw center loosens	Mounting fault	Be sure screw is heavy enough for application. Use screw center only when work can't be mounted on a faceplate or between centers

IX. DISC SANDER

General Sanding

Problem	Possible Cause	Solution
Work lifts from table	Using wrong side of disc	Apply work against "down" side of disk
Miters not accurate	Misalignment (if miter gauge used)	Adjust miter gauge and reset auto-stops
	Work habit	Mark miter line with combination square; make and use a mitering jig
	Misalignment	Disk and slot in table must be parallel
Slight bevel on sanded edge	Misalignment	Angle between disk and table must be 90 degrees; check auto-stop
Bevels not accurate	Misalignment	Make settings carefully; check them with bevel gauge
Burn marks on work	Excessive feed pressure	Don't force work against disc
	Work held stationary	Move work across "down" side of disc
	Using center of disc	Outer edge of disc sands more freely than center
	Problem with sandpaper	Replace sandpaper when worn; don't use fine grits for heavy stock removal
Thin work jams between disc and table	Misalignment	Gap between disc and edge of table must not be more than $1/8$ inch
Sandpaper tends to loosen or has bubbles	Poor application of sandpaper	Attach abrasive discs very carefully; follow manufacturer's instructions
	Problem with sandpaper	Don't use sandpaper if distorted; salvage it for other applications
	Problem with disc	Be sure disc is clean and dry before attaching abrasive paper
Obvious sanding marks	Work held stationary	Keep work moving across "down" side of disc
	Problem with sandpaper	Use abrasive grit that is suitable for the job
	Sanding cross-grain	Progress to fine grit when surface-sanding; it may be necessary to finish by hand or with portable sander

DISC SANDER CONTINUED

General Sanding (continued)

Problem	Possible Cause	Solution
Inadequate results on metal	Problem with sandpaper	Use abrasive designed for metal working
Abrasive clogs too quickly	Feed pressure	Light pressure always best; allow abrasive to cut at its own pace
	Finished-painted surface	Use open-grain abrasive; it is better to remove paint with proper solvent
	Problem with wood	No cure if wood is wet or gummy
	Work habit	Use abrasive "eraser" product frequently
Chatter	Inadequate support	Supply support for work as close to disk as possible; hold work firmly

X. DRUM SANDER

General Sanding

Problem*	Possible Cause**	Solution
Sleeve slips and moves off drum	Problem with mounting	Tighten drum-expansion nut (check owner's manual)
Sanded edges not square	Problem with operation	Freehand sanding hard to control; use table to support work square to drum
	Misalignment	Angle between side of drum and table (or jig) must be 90 degrees
Edge of work indented	Work practice	Keep work moving to avoid concave flaw
Drum distortion	Feed pressure	Don't force work; light pressure is always best
Sleeve clogs in one area	Work practice	Move drum vertically to make use of entire abrasive area

* Many of the problems listed in this chart also apply to belt sanding

** Assumes that drum sanding is being done on a drill press

XI. BELT SANDER

General Sanding

Problem*	Possible Cause	Solution
Belt moves off drum	Misalignment	Adjust upper drum to center belt
	Belt tension	Adjust tension to keep belt taut
Belt slips	Feed pressure	Light pressure is always best; don't force feed
	Belt tension	Adjust to keep belt taut
Curves not square to surfaces	Work practice	Freehand application is poor habit; use an extension to support work and keep it square to belt
Floppy belt or bubbles	Work practice	Do not apply work in only one area; use entire width of belt

* Many of the problems listed in this chart also apply to the drum sander.

Metric Conversion Table

INCHES TO MILLIMETERS AND CENTIMETERS

MM—millimeters   *CM—centimeters*

Inches	MM	CM	Inches	CM	Inches	CM
⅛	3	0.3	9	22.9	30	76.2
¼	6	0.6	10	25.4	31	78.7
⅜	10	1.0	11	27.9	32	81.3
½	13	1.3	12	30.5	33	83.8
⅝	16	1.6	13	33.0	34	86.4
¾	19	1.9	14	35.6	35	88.9
⅞	22	2.2	15	38.1	36	91.4
1	25	2.5	16	40.6	37	94.0
1¼	32	3.2	17	43.2	38	96.5
1½	38	3.8	18	45.7	39	99.1
1¾	44	4.4	19	48.3	40	101.6
2	51	5.1	20	50.8	41	104.1
2½	64	6.4	21	53.3	42	106.7
3	76	7.6	22	55.9	43	109.2
3½	89	8.9	23	58.4	44	111.8
4	102	10.2	24	61.0	45	114.3
4½	114	11.4	25	63.5	46	116.8
5	127	12.7	26	66.0	47	119.4
6	152	15.2	27	68.6	48	121.9
7	178	17.8	28	71.1	49	124.5
8	203	20.3	29	73.7	50	127.0

Index